# 'ALONE ON A WIDE, WIDE SEA'

# 'ALONE ON A WIDE, WIDE SEA'

The Story of 835 Naval Air Squadron
in the Second World War

by

E. E. Barringer

LEO COOPER
LONDON

First published in Great Britain in 1995 by
LEO COOPER
190 Shaftesbury Avenue, London WC2H 8JL
an imprint of
Pen & Sword Books Ltd,
47, Church Street, Barnsley, South Yorks, S70 2AS

ISBN 0 85052 278 1

A CIP record for this book is available from the British Library


Typeset by Phoenix Typesetting, Ilkley, West Yorkshire.
Printed by Redwood Books Ltd,
Trowbridge, Wilts.

# *CONTENTS*

# ILLUSTRATIONS

# ACKNOWLEDGMENTS

Passages from *Wings of the Morning* by Ian Cameron and *Bring Back my Stringbag* by Lord Kilbracken are reproduced by kind permission of the authors.

Photographs 6, 8, 9 and 46 are reproduced by permission of the Fleet Air Arm Museum. Photographs 42, 43, 45, and 47 are reproduced by permission of the Imperial War Museum (London). I should like to thank both museums for tracking down these wartime pictures. All the photographs belong to members of the Squadron, who have been remarkably generous and patient in letting me use them. My grateful thanks to you all.

My thanks too to our 'resident artist', Jock Bevan, who supplied the original cartoons (drawn in '44 and '45), and who also designed the squadron crest of which we are all very proud. What a team effort this has been!

# INTRODUCTION

You may wonder why, in the mid-1990s, this story of a Naval Air Squadron in the Second World War has been so belatedly written.

It has been written first because, even after all these years, it is a good story: a story of brave men in outdated aircraft who carried out combat missions in conditions as difficult as airmen have ever had to fly in. To quote the Official Naval History: "Aircraft operating from escort-carriers, often in heavy seas and appalling weather, played a vital role in defending our convoys in the North Atlantic. Without the protection provided by these carrier-based aircraft many convoys would never have reached the British Isles with their vital supplies, or Russia with their vital equipment." Convoy protection was the *raison d'être* of our being. For three years this is what we trained for and what we did, and it seems to me the story of how we did it is worth telling.

Another reason for writing the story of 835 Squadron is that it fills a niche in history. There have been books before about Fleet Air Arm carriers like *Illustrious*, and Fleet Air Arm achievements like helping to sink the *Bismarck*, and crippling the Italian fleet at Taranto, but the story of a Fleet Air Arm squadron from start to finish has never been told.

My final reason for writing *Alone on a Wide, Wide Sea* is that everyone who served in the squadron during the war has now passed his allotted three-score-years-and-ten; the feeling is that if we don't reminisce today, we may not have the chance tomorrow! So as the C.O. and one of the longest-serving members of the Squadron, I decided to get writing!

★    ★    ★

I believe that an Introduction is the proper place to say one's "thank yous".

Many pilots, observers and air-gunners who served in the squadron during the war have sent me reminiscences from addresses as disparate as New Zealand, Canada, the United States, France, Ireland, Scotland, Wales, Thames Ditton and the House of Lords. This is their story, told as far as possible in their words. Without their help it could not have been written. So thank you all. And special thanks to Bob Selley, who spent so much time behind the scenes bringing us all together after a gap of more than 40 years.

I am also grateful to the staff of the Public Record Office at Kew, to David Brown, head of the Naval Historical Branch in the Ministry of Defence, and to my wife Lesley for her encouragement and help and for typing what must have seemed like an endless succession of drafts.

Finally, I should like to thank those ship's officers of HMS *Nairana* who have given me help. In the latter part of the war our fortunes were linked to those of the escort-carrier *Nairana*. She was our ship. We were her squadron. This is our story.

E.E. Barringer
Dunedin, New Zealand
1994

# I

# CONCEPTION

I was on my way to join 835 Naval Air Squadron, with orders to "repair forthwith to HMS *Raven*". *Raven*, I knew, was not an aircraft carrier but a somewhat nondescript shore establishment near Eastleigh, at the south-west tip of the Downs.

It was snowing when I got off the train at Eastleigh. The date was 20 January, 1942. I remember that because the next day was going to be my 21st birthday. I was cold and tired, having spent the previous night travelling south from Liverpool; someone with local knowledge got to the one and only taxi before me, and by the time I arrived at HMS *Raven* I wasn't exactly full of *joie de vivre*. My spirits were not revived when I discovered nobody was expecting me, and nobody had ever heard of 835 Squadron. However, I was given a cabin, and when I'd unpacked I made my way to the wardroom. Alas, it was deserted and the bar locked. After a solitary meal, I decided the only option was bed.

I remember telling myself, before I dropped off to sleep, that everything would be OK tomorrow when the rest of the squadron turned up. That is the way it always seemed to be in the Fleet Air Arm. Our planes might look like relics from the First World War; our *modus operandi* might have serious affinities with the fleet orders issued before Trafalgar; but there was nothing wrong with the air crew. And they, after all, were what mattered. For as the old Greek historian put it, "it is not walls that make a city but the men who man them."

Yet looking back after fifty years, I can't help thinking how much less costly the war at sea would have been for the allies, and how many ships and how many lives would have been saved, if we had been given decent equipment.

To understand why we were denied such equipment and why, throughout the war, we were tied as by an umbilical cord to our antediluvian past, we need to know something of the early history of the Fleet Air Arm.

*   *   *

During the First World War the Army and the Navy each controlled its own individual "wing" for flying; Army flying was carried out under the aegis of the Royal Flying Corps, Naval flying under the aegis of the Naval Air Service. This was a sensible arrangement, and one which most other countries, including America and Japan, have adhered to from that day to this. However, on 1 April, 1918, the two "wings" of the Army and the Navy were combined to form a single new service, the Royal Air Force.

The date of this amalgamation – All Fools' Day – might be thought significant. For in a moment of self-abnegation, which for the Navy was to prove tragic, the Sea Lords handed over 2,949 aircraft, 126 aerodromes and 67,000 officers and men. And, what was worse, they lost control over the future of their air arm.

So throughout the 1920s and most of the 1930s it was the RAF who provided planes, aircrew and maintenance personnel for the Navy. In times of retrenchment and financial parsimony, the RAF had little enough to spend on its own requirements and even less to spend on the Navy's. So when eventually a growing body of opinion in the Navy began to ask for its air arm to be upgraded, they got a chilling response: "the Air Ministry favours not the expansion but the drastic reduction of the aircraft-carrying capacity of the Fleet." If the Navy wanted a carrier they were told there was no money to build one; they had to adapt an existing warship. If they wanted a plane there was no money for that either; they had to make do with an RAF castoff.

This unhappy state of affairs may have been aggravated by inter-service rivalry; but the root of the trouble lay deeper. The unpalatable truth is that in the Navy itself those responsible for the development of the service looked backward rather than forward. They failed to appreciate the potential of aircraft as weapons of war – "the aeroplane," reads a Sea Lord's memo of the '20s "will be of little practical use to the Fleet." High-ranking naval officers continued to put their trust in the heavy guns of their battleships which had for so long maintained Great Britain's naval supremacy throughout the world; they had no time for new-fangled weapons which took them out of their traditional element. There are none so blind as those who do not wish to see.

So between the wars the Fleet Air Arm stagnated in the doldrums.

There was, however, one bright spot. Flying with the Navy was never popular with RAF aircrew; and in 1924 it was decided to send a small number of naval officers – there were never more than forty in any one year and sometimes as few as twelve – to train as pilots at Netheravon and as observers at Lee-on-Solent. The men who volunteered for this training *had* to be fanatics. For the Air Arm in those days was considered a backwater; it was unpopular with senior officers; promotion was slow and pegged to a low level; planes lagged at least five years behind their RAF counterparts, and flying from carriers involved a constant battle with the forces of reaction. However, the men who trained at Lee and Netheravon had a point to prove; they were determined to show the powers-that-be that naval aviation *had* a future, and that this future lay not with the RAF but with the Navy. To do this, they found it necessary to achieve an exceptionally high standard of flying: to fly in all weathers and never crash on take-off or landing, never to get lost, never on fleet manoeuvres to mistake a battleship for a cruiser. It is of course more difficult to land-on and take-off from a carrier than an airfield; it is more difficult to drop a torpedo than a bomb, and navigation over the featureless sea is far more difficult than over land. Those able to meet these demanding standards found themselves sharing a special *esprit de corps*, and bonded into what might be described as an unintentionally *élitist* club. And in 1937 the dream of these "fanatics" was realized. The Fleet Air Arm was handed back to the Navy.

This came about not because the Sea Lords suddenly woke up to the importance of air power, but because they couldn't stomach the thought of Lord Trenchard getting hold of their carriers and aircrew. In 1936 Lord Trenchard, "the father of the modern RAF", made a succession of speeches in which he claimed dominion for the RAF over everything remotely connected with the air – including the Fleet Air Arm. This so incensed senior naval officers that they clutched their hitherto unwanted child to their bosom and insisted on taking control of all aspects of naval aviation.

The years of bondage were over. But their legacy remained.

In 1937 the Navy embarked on a crash programme of building carriers, updating its aircraft and training its personnel. But eighteen months of frantic activity couldn't compensate for eighteen years of neglect. The war, for the Fleet Air Arm, came too soon; and to quote the official *Naval Staff History:*

> "*In 1939 the air component of the Fleet had not reached that stage of development which world progress in aviation justified . . . Not only was the Navy deficient in the numbers of its aircraft and their*

*technical development, it was lacking in personnel with experience in carrying out its aviation activities."*

To confirm this we need only look at the seven carriers, 232 aircraft, and 2,000-odd personnel with which the Fleet Air Arm went to war.

The carriers were a job lot. Only one, the *Ark Royal*, had been specially designed to operate aircraft; the others were interwar conversions or First World War museum pieces. The *Ark Royal* was a fine ship; but being the first of her class she had teething troubles; her lifts were too small and wrongly positioned; she had no radar, and could operate fewer aircraft less efficiently than her American and Japanese counterparts. Of the others the *Glorious* and *Courageous* were inadequately armoured and alarmingly top-heavy (in any sort of sea they rolled so heavily they couldn't operate their aircraft); the *Furious* spouted smoke like a blowing whale through her deck-plates, while the *Argus* was described by one spotter as "a small dismasted hulk, on fire aft", and by another as "a wreck floating bottom up". It is true that five new fleet carriers of the *Illustrious* class were being built, but none was ready for service in 1939. Significantly, no thought had been given to building escort-carriers: i.e. carriers that could be used to escort and protect convoys.

The aircraft were as bizarre as the carriers. They consisted of 140 torpedo-bombers-cum-reconnaissance planes, thirty dive-bombers-cum-fighters, twenty-four fighters (nearly all of them biplanes) and thirty-eight seaplanes. With a single exception, none of these aircraft was capable of efficiently carrying out the purpose for which it had been designed. One reason for this was that between the wars the Fleet Air Arm had been so starved of aircraft that it had tried to make do with multi-purpose planes: for example the Skua, which was supposed to act as both dive-bomber and fighter, an unlikely combination which resulted in it being a disaster in both roles. Another reason for the poor performance of naval aircraft was that senior officers insisted that carrier-based planes had to carry an observer (or navigator), the thinking being that pilots flying over the sea by themselves were bound to get lost. An extra passenger meant extra size; extra size meant extra weight. The result was that when the Fleet Air Arm's latest fighter, the two-seater Fulmar, at last came into service, it turned out to be slower and more cumbersome than the German and Italian bombers which it was supposed to shoot down. For those who are technically minded, it would be possible to go on listing the shortcomings of British naval aircraft for page after page. For the average reader, it is enough to know that 90 per cent of them were biplanes with fabric wings, no flaps, constant-pitch propellors and fixed undercarriages; in most cases their top speed was lower than that of many planes in the *First* World War! What a contrast to the thousand-odd aircraft of the U.S. Navy: all, in 1939, monoplanes, all with retractable undercarriages, and many able to fly at double the speed of their British counterparts.

Among this tatterdemalion rabble there was, however, one aircraft which was to prove an unexpected success; indeed it would be no exaggeration to say it became something of a legend. The fleet's torpedo-bomber-cum-reconnaissance plane, the Fairey Swordfish, *looked* out of date in 1939, yet it turned out to be so successful that it was the only aircraft of any of the combatants to remain in service throughout the war – indeed more Swordfish were operational on the last day of hostilities than on the first.

These remarkable aircraft were the work-horses of 835 Squadron. We flew them from the day we were formed until the day we were disbanded; so a few facts about them are not out of place.

Swordfish were the brain child of Captain (subsequently Admiral) H.C. Rawlings, who in 1930 put forward the idea that the Navy needed a plane which could not only spot and reconnoitre but could also deliver a torpedo attack: "a plane with a sting in its tail". The Sea Lords were unresponsive; so Rawlings took his idea to Fairey, whose chief designer, Marcel Lobelle, drew up the specification for a prototype. In 1933, on only its second flight, Lobelle's creation went into a flat spin that it couldn't get out of, crashed and was burned to the proverbial cinder. It says much for Rawlings's tenacity and Fairey's commitment that they didn't give up. After eighteen months of redesigning and restructuring, a second prototype took to the air, and its trials proved so successful that an order was placed, and in May, 1935, the first Swordfish were delivered to the Navy. Nine and a half years and 2,399 aircraft later, the last was delivered.

What qualities, you may ask, did these archaic-looking biplanes possess that they were used so long and with such success? (And there can be no doubt about the fact that they *were* successful; for it was Swordfish which crippled the Italian fleet at Taranto, Swordfish which found and helped to sink the *Bismarck*, Swordfish which kept the U-boats at bay from our vital Atlantic convoys, and Swordfish which sank a greater tonnage of enemy shipping than any other type of aircraft.)

It was certainly not their speed that commended them; for the only time they could "do a ton" was in a dive or with a gale behind them. It was certainly not their fire-power; for their defensive armament was a solitary hand-operated Vickers gun, and their offensive armament no more than a few bombs or a torpedo, or eight rocket projectiles or four depth charges. And it was certainly not their beauty of line; for they looked as though they were glued together by a cat's cradle of struts and wires – hence the epithet "Stringbag". They had open cockpits, and their engines, like those of a vintage car, had to be started by hand-cranking. However, on the plus side they were robust, reliable, manoeuvrable, without vice, forgiving and above all ideally suited to flying from carriers. It was this last quality which endeared them to a decade of Fleet Air Arm pilots. Aircraft operating from carriers often suffer heavier losses from accidents than from enemy action – Seafires covering the allied landings in Italy for example lost twenty planes taking-off or landing for every one lost in combat. Swordfish, with their short take-off run, slow landing speed and sturdy undercarriage were able to operate from carriers by night, in heavy seas and in weather conditions no other aircraft could have survived in. If 835 Squadron had been flying any other type of plane, the odds are we wouldn't today be telling our story.

With few carriers and outdated aircraft the Fleet Air Arm at the start of the war depended heavily on it personnel. And they, like the curate's egg, were good and bad in patches.

To start at the bottom of the naval hierarchy . . . The maintenance crews, whose job was to keep the Air Arm's planes fuelled, armed and airworthy, started off with a disadvantage that *could* have been crippling. Between the wars, naval aircraft had been serviced by RAF ground crew. It was therefore inevitable that when in 1937 the RAF severed its connections with the Air Arm, most of those engineers, riggers and fitters who had been looking after the Navy's planes returned to service on RAF aerodromes. This left the Navy bereft of those artisans without whose skills its aircraft couldn't be kept in the air; and in particular it left them bereft of those long-service non-commissioned officers who have worked their way up through the ranks and are the backbone of every effective fighting force. The Navy embarked on a crash programme of training riggers and fitters; but, as was the case with its carriers, eighteen months of activity couldn't make up for eighteen years of neglect; and in 1939 the majority of Fleet Air Arm groundcrew had little in the way of experience, and nothing in the way of tradition to fall back on. Bearing this in mind, the high standard of maintenance achieved in carriers and shore establishments throughout the war was remarkable. And this perhaps is the place to pay tribute to the unsung heroes of 835 Squadron.

It has been estimated that when a carrier is operating in difficult con-ditions – bad weather and heavy seas – for every hour a plane is airborne, it takes two hours to get it onto and off the flight deck, fuel it, arm it and carry out essential inspection, maintenance and repairs. Our squadron riggers and fitters had a heavy work load, and their task was complicated by the fact that it is a great deal harder to keep planes serviceable in a carrier than on an airfield. Safety precautions have to be more rigorous, working conditions are more cramped, more malodorous and in heavy seas more dangerous; because of lack of space, spare parts are always in short supply, and there isn't the option of simply lifting the phone to order a replacement. In view of these difficulties the wonder is not that some of our planes were sometimes unairworthy, but that any were ever airworthy at all.

Next step up in the hierarchy were the aircrew. The small core of RN observers and pilots who had learned their trade at Lee-on-Solent and Netheravon were the *crème de la crème*. In 1939 many of these dedicated men were given the job of training their RNVR successors, and they managed to pass on to their pupils something of their own commitment, expertise and *esprit de corps*. Although it may seem conceited to say so, there was not much wrong with the standard of flying in the Air Arm at the beginning of the war, or for that matter at any time during the war.

The situation was not so roseate in the next echelon of the hierarchy; for the Air Arm was bereft of officers of flag or even captain's rank who had experience in operating aircraft carriers. It was a different story in the American and Japanese Navies; they had large numbers of senior officers who had graduated to their position through the ranks of naval aviation; but because the Fleet Air Arm had been controlled until 1937 by the RAF, it had virtually no officers who were senior enough to fill key positions in an aircraft carrier. This was a serious lack. It was felt throughout the whole duration of the war – witness the fact that when, in 1944, a new captain was appointed to command our aircraft-carrier HMS *Nairana*, the man chosen for this not unimportant job had previously served only in cruisers and destroyers, and had no personal experience of what aircraft could do or how to operate them.

With such a conception, it is hardly surprising that the birth of 835 Squadron was a low-key, almost apologetic affair. Indeed it seemed for quite a while that it wasn't going to take place at all.

## 2

# *BIRTH*

On my second day at Eastleigh I resumed my search for colleagues or aircraft, but to no avail. The snow continued to fall. The wardroom remained deserted.

That evening I walked into the town in search of the Station Hotel, which I'd caught sight of as I got off the train. Everything was blacked-out; but when it came to locating pubs I seemed to have a built-in homing instinct – enhanced perhaps by my training as a navigator. Getting to the Station Hotel was no problem. Getting a beer was another story. I asked for a pint of bitter, and was told I could have a half. (Beer was not officially rationed during the war; but it was often in short supply, and some pubs had a "locals only" or "no more than a pint" rule.) At first I was the only person in the bar, but after a while a middle-aged man came in. We wished one another "good evening", and, thinking this was going to be the only chance I'd have to celebrate my 21st birthday with a companion, I asked him if he'd like a drink. The statutory half-pint was duly poured and drunk. But, alas, when my new-found friend said it was his round, we were told we had had our ration!

As I walked back to HMS *Raven* the snow had stopped and the sky was bright with stars. It was a beautiful evening. All the same, I could think of more exciting ways of spending one's 21st birthday.

Next day, finding I was still a one-man squadron without aircraft, I approached the captain's secretary. What I had in mind was a bit of belated celebrating. What I asked was: "Why don't I go to the Admiralty and find out what's happening?"

Returning to Eastleigh a few days later, after various episodes in London which did indeed include a brief visit to the Admiralty, I found that over the weekend five somewhat bewildered sub-lieutenants (A) RNVR had arrived at HMS *Raven*, all looking for 835 Squadron. Three of the newcomers were pilots. There was "Taffy" Jones from Llanelly: fair haired, shrewd and exuberant. Robin Shirley-Smith, an architect by profession: reserved but unfailingly even-tempered and considerate. And Johnny Hunt from north London, one of those gifted, easy-going and modest men who are liked by everyone. The two observers were Jackie Parker: a delightfully innocent young man, anxious to do his bit and full of admiration for anyone who had already done theirs. And Jack Teesdale, who was soon to become not only a personal friend but – as Stores Officer – quite literally the prop and stay of the Squadron.

About the last to arrive was our squadron CO, Lt-Cdr Mervyn Johnstone, DSC, RN. Nobody dared ask if he was late or we had been early!

Johnstone was a maverick. Important things he did very well; routine things he got someone else to do; trivia he ignored. First, he talked to each of us individually. I was rash enough to volunteer the information that I'd previously served in HMS *Eagle* in the Mediterranean. On hearing this, he promptly appointed me Senior Observer and Squadron Adjutant. He then assembled the whole squadron – all six of us – and told us why we'd been brought to Eastleigh.

835 Squadron, he said, was going to consist of four Swordfish, four pilots, four observers, four telegraphist air gunners and thirty-four maintenance personnel. Our objective would be to carry out convoy protection duties, flying from one of the small escort-carriers currently being built in the United States. We would go first to the Royal Naval Air Station at Palisadoes, near Kingston, Jamaica. Here we would pick up our aircraft. Then, as soon as one of the carriers under construction in the yards of Norfolk, Virginia was ready, we would fly north and embark in her.

We were not sure what to make of this. So far in the war Swordfish had been used mostly as torpedo-bombers – they had crippled half the Italian fleet at Taranto and been instrumental in sinking the *Bismarck* – and most of us, I fancy, had secret dreams of emulating these great feats. Convoy protection would, we knew be different: not the occasional dramatic sortie, but long hours of circling a slow-moving convoy on anti-submarine patrol. Valuable, yes. Exciting, no. In retrospect, I wonder we didn't ask ourselves the obvious question: why was the squadron to consist of no more than four ancient biplanes, and why was there no British escort-carrier from which we could operate? These questions *did* occur to some of us later. But at the time we were simply delighted at the prospect of exchanging the snow, cold and gloom of Eastleigh for the sun, warmth, palm trees, rum and limbo dancing of the Caribbean.

And suddenly it was all happening. Next day the CO told me to prepare a movement order to take the squadron first by train to Glasgow and then to the SS *Andalucia Star*, at anchor in the Clyde.

Johnnie Johnstone then disappeared into the best hotel in Winchester to enjoy a few days of unofficial leave with his wife. I wasn't sure then (and I'm still not sure now) whether to be flattered that he trusted me to do everything that had to be done, or disgruntled at being landed with all the work.

We left Eastleigh with few regrets on the afternoon of 29 January, the last of our observers, Sub-Lt(A) S.W. Thomas, joining us literally only a few hours before we got on the train. For those with romantic connections in the south there was a last rendezvous with loved ones at Victoria Station, for those with romantic connections in the Midlands a last rendezvous at Crewe. Those with romantic connections in Scotland were unlucky. There was no time for any sort of rendezvous in Glasgow. Within a couple of hours of de-training we were aboard the *Andalucia Star*, and next day the ship moved downriver to the Tail O' The Bank at Greenock.

It was dark and cold as, a little after 1 am in the morning of 4 February, a small convoy stood silently out of the Clyde. Apart from the *Andalucia Star* there were only two other merchantmen in the convoy, and we were escorted by just two destroyers. The latter saw us safely through the sea-lanes north of Ireland, which in those days were a happy hunting-ground for the U-boats; then on 7 February they left us, and the three merchantmen split up, each heading at top speed for its destination.

And speed, on these solo voyages, was a matter of life or death.

Luckily for us, the *Andalucia Star* was a fine, fast vessel. One of the élite of the Blue Star Line, she had been launched in 1936 and had a displacement of 15,000 tons and a cruising speed of 16 knots – in other words she was just about as fast as a U-boat on the surface. She was well, indeed luxuriously, appointed, and remarkably well stocked with food and pre-war vintage wines; so our passage across the Atlantic had all the trappings of a pleasure cruise.

The squadron telegraphist-air-gunners and maintenance personnel travelled third-class: not uncomfortable but by no means luxurious. With them there happened to be the leading airmen of the 50th Observers Course on their way to Trinidad to complete their training, and among these trainee observers were A.R.J (Johnny) Lloyd and A.C. Arber who were later to join the squadron.

The pilots and observers travelled first-class, and, conforming to the practice of the day, we were strictly segregated from our companions below decks. Also travelling first class were a number of ladies, most of them officers' wives, on their way to join their husbands in the West Indies, Canada or the United States. It didn't take us long to wake up to the fact that several of our travelling companions were most attractive, especially a young lady of French extraction with the name of Marianne. Taffy Jones did his best to zero in on her; but, having surveyed the field, it was Johnny Hunt whom she invited to sit at her table. Other pairings followed, it being generally felt that Shirley-Smith's might be the least successful, since his American girl friend insisted on carrying her handbag with her wherever she went, and in it a small revolver.

As we headed south the weather got warmer. Tropical rig became the order of the day; deck-tennis and quoits became increasingly popular; the food seemed to get better and better, the wine to flow ever more freely, and the dancing to go on ever later into the small hours of the morning. It was an idyllic interlude: ten days of the sort of cloistered luxury that first-class passengers on first-class liners took for granted between the wars. Some of us, when we weren't dancing away the night, found ourselves watchkeeping; and it could be that the ever-present threat of U-boats gave our *amours* an urgency that made them the more memorable.

But all good things come to an end. On 16 February we sighted Jamaica. It was an evening for parties, a night for farewells; and on the morning of 17 February the *Andalucia Star* nosed up to one of the long wooden jetties in Kingston harbour.

Maybe the wind was gusting, maybe the tide was exceptionally strong, maybe the ship's officers had been kept awake by our farewell party. Whatever the cause, the *Star* came alongside with an almighty crash which not only buckled the jetty but so terrified a group of Jamaican dockers that they dived headlong into the sea!

After this somewhat inauspicious arrival, we disembarked and were taken to Palisadoes, in those days a naval airfield a little to the south-east of Kingston. Here we were given a warm welcome and fine airy cabins; and that afternoon the CO, Jack Teesdale and I took charge of our four Swordfish (numbers W5966, W5968, W5973 and V4719) and the squadron's mobile equipment. These aircraft and their accoutrements – bombs, torpedoes, spare parts, spare compasses and servicing apparatus etc. – had been left for us several months earlier by HMS *Furious* when she had called at Kingston, *en route* to Norfolk, Virginia, where she was due for a refit.

At last we were a proper squadron, with aircraft. And it seemed we were in the right place at the right time. For that evening we were told that U-boats were shelling the oil installations at Aruba, in the south of the Caribbean.

In fact our short stay in Jamaica turned out to be more enjoyable than eventful; though, as far as the U-boats were concerned, our mere presence may have been a deterrent – a state of affairs to be repeated many times in the years to come.

February 18 was a busy day for the ground crew. They worked flat out to get our four aircraft not only serviceable but operational. Airframes were tested, engines tuned, compasses swung, radios and machine guns checked. And the squadron's Fair Flying Log records that next day we ventured for the first time into the air: not anything dramatic or even useful, just the CO leading his four Swordfish on a "familiarization flight" over Kingston and its environs.

The sun, I remember, was warm, the sea a deeper-than-Mediterranean blue, the Jamaican jungle a brighter-than-emerald green. It was a different world from the cold grey reaches of the North Atlantic which were to be our stamping ground in the years to come.

Next day, 20 February, 1942, Taffy Jones and I flew the squadron's first operational sortie: an anti-submarine patrol.

Since anti-submarine patrols were what most of us would be doing over the next three years, some explanation of why they were so important and how they were carried out seems to me to be called for.

To say our job was to sink U-boats would be not only simplistic but misleading. Our theatre of war was the North Atlantic. This was the setting for a Homeric conflict on which the outcome of the war depended. "The battle of the Atlantic," wrote Churchill, "was the dominating factor all through the war. If we had lost that we would have lost everything." So the work we were called on to do was of some importance. This is worth emphasizing because much of our flying seemed at the time (and indeed seems in retrospect) unexciting, uneventful and apparently unrewarded: ever circling ships that we seldom saw, protecting them from an enemy we never met, most of our anti-submarine patrols were carried out either at night or out of visual range of the convoy we were guarding, while many of our aircrew never so much as sighted a U-boat during the whole of their active service. Nothing here, you might think, to fire the imagination! Nevertheless, it was squadrons like 835 operating from escort carriers which tipped the scales in our favour in the Battle of the Atlantic. For early in 1943, at a time when things were going badly, it was carrier-based aircraft which helped to turn the possibility of defeat into the certainty of victory.

To understand why our contribution was so vital – and so tardy – we need to know a little about the background to the Battle of the Atlantic.

In 1939 the Navy was ill-prepared to cope with the threat posed by German U-boats. There were several reasons for this. Between the wars senior naval officers had had a battleship, as distinct from a little ship, mentality. This is reflected by the fact that there were, in the words of the naval historian Captain Roskill, "voluminous instructions for the operation of the battle-fleet, but no instructions whatsoever for the defence of mercantile convoys". There seemed to be a general feeling that the introduction of a convoy system would be enough *per se* to keep the U-boats at bay; and this over-optimistic view was reinforced by the Navy's faith in its Asdic (now known as Sonar), an acoustic device for detecting and homing-in on underwater objects. Asdic was indeed a key weapon – if we hadn't had it, the U-boats would have run rampant – but it had limitations; it was difficult to operate in bad weather, it had a relatively short range, contact was lost at close quarters, and the depth of the object detected was hard to estimate. In short, although the Navy recognized that in the event of war a convoy system would be needed, they lacked the warships, the commitment and the training to ensure that convoys were adequately protected; in particular they lacked even a single purpose-built escort-carrier to provide a convoy with air cover.

If the allies were ill-prepared in 1939 to defend their merchant ships, the Germans were equally ill-prepared to attack them. It is now known that Hitler hadn't expected war to break out until 1943. On this assumption, he had authorized the building of a high seas fleet (two superbattleships, two battlecruisers, three pocket battleships and an aircraft carrier) in the hope of challenging British Naval supremacy. U-boats were accorded a low priority. Few were built; and when war did break out – prematurely from the point of view of the German Navy – they had no more than twenty-two operational submarines, several of which could be used only in coastal waters.

On the first day of war a U-boat, contrary to orders, attacked and sank the passenger liner *Athenia*; the Admiralty at once introduced the convoy system, and the protagonists settled down to a period of low-key skirmishing which bore little relationship to the holocaust to come. The Germans had so few U-boats and such unfavourably-placed bases that they were unable to mount a sustained offensive. The allies had so few warships they were hard-pressed to defend their convoys against even such spasmodic attacks as were mounted against them. During this stage of the "phoney" war many merchantmen preferred sailing solo to sailing in convoy, and it is easy to see why. Ships like the *Andalucia Star* were fine fast vessels, and their captains were experienced seamen used to operating on their own initiative, and impatient of the slow speed and loss of freedom which were the price of sailing in convoy. During the winter of 1939/40 allied ships in the Atlantic got away with the sort of solo voyages and lightly defended convoys which would have been suicidal a year later. It would perhaps be unfair to say that the

Admiralty was lulled into a sense of false security by this; it *would*, however, be fair to say that they failed to address the problem of convoy-protection with the urgency which subsequent events were to prove was called for.

The skirmishing gave way to something more serious when France fell and the allies withdrew from Norway. For then the U-boats, which had been steadily increasing in number, found themselves presented with a whole chain of ocean-facing ports from the Barents Sea to the Bay of Biscay. To reach allied shipping lanes they no longer had to make long and hazardous voyages from ports like Wilhelmshaven, they were able to get there safely in a matter of hours from ports like Brest. The U-boats stepped up their attacks. Allied losses escalated. And the Navy was now made to pay for the low priority it had accorded convoy-protection duties between the wars. When it was realized that solo-sailing merchantmen were being picked off one by one, all ships were ordered to sail in convoy. This meant that the size and number of convoys increased; and this in turn resulted in an added workload being placed on the escorting warships which were already stretched to breaking point. There simply weren't enough destroyers and corvettes to do the job. During the winter of 1940/41 the situation became so bad that if a warship guarding a convoy located a submerged U-boat it couldn't stay behind to hunt it for fear of leaving a gap in the convoy's threadbare defences. Between July, 1940, and March, 1941, U-boats in the Atlantic sank over two million tons of allied shipping. No wonder German submariners called this "the Happy Time"!

However, both the Royal and Merchant Navies have a long tradition of resilience. They weathered the storm, albeit at a terrible price, and the Battle of the Atlantic settled down into a long bruising war of attrition. To start with the U-boats had the upper hand; but towards the middle of 1941 counter-measures taken by the allies began to have effect. A special command – Western Approaches – was set up to co-ordinate both an overall strategy against the U-boats and day-by-day tactics. The Ultra cryptographers at Bletchley deciphered the German code, so that transmissions between the U-boats and their headquarters could be not only intercepted but understood and acted on. Corvettes and destroyers (and in particular the Flower-class corvettes) which had been laid down at the start of the war began to come into service. And, perhaps most important of all, Coastal Command was placed under the jurisdiction of the Navy, and long-range Catalinas and Liberators were soon carrying out anti-submarine patrols not only offshore but deep into the Atlantic.

The Germans also had their successes. They captured two French destroyers which were equipped with Asdic, and this enabled them to assess the equipment's weaknesses. They altered their transmitting code, and it was some time before Bletchley were able to crack the new one. They brought improved U-boats into service. Some of the latter, like the Type IXc, were able to dive to over 1,000 feet, although the British remained convinced they could only go to 550 feet and continued to set their depth-charges to explode at this maximum depth. As the battle ebbed and flowed both combatants suffered heavy losses.

Then, at the end of 1941, the killing-ground shifted. America entered the war.

The US Navy were reluctant to introduce convoys, and throughout the early months of 1942 their warships and merchantmen continued to sail individually. For this they paid a terrible price. The U-boats flocked to the eastern seaboard of the United States and picked off the unprotected vessels one by one. Tankers were an especially favoured target, many of these great ships going down in flames within sight of the shore. When the Americans did at last bring in a convoy system in the North Atlantic, the U-boats moved south into the Caribbean and the estuary of the River Plate, where the slaughter continued. This was known to German submariners as "the Second Happy Time".

By the middle of 1942 virtually all allied ships in virtually all parts of the world were sailing in convoy. This had the effect of concentrating the war in the Atlantic into a succession of running battles, with "wolf-packs" of German U-boats (sometimes as many as forty at a time) attacking convoys which were relatively well defended. The result was a bitter, protracted, seesaw battle, fought without mercy but also for the most part without rancour, often in appalling weather, and for high stakes. If a convoy became scattered, it could be virtually annihilated; this is what happened to the ill-fated PQ17, which lost twenty-three out of its thirty-six merchantmen *en route* to Russia. If, on the other hand, the escorting warships and aircraft managed to keep the U-boats at bay, then the entire convoy might get through without loss. And this, rather than the actual sinking of a U-boat, was the overriding objective of the convoy escorts. They were, to quote C.S. Forester's analogy, "good shepherds guarding their flock".

So when our squadron did, at last, get round to providing air cover for convoys, we saw the merchantmen we were circling as *"our"* merchantmen, *"our"* flock to be protected at all costs from the marauding wolf-packs.

So much for the nature of the work we would soon be doing. But what, specifically, did this work entail? What *was* an anti-submarine patrol?

From our first operational sortie to our last, the aircraft we used for our patrols were Swordfish: initially the Swordfish Mark II with a crew of three, latterly the Swordfish MKIII with a crew of two. Mark II Swordfish lacked the sophisticated equipment which, in the final stages of the war, enabled us to home on U-boats and circle convoys in the dark relying almost entirely on instruments. Everything at first had to be done visually, and in the early days each of the three aircrew had his specific duties, which included keeping a lookout for surfaced U-boats.

The observer was very often captain of the aircraft. This was a legacy of the inter-war years when it was thought, with some justification, that pilots needed a navigator when flying over the sea to stop them getting lost, and that, as it was the observer who decided the aircraft's movements, it was he who should be in command. All Fleet Air Arm observers went through a thorough and demanding training, the basic objective of which was to enable them to keep a dead-reckoning plot: i.e. a chart on which they recorded their aircraft's course, track and speed, so at any one moment they could tell exactly where they were and their bearing and distance from base. Keeping such a plot was a lot easier said than done. One variable was the wind, which could blow an aircraft – and especially a slow-moving Swordfish – way off course. Another variable were the compasses, which were affected by the aircraft's individual magnetic field and had to be constantly corrected. Yet another was the pilot, who, through indolence or incompetence, might not be flying the precise course he had been told to. Among an observer's other duties was wind-finding; this involved dropping a smoke float, flying round it on the four sides of a rectangle, then calculating the wind's strength and direction from the amount by which the plane had been blown off its starting point. It was also an observer's job to operate the aircraft's homing beacon and, on Mark III Swordfish, the radio and the invaluable air-to-sea radar. At first the observer's cockpit, though open to the elements, was reasonably roomy. However, as more and increasingly sophisticated equipment was loaded into it, the unfortunate observer found he had barely room to sit down and was surrounded by so many devices that he needed double-jointed arms and backward-facing eyes to operate them – hence the evolution of a new species *Homo Swordfish (O)*.

The pilot was responsible for handling the aircraft and its offensive armament (bombs, torpedos, depth-charges or rocket-projectiles). Swordfish were easy to fly, being robust and reliable – the antithesis of their intended successor, the Barracuda. Although they were slow and had virtually no defensive armament, they were regarded with affection by their pilots: an affection epitomized in *The Stringbag Song*, sung at many a wardroom party to the tune of *My Bonnie Lies over the Ocean*:

*Homo-Swordfish (O)*. Fur, bladder and diet as Homo-Swordfish (P). Has vast brain for storing courses, winds, speeds, codes etc. Its eyes revolve on small cranks: a for'ard eye to follow rotations on radar screen; an aft eye (on tip of tail) to enable radio to be tuned. Ears supersensitive to pick up even non-existent signals. Vocal cords well developed to yell at mentally deficient Homo-Swordfish (Ps). Left arm is double-jointed, usually hooked behind back to play with 1460. Right hand has two pointed fingers to form dividers. Legs very short, enabling it to hop round cockpit. Left leg telescopic, armed with heavy boot for kicking ASVX. This species faces extinction.

"My Stringbag flies over the ocean,
My Stringbag flies over the sea.
If it wasn't for King George's Swordfish
Where the hell would the Royal Navy be?"

Torpedo-dropping requires precision flying and considerable skill; dropping bombs, depth-charges and rocket-projectiles, on the other hand, is mainly a matter of practice. The staid old Swordfish was simply put into a not-too-steep dive and aimed at its target; the weapons were then launched by the press of a button. However, we soon found there was one big disadvantage to this type of attack. The Swordfish was so slow that most U-boats detected our approach on their Metox-tube radar and submerged to a safe depth before they were even sighted. The pilot's cockpit, like the observer's, was open; this made flying in the Caribbean extremely pleasant, but flying north of the Arctic Circle less so. The layout was good. Nonetheless in the Swordfish Mark III the pilot, like the observer, eventually found himself with more apparatus than he could comfortably reach. Also, because the later models of the Swordfish were so festooned with equipment, they were aerodynamically less efficient and had to be landed in a "nose-up" attitude; this meant that, approaching the aircraft-carrier, the engine cowling tended to get in the pilot's line of vision, and to have a clear view of the batsman (the deck-landing officer controlling the plane's approach) the pilot had to lean out and peer into the slipstream. Hence the evolution of another new species *Homo Swordfish (P)*.

The telegraphist air gunner occupied the rear cockpit. His most important job was to maintain W/T or R/T communication with base, be it airfield or carrier. For this he was equipped with a T1155/R1154 transmitter-receiver, which was crystal controlled and could be fine-tuned by varying the length of its trailing aerial. In theory this somewhat Heath Robinson apparatus had a range of 100 miles, but in practice it was usually a good deal less. His other piece of equipment was even more archaic: a single gas-operated 303 machine gun. With this cumbersome relic from the First World War he was expected to keep down the heads of the U-boats' gun-crews as the Swordfish dived in to the attack. Since whenever he fired forward he was liable to shoot off his Swordfish's wings, if not his pilot's and observer's heads, the feasibility of this is questionable!

A TAG's training involved learning the Morse Code and flag and semaphore signalling; he had to be proficient in transmitting and receiving all types of radio signals, and was responsible for the maintenance of his equipment. Most TAGs were leading airmen. They faced all the dangers and discomforts of operational flying without enjoying any of the

*Homo-Swordfish (P)*. Fur-covered to keep out cold. Three gallon bladder for long patrols. Diet: cold ersatz coffee and bully beef (when permitted by "Fat Jack".) Streamlined head situated on left shoulder to see over oiled-up windscreen. For deck-landing, left eye goes out to port to watch batsman, right eye lowered to watch air speed indicator. Ears have built-in volume controls to eliminate unwanted noise (i.e. Homo-Swordfish (O)). Left foot enormous to cope with Oscar. Left arm 5′6″ long and treble-jointed so that RATOG-jettison, oil heater etc. can be operated as well as bomb distributor, throttle etc. Right arm double-jointed to reach fire extinguisher and IFF. This species too is in danger of extinction.

privileges of officer-status. About halfway through the war it was realized that, in Swordfish, they were somewhat *de trop*; for their radio could be operated by the observer, and their cumbersome machine gun frightened only their fellow aircrew. By 1944 most squadrons were equipped with Mark III Swordfish, in which the TAG's cockpit was integrated with the observer's and the TAG himself had been superseded by a complexity of air-to-sea radar equipment. In retrospect it seems a pity that these young men, the cream of the lower deck, all of whom had volunteered for flying duties, were not given greater opportunities. As one of them put it, "With a little training in the essentials of Air Navigation, we could have helped the observers a lot."

So our anti-submarine patrols from Palisadoes were like the simplest of the exercises we had done in training. We were given an area somewhere off Jamaica to search; I projected the area on to my chart and worked out the courses we needed to fly and the times we needed to fly them; and Taffy Jones could have done the required flying (metaphorically speaking) with his eyes shut. Visibility was nearly always good. The sun was nearly always shining. Jamaica is a large island, a base which even the most incompetent navigator could hardly fail to return to. The German U-boats were conspicuous by their absence. Few squadrons can have had a more idyllic initiation to war.

As far as I was concerned, my only moments of danger were a little after take-off and a little prior to landing. For Taffy Jones discovered that on the suburban patios of Kingston young ladies could frequently be seen sunbathing *déshabillé*, and mindful of Nelson's dictum that naval officers should ever engage their targets more closely, he felt duty bound to try some low-level reconnaissance. On one occasion, the sight of a lumbering Swordfish piloted by a libidinous Welshman coming straight at her at a height of less than 15 feet was too much for a pregnant mother; it precipitated a premature (but happily safe) birth. An official complaint brought an official reprimand, and the end of Taffy's low flying.

Other members of the squadron found other dangers in Kingston. Taffy Jones, Johnny Hunt and the two Jacks (Teesdale and Parker) went ashore there one evening to settle a bet: to see who could get the best offer from the ladies of the Red Light area. Taffy won at a canter, with an offer to accommodate him for 6d. Only after the bet had been paid did he reveal that the offer had been conditional – a sort of bulk discount: his three colleagues were expected to participate on the same terms!

I avoided these dangers, though not for a reason I would have wished. And if the incident I am about to recall seems petty, I only mention it

1. The original Squadron, February, 1942, taken at HMS *Buzzard*,
RN Air Station, Palisadoes, Kingston, Jamaica.
Back Row L. to R.: Jack Teesdale, Stan Thomas, Barry Barringer,
Jack Parker.
Front Row L. to R.: Johnnie Hunt, Gwynne Jones, the C.O. Johnnie
Johnstone, and Robin Shirley-Smith.
Barry Barringer is the only survivor of this group.

2.  The Squadron, November, 1942; taken at HMS *Landrail*, RN Air
Station Machrihanish.
Back Row L. to R.: Bob Selley, Jimmy Urquhart, David Newbery,
John McCormick, George Sadler, Johnny Hunt, John Winstanley.
Front Row L. to R.: Jack Teesdale, Jack Cramp, Gwynne Jones, Hank
Housser, the C.O. J.R. Lang, Robin Shirley-Smith, Barry Barringer,
Stan Thomas, Jack Parker.

3.  The fighter pilots of 835 Squadron — early 1945.
L. to R.: Pete Blanco, George Gordon, Sam Mearns, Al Burgham,
Bill Armitage, Ken Atkinson.
Squatting: D.J. Edwards, Norman Sargent.

4. HMS *Nairana* with four
white Sea Hurricanes ranged
for'ard of the barrier.

5. HMS *Battler*.

6. HMS *Furious* in heavy seas.

Some of the aircraft flown by the Squadron:

7. Fairey Swordfish II.

8. Hawker Sea Hurricane II c.

9. Grumman Martlet II (Wildcat).

because it shows the antipathy that sometimes existed between RN and RNVR(A) officers.

One evening Taffy Jones and I had been flying an anti-submarine patrol. On landing, I supervised the securing of the aircraft, cleared the signals log and hurried into the wardroom for dinner dressed in informal but immaculately clean white tropical rig. About the first person I almost bumped into was the duty officer, a Lieutenant RN, dressed in the formal stiff-necked No. 10 white dress-uniform, known to the initiated as "death by choking". He told me I was improperly dressed, and ordered me to "get into the proper rig". In the argument that followed he got more and more pompous and I got more and more angry until I was rash enough to tell him to "bugger off". Next morning, inevitably, I was summoned to the Captain's office. I could detect some sympathy in Captain Hawkins's eyes; but I *had* been grossly insubordinate, and he had no option but to punish me. I found myself duty officer for the rest of our stay in Palisadoes, barred from leaving the airfield.

Luckily this was by no means an arduous chore. Nor did it last long. For on 12 March we received a signal ordering us to Norfolk, Virginia.

Our first thought was that we would be embarking on one of the newly built US escort-carriers.

Then we saw that the signal ended: "and proceed HMS *Furious*".

★   ★   ★

Moving a squadron lock stock and barrel (aircraft, personnel, equipment and weapons) 1500 miles by sea and land over unfamiliar terrain calls for careful planning. Since our CO had ensconced himself in the luxury of the Myrtle Bank Hotel in Kingston, the move was master-minded by our more than competent Stores Officer, Jack Teesdale.

Jack and I decided that we needed a sea-and-land contingent and an air contingent. The former, consisting of two observers, most of the squadron's ground crew and all of its weapons and stores, would proceed to Jacksonville on the coast of Florida by sea, and thence to Norfolk by train. The latter, consisting of four pilots flying the Swordfish, with two observers, two TAGs and four maintenance personnel as passengers would fly to Norfolk via Puerta Camaguey, Havana, Miami, Jacksonville, Charleston and Pope Field.

If any of the sea-and-land party had visions of another *Andalucia Star*-style cruise, they were quickly disillusioned. They were told they would be sailing in the SS *Allister*, a very small and very ancient merchantman which had been built on the Clyde a good many years before the *First* World War. The *Allister* had ended up in the Caribbean, ferrying soft fruit between the islands and the mainland of the United States. Since Pearl Harbor and the entry of America into the war, she had lain at anchor off Kingston, becoming filthier and filthier because the harbour authorities refused her permission to dump rubbish into the harbour. She had recently been chartered by an American speculator to run a cargo of bananas to Florida, and 835 Squadron had been added to her manifest as an afterthought.

The Squadron stores were packed into twenty-seven crates and given a bill of lading. Jack then discovered to his dismay that he was also expected to take with him four torpedoes, which had been left behind by the *Furious*. He was given a crash course in handling, slinging and storing torpedoes and their warheads, and the fearsome-looking "fish" were loaded into special cases. For security reasons, these cases were labelled "Request 137", which was the US Navy's job number for the refit of the *Furious*; they were not mentioned in the bill of lading, an omission which was soon to cause some panic.

On 18 March Jack and I went to the docks in Kingston to supervise the loading of our stores onto the *Allister*, only to find our way blocked by decidedly militant pickets who told us the dockers were on strike. My reaction was to enlist the help of an RN Chief Petty Officer – a species well able, if the need arises, to eat pickets for breakfast – and six able seamen. However, by the time my reinforcements had arrived, Jack had had a good-humoured chat with the dockers' union leader and had been given permission to bring the stores onto the quay and load them ourselves. The union leader, Jack said, was "a very pleasant fellow called Mr Bustamente" – he later became Prime Minister of Jamaica.

The stores were swung aboard, the sea-going party embarked, and at dawn next morning the *Allister* set course for Jacksonville. At the last moment Jack was handed a somewhat inauspicious signal. It read: "You are to organize anti-submarine lookouts to keep watch in whatever West Indian ports you touch, and at sea."

The moment the *Allister* cleared Kingston harbour Jack Teesdale and his second-in-command Jack Parker set about cleaning up their cabins; the maintenance personnel set about cleaning up their quarters in the fo'c'sle, and by the end of the day the ancient merchantman was looking positively spick and span. The squadron then settled down to a leisurely six-day passage to Jacksonville.

The sun was warm; the sea was sapphire-blue, the passing islands emerald-green. What could have been more pleasant? Although the round-the-clock watch for U-boats was a reminder of potential serpents in paradise.

Jack Teesdale got on particularly well with the *Allister*'s captain, who, like all his crew, was a Cayman Islander. They spent long hours together on the bridge, with Jack learning navigation the practical way. To his amazement the captain used neither charts nor sextants; nor did he have a radio;

he said he simply "knew the way". And his lack of conventional aids certainly didn't impair his efficiency. For he made accurate landfalls off Port Morant and Port Antonio to take aboard more bananas, and a couple of days later off the southernmost keys of Florida. Jack admitted later that, as they headed up the Florida coast, he was extremely nervous. For in the seaboard towns there was no sort of blackout; life appeared to be going on as though the war was 1000 miles away; and as the *Allister* wallowed slowly northward she must have been silhouetted against a blaze of neon and arc lights. Jack could only assume she was too small a target for the U-boats to waste a torpedo on her.

The squadron were thankful to arrive safely at Jacksonville on the Florida/Georgia border.

What followed was the stuff of comic opera. First to come aboard was the British Consul, an excessively polite young man who said he had not the slightest idea what Jack Teesdale's orders were but that he had been told to give him as much money as he needed to carry them out. Jack was sorely tempted to tell him the Squadron was *en route* for Sydney!

Next to arrive were a gaggle of US officials who began asking somewhat awkward questions about the *Allister*'s cargo. Jack told them firmly that he was on operational duties and needed to get his personnel, his stores and his torpedoes unloaded without delay. The mention of torpedoes caused consternation – indeed panic – since they had not been included in the Bill of Lading. The head of the local fire department was hastily summoned, and the *Allister* was even more hastily moved to the remotest possible berth. This, however, caused a problem. The dockers working at the remote berth belonged to a different union to the dockers working at the original berth; neither was pleased by the altered arrangements for unloading, and both downed tools and went on strike. The weather got hotter and hotter and more and more humid. The bananas started to rot. This was the cue for the Port Health Officer to get in on the act. He declared the bananas a potential health hazard and ordered the crew to unload and destroy them. Eventually the *Allister*'s deck was sufficiently clear for Jack to get at his torpedoes, which by this time were awash with molten banana. Surrounded by great clouds of flies, the torpedoes were swung ashore, while the local fire brigade stood apprehensively by, hoses at the ready. Jack then had the dreaded "fish" hosed down and loaded on to a specially chartered train.

The squadron maintenance personnel, meanwhile, had been given forty-eight hours leave, and had descended en masse on Jacksonville, where the good citizens feted them right royally, under the misapprehension they were fighter pilots. For that evening the local newspaper had a headline reporting that "a flight of British Spitfires" was passing through *en route* to Norfolk – probably the only time in the war our ancient biplanes were mistaken for the world's most elegant monoplane fighter!

Next morning the ground party, some of them decidedly the worse for wear, left by train for Norfolk, with Jack Parker in charge. Jack Teesdale tidied up the bureaucratic odds and ends, made sure the British Consul had paid all the bills, then – taking a leaf out of the CO's book – followed his ground crew on the same train journey but in the comfort of a Pullman coach.

While this saga was unfolding, the air party were getting ready to fly from Kingston to Norfolk.

Our route lay via Camaguey and Havana (in Cuba), across the Straits of Florida to Miami, then via Jacksonville, Charleston and Pope Field to Norfolk. My first job was to try and get hold of an Admiralty chart for the Caribbean part of the flight. However, much to my consternation, I was told no such charts were available. I had therefore to borrow an atlas from the local school and project from it an extremely elementary map by which to navigate. As a back-up, I told our telegraphist-air-gunner to establish contact on a commercial wavelength with Pan American Airlines who I knew operated out of Camaguey and Havana.

With these somewhat tentative arrangements, our four Swordfish took off in the early hours of 22 March and headed in loose V-formation for Cuba.

It was a sunny but hazy morning, made hazier still by the CO's addiction to chain-smoking while he was flying – which was not only against regulations but highly dangerous. Nor was my concentration helped by our eccentric TAG, Petty Officer Duggan, who insisted every now and then on taking off his flying boots and sticking his bare feet out of the cockpit and into the slipstream. This, he said, was good for his "desert feet": an euphemism, I suspected, for athlete's foot. In spite of these distractions, I had no difficulty finding Cuba. Finding Camaguey, which was somewhere in the middle of the island, was another matter. The haze seemed to be thickening; my primitive chart was useless, and since there seemed to be neither roads nor towns I had little idea over which part of Cuba we were flying; it all looked depressingly similar – mountainous and heavily wooded – not the place for an emergency landing. I asked Duggan to request bearings from Camaguey, but he got no reply. I was beginning to get a bit worried when I spotted an airliner above the haze. It seemed to be losing height and I reckoned it might be making for Camaguey. We followed it, and ten minutes later the airport emerged out of a miasma of cloud and mist.

A quick lunch, while the Swordfish were refuelled, then we were on our way to Havana.

This was an easier, though slightly longer, flight. All we had to do was follow the north coast of Cuba until the capital appeared over the rim of our engine cowlings. We landed a little before dark, to find ourselves metamorphosed by the local press and radio to "a squadron of Spitfires". This was almost certainly the origin of the misconception about our maintenance personnel when they arrived a couple of days later in Jacksonville. Anyhow, the CO now came into his own. He gave curt instructions to the Cuban airport officials to look after our planes, disdainfully waved away the customs officers and told the British Consul that only the best accommodation was good enough for his aircrew. So we found ourselves ensconced in the luxurious Hotel Nacional, in those days undoubtedly the best in Havana. It was Sunday. There was, inevitably, a festival. The streets were full of cafés, people, processions, floats, music, dancing, girls. Perhaps it was our transformation to Spitfire pilots. Perhaps it was our unfamiliar and exotic uniform. Perhaps it was simply Cuban *joie de vivre*. It was a night to remember.

Next day we crossed the Straits of Florida and landed at a US training aerodrome near Miami. The monoplanes which the US pilots were learning to fly were a good deal faster and more modern-looking than our archaic biplanes, and as our four aircraft waddled round the perimeter-track they were subject to the sort of incredulous stares accorded to the dinosaur skeletons in a museum. That evening, however, we pointed out to our hosts that a Swordfish could carry almost as heavy a bomb-load as a Flying Fortress, and that twenty of them had crippled half the Italian fleet in Taranto Harbour. Since the American fleet had just suffered a similar mauling at the hands of the Japanese in Pearl Harbor, this silenced criticism.

We spent 48 hours in Miami, staying in yet another luxury hotel. It was called the McAllister; and as though to underline the coincidence, on the night we stayed there the rest of the squadron were only a couple of miles away *en route* to Jacksonville in their old banana-boat the *Allister*. The names may have been similar, but the standard of accommodation could hardly have been more different.

The penultimate airfield we touched down at was Pope Field, a US Army Air Force base devoid of both character and comfort. We could only get into our rooms – which were dusty and poorly ventilated – by inserting coins through a slot in the door, and everything had to be paid for on the spot in US dollars. Maybe we had been spoiled by the luxury of the Nacional and the McAllister, but we left Pope Field without regret, and that evening arrived at our destination.

Norfolk, Virginia, lies at the entrance to Chesapeake Bay and is one of the older and more attractive home ports of the US Navy. Its ship-building and repair yards are among the finest in the world, and in 1942 they were working at full capacity. Many allied warships in the Second World War – like the *Furious* – limped into Norfolk crippled and left whole. Virginia has a tradition of hospitality; and certainly the naval officers with whom we liaised couldn't have been kinder or more helpful. They went out of their way not only to see we had everything we needed but to make us feel at home.

Our ground party and stores had reached Norfolk the day before. We were glad to have the squadron reunited and once more a coherent unit. And on 29 March we were ordered to embark in the *Furious*.

The carrier lay berthed in the repair yards, the contractors' scaffolding still clinging to her like matchsticks to a leviathan. There was clearly no possibility of flying-on the Swordfish; they would have to be hoisted aboard by crane; and the supervision of this somewhat complex operation was entrusted to Jack Teesdale. For once he made a mistake. And what a mistake!

It was agreed that the Swordfish (with wings folded) would be taxied to a nearby quay and lowered into a lighter; the lighter would then be towed alongside *Furious* and the aircraft hoisted aboard. Jack was ordered to beg, borrow or steal a lighter and crane to carry out this move. Logically enough, he decided that the ideal thing would be to get hold of a lighter-and-crane combined; so this is what he asked the Americans for. He had a hard time persuading the US admiral in charge of the dockyard to provide this particular equipment, but eventually a huge floating-crane which had been installing gun-turrets into a US battleship stopped work and was towed by five tugs halfway across the harbour to the quay where the Swordfish were waiting. When the captain of the *Furious* saw what was happening he nearly had a fit. What he had expected Jack to get was a small (or in technical terms a "dumb") lighter, and to use a small (or dockside) crane to lower the Swordfish into it, then to use the carrier's own crane to swing the Swordfish aboard; but our unfortunate stores officer had produced an extremely large sledge-hammer to crack a very diminutive nut! Happily the captain was fair-minded enough to blame not Jack but the lack of technical clarity in his orders. How he placated the US admiral, the captain of the battleship *sans* turrets, the captain of the floating-crane and the captains of the five tugs is not known. However, since no formal complaint was recorded, it seems that these gentlemen must have had a sense of humour!

While the squadron settled down into what for most of us was our first operational carrier, the contractors' débris was cleared away. On 2 April *Furious* did a test run in the Norfolk Roads. Next day we put to sea.

It looked as though our participation in the battle of the Atlantic was about to begin.

★　★　★

Our new home could best be described as "historic".

*Furious* had been laid down in 1915 as a giant cruiser. However, after a couple of years her gun turrets were replaced by a wooden flight-deck and she was handed over to the Royal Naval Air Service for trials. On 3 August, 1917, Squadron Commander Dunning successfully landed his Sopwith "Pup" on her flight-deck – the first ever landing to be achieved on a ship underway. One might have thought that, having pioneered this basic step in naval aviation, *Furious* between the wars would at least have been able to keep abreast of progress in her specialized field. Unfortunately the RAF, who controlled the purse strings, wanted to see naval aviation downgraded not upgraded; no funds were made available for new equipment; and in the early 1930s, at a time when all US carriers were fitted with efficient arrester-wires, the Navy's premier carrier was having to put sandbags across her flight-deck to stop her aircraft, on landing, from toppling over the bow. She was downgraded to training and in 1939 had aboard only six Swordfish and four Skuas.

Nevertheless and in spite of her age, *Furious* had a fine record in the Second World War. She helped in the search for the *Graf Spee*, took part in operations off Norway, escorted a quite incredible number of Atlantic, Russian and Malta convoys, ferried aircraft to Africa and played a leading role in air strikes against the *Tirpitz*. It has been claimed that she covered more miles on active service than any other allied warship: all things considered a remarkable achievement, although you may think it a reflection on the Navy's planning that their most overworked warship in the Second World War was a makeshift aircraft-carrier which had been cobbled together from an unwanted cruiser in the First.

How much easier the Battle of the Atlantic would have been, and how many thousands of ships and tens of thousands of lives would have been saved, if we had had half as many battleships and twice as many aircraft-carriers.

835 Squadron played only a very minor role in the exploits of the *Furious*: we were with her for just the one convoy. But this convoy was, for most of us, our first taste of serious operations – and for Johnnie Johnstone and me it was very nearly our last.

We rendezvoused with part of our convoy during the night – several troopships and three destroyers. We then headed south for the Caribbean, where we expected to pick up more ships before proceeding to the British Isles.

The CO and I took off at 0645 on the dawn patrol. It was fine but misty, and we knew the forecast was not good. As we circled the convoy we eyed our merchantmen much as a sheepdog might eye a flock to be driven, looking for potential troublemakers: the sort of ancient vessel whose top speed was a couple of knots less than everyone else's, and who was liable to belch out great globules of telltale smoke. However, it looked as though on this occasion we were lucky; the merchantmen all seemed to be large and fast, and we were heading south at a fair rate of knots, each ship leaving behind it a straight well-defined wake.

I liked the dawn patrol; apart from the pleasure of seeing the sunrise, which often seemed more spectacular from 500 feet than from sea-level, it always seemed to give me a good appetite for breakfast. This first patrol was uneventful, and we landed back on the *Furious* at 0915.

The CO and I were about to sit down to our bacon and eggs when we were called to the bridge. A garbled SOS was being picked up. It seemed that a tanker, about 100 miles to the north, was being shelled by a U-boat. It was decided to send a Swordfish to the rescue; and since none of the other aircrew had experience in this sort of mission, the job was given to the CO and me.

While our plane was being quickly refuelled, I was briefed by the Senior Operations Officer. It seemed to me that since the U-boat was way to the north and the convoy was heading rapidly south, we would need to be especially careful (a) that we didn't run out of fuel, and (b) that we always kept track of exactly where the *Furious* was. I therefore asked the SSO if, as a back-up to my dead reckoning plot, *Furious* would transmit radio bearings (if we asked for them) so that on our return we could get an accurate fix on the carrier's position. This he said he would do. So we took off and flew north.

After about an hour we arrived in the area where we ought to have found a tanker, but there was nothing to be seen except sea, low clouds, mist and sky. We decided to carry out a square search: i.e. to fly along the four sides of an ever-expanding square, the length of the sides being determined by the limits of visibility. After some forty minutes of fruitless searching, I shifted the axis of our square to the east and tried again, but again without success. It seemed unlikely that in so short a time the tanker could have gone down without trace; so we could only assume her position had been reported incorrectly. Since we had the promise of radio bearings, should we need them, to help us find the carrier, I continued the search until the last possible moment; but eventually a combination of worsening weather and dwindling fuel obliged us to return. I had every confidence in my navigation, and didn't anticipate my difficulty finding the *Furious*; but when, at the end of four hours' flying, we got back to the spot where we expected to find the convoy, it wasn't there. Once again, we could see nothing but sea, low cloud and ever-thickening mist. For the first time in my career as a navigator, I had to admit I was lost.

Duggan called up the carrier to request the radio bearings we had been promised, but there was no reply. He tried again and again and again, but each request met the same depressing silence.

We threw an aluminium seamarker over the side, and while the CO circled it and Duggan continued his transmissions, I checked and rechecked my navigational calculations. I could find no error. *We* were where we ought to be. The convoy wasn't.

To say I was worried would be an understatement. We now had fuel for only about twenty-five minutes' flying and, while Duggan continued his plea for bearings, and the CO lit yet another cigarette, I had to make up my mind what to do. I decided our best bet would be to head south-east for Bermuda. We hadn't a hope of getting there; but, assuming we ditched, survived and managed to get into the aircraft's emergency dinghy, every mile we now covered would be a mile less to paddle.

We had been heading towards Bermuda for about ten minutes when, through the thickening haze, we unexpectedly sighted the convoy, steaming not south but east. We landed-on, after a flight of four hours and twenty-five minutes; and our groundcrew told us, later that evening, that when they checked the tanks there wasn't enough fuel in them to cover an upended sixpence.

At the end of our debriefing I said to the Senior Operations Officer, "Didn't you hear us? Asking for radio bearings?"

"Yes," he said. "We heard you."

"Then why the hell didn't you answer?"

He was very matter of fact. He offered no apology – and indeed when I'd calmed down and thought about it, I realized none was called for. "There was a U-boat," he said, "dead ahead. The convoy had to alter course."

And Johnstone and I saw at once that, if the *Furious had* answered our call, she would have revealed the convoy's position and altered course to the U-boat. The captain was absolutely right not to jeopardize his vessels for the sake of a single plane. This we accepted, but it didn't make us feel any the less expendable. By coincidence, only a few weeks later, on another convoy, two Swordfish of 836 Squadron, flying from HMS *Avenger*, were lost in exactly the same circumstances. We were lucky. They were not. War is seldom fair.

During the rest of the day close anti-submarine patrols were flown round the convoy, with Taffy Jones, Robin Shirley-Smith and Johnnie Hunt making their first deck-landings without difficulty. And our constant patrolling evidently kept the U-boats' heads down, for there were no attacks on the convoy. It is worth recording that only a month earlier, in much the same area, one of our convoys sailing *without* air cover suffered heavy losses.

Late that night we entered St George's Harbour in Hamilton, Bermuda, where we remained at anchor for forty-eight hours. Although there may have been U-boats within a few miles of the island, the war might have been taking place on another planet. The beaches were crowded with sunbathers, the restaurants had obviously never heard of rationing, and the shops were well stocked with luxuries – though rather less well stocked with silk stockings and perfume by the time we sailed.

Last to leave the island, as befitted his rank, was our elderly and slightly tipsy Paymaster Commander. As he boarded the pinnace he failed to notice that the bottom rung of the landing-ladder was missing and dropped with an almighty splash into the harbour. The boat's crew hauled him out and sat him streaming-wet in the stern. One of them handed him his cap and, although this was full of water, in accordance with the demands of naval etiquette, he put it on. It says much for his adherence to the tradition of the stiff upper lip that all the way to *Furious* he sat rigidly in the sternsheets, apparently oblivious to the ever-deepening pool of water in which he was sitting.

We sailed on 6 April, rendezvoused off the island with our now fully assembled convoy and set course for the Clyde.

We had an uneventful passage to the United Kingdom: uneventful, that is, as far as U-boats were concerned. The weather was another matter.

For three days the squadron flew continuous anti-submarine patrols, circling the convoy at a radius of either 15 or 20 miles, the first plane take-off half an hour before sunrise, the last landing-on in the twilight. We sighted no U-boats. But we soon had another adversary to contend with: the weather. Slowly the wind increased: 30, 40, 50 knots. The waves steepened, until huge rollers half-a-mile from crest to crest and 30 feet in height were thundering down on us out of the north. By 10 April conditions had become so bad that flying had to be cancelled.

*Furious* was not a good ship to be in in bad weather. Her flight-deck made her top-heavy, accentuating her every pitch and roll, while, because of her curious open structure, she took aboard vast quantities of water. Soon we were "shipping it green"; several of our ship's boats were crushed by waves breaking flush on top of them; water came swirling into our cabins, and at times the wardroom was literally awash. But worse was to come. Lashed down in the hangar were a number of American fighters – Corsairs and Wildcats – and the first of the American Avenger torpedo-bombers, being brought to the United Kingdom for trials. A ring-bolt securing one of the Wildcats to the deck of the hangar sheared under the strain and the plane began to break loose. As the maintenance crew rushed to secure it, an oil drum came cartwheeling across the deck, smashed into one of the aircraft and burst open. For several minutes the deck was like a nightmare skating rink as the maintenance crew fought to prevent the Wildcat breaking loose and turning the hangar into a scrap-yard of shattered aircraft. They did it. Luckily our four Swordfish escaped damage. And luckily none of our maintenance personnel was seriously injured.

That evening we passed through the heart of the storm and by the following morning, although conditions were difficult, we were able to resume flying. This was as well, for we were now coming up to the sea lanes north-west of Ireland, a happy hunting ground for the U-boats.

However, once again our Swordfish proved an effective deterrent. No attack was made on the convoy and the only excitement came when, in the middle of a patrol, the CO suddenly found to his horror that our Swordfish wasn't answering its controls. Somehow he managed to get back to the carrier and land-on. It was then discovered that, while the aircraft had been serviced, a roll of wing-fabric had been carelessly left beneath the floor of the pilot's cockpit and this had been spasmodically jamming both ailerons and elevators.

In my two-and-a-half years with the Squadron this is about the only case I can remember of our groundcrew letting us down.

In the early hours of 15 April the convoy dropped anchor in the Clyde and our first carrier-based operation came to an end.

We would have been more than happy to stay with the *Furious*, but it seemed as though the powers-that-be had other plans for us, for we were ordered to RNAS Lee-on-Solent, near Gosport in Hampshire.

The Swordfish flew there via Machrihanish and Sealand; the groundcrew followed by train via Glasgow, London and Portsmouth. The Squadron was then given a week's leave.

In view of what happened next, it might be stressed that our first taste of operations had been successful. Although 75 per cent of our aircrew had no previous experience of operational flying, we had carried out over 30 anti-submarine patrols from Jamaica and about the same number from *Furious* (many of the latter in difficult flying conditions) without sustaining the slightest injury to our aircrew or damage to our aircraft. And, what is more to the point, while the Squadron had been flying not a single warship or merchantman in the vicinity had been attacked, let alone damaged or sunk. These were not great achievements, but we reckoned they ought to guarantee us a continuing role in the Battle of the Atlantic – which in the spring of 1942 was not going well.

This, however, was not to be.

# 3

# *ADOLESCENCE*

Adolescence is often reckoned to be a frustrating time. Ours was. For between May, 1942, and November, 1943, the squadron was moved from place to place no fewer than sixteen times, and only once did we find ourselves aboard a carrier and actually doing the job for which we had been trained – escorting a convoy. The rest of the time we were "working up".

Working up is an euphemism for advanced specialized training, the idea being that aircrew should polish up their general flying and practise those special skills which are likely to stand them in good stead on forthcoming operations. Many great feats of flying in the Second World War owed their success to meticulous working up – the Swordfish attack on the Italian fleet in Taranto for example, or the Lancaster attack with bouncing bombs on the Möhne dam – and by and large this training was a great help to squadrons about to embark on carrierborne operations. However, working up *per se* achieved nothing; it was the means to an end, not an end in itself; for there is little point in perfecting one's skills if one is never given the opportunity to use them. And this is exactly what happened to 835 Squadron. For, the rest of 1942 and the better part of 1943 we were kept, like theatrical extras, ever "waiting in the wings", at a time when the Battle of the Atlantic was going badly, and we could have made (and knew we could have made) a valuable contribution.

However, in the spring of 1942 we had no idea of what was in store for us. Indeed we rather fancied the prospect of a little working up so that we could turn our reconstituted squadron into an effective fighting unit.

"Reconstituted" because, when we returned from leave to Lee-on-Solent, we found waiting for us six new aircraft, six new aircrew and a new Commanding Officer.

Our four original Swordfish, before we took them over, had been operating from *Furious* since the early days of the war. Our six new ones were the same Mark but more recently off the assembly line and powered by a Pegasus 30 engine rather than a Pegasus 3. Their numbers were DK 771-A, 769-B, 770-DE, 714-G and 684-H; and glancing, fifty years later, through the Squadron's Fair Flying Log, I see that we were flying the same faithful old aircraft in the autumn of 1943 as in the spring of 1942, a tribute to their sturdy construction and pilots' skill. As far as possible, each crew had their own plane, which helped to create a bond between aircrew and maintenance crew.

Our new pilots were, in alphabetical order, Harry (Hank) Housser, a large, flamboyant, somewhat opinionated lieutenant on loan from the Royal Canadian Navy. A barrister by profession, Harry had a slow drawl and a quick wit, and was one of those irrepressible, highly intelligent characters destined to make their mark any time, any place, in any company.

George Sadler was a straightforward down-to-earth Lancastrian who could be blunt to the point of rudeness, but whose judgement could seldom be faulted and who probably had more sound commonsense than the rest of the squadron put together. It was typical of George's sensible and practical approach that, when he was put in charge of aircrew parachutes, he insisted on going on a training course and becoming himself a most proficient parachute-packer.

Bob Selley was a small unsophisticated Devonian, whose first reaction to the goings-on in 835 Squadron was a breathless "Crumbs!" Harry Housser promptly christened him "Crumbie", and the name stuck. Bob turned out to be an outstanding pilot, surviving both the boredom of 1942/43 and the hazards of 1944/45. He flew more hours while serving with the squadron and did more deck-landings than anyone else – 562 hours and 207 deck-landings, many of the latter at night and in the most appalling conditions.

Jimmy Urquhart, a Scot, had been brought up in Lima, Peru, where his father was British Consul, and educated at Aberdeen Grammar School. Jimmy was generous to a fault, happy to lend his last penny to any of his large circle of friends. The trouble was he seemed invariably to have spent his last penny, and was forever raising loans on the security of his magnificent Urquhart kilt, which spent most of its life in hock awaiting the next pay day!

Our observers, again in alphabetical order, were John Lang, who was also our new Commanding Officer, a short, chubby-cheeked product of Dartmouth. Lt John Lang RN had seen service off Norway, on Atlantic convoys and in the Mediterranean, and as a result of more than eighteen months' continuous operational flying he had developed a twitch in his right eye, which led, unkindly but inevitably, to his being christened "Blinkie".

I have to admit that he and I got on about as well as oil and water. I saw him as the personification of those old-fashioned traditions of the Royal Navy which "hostilities only" aircrew like myself found irksome. He probably saw me as the personification of those brash young men of the Royal Naval Volunteer Reserve who preferred beer to pink gin and were prone to pass the port in the wrong direction. If the squadron had been kept busy with operational flying these differences would almost certainly have been recognized as trivial and disappeared. As it was, during long spells of enforced idleness, they festered. To put it mildly, we got on each other's nerves.

David Newbery was a quiet, handsome young man who, like myself when I first joined a squadron, had to suffer the indignity of being a Snotty or Midshipman. For if a pilot or observer completed his flying training before he was twenty he was commissioned not as a sub-lieutenant but as a temporary acting midshipman. This meant he often had to take orders from men with less flying experience than he had, simply because (in the words of Pitt the Elder) he "was guilty of the atrocious crime of being a young man".

Last but by no means least was John Winstanley, whose eyes were of a different colour. His comic appearance was something he played up to, pretending to be a buffoon, whereas in fact he was extremely shrewd and a born survivor. As evidence of the latter, he was found one morning after a party fully clothed in a bath of cold water. This was less disastrous than it might have been, because Winnie had almost as many items of uniform as the rest of the squadron put together, including a tropical pith helmet. The existence of this unusual piece of sartorial extravagance was revealed at another and particularly riotous party. Its owner was persuaded to bring it into the wardroom, where it was used for purposes other than that for which it had been designed – "after all," as someone said with a lisp, "it is a pith helmet, isn't it!"

To start with working up was fun. With the Battle of the Atlantic going badly, we were keen to achieve maximum operational efficiency so that we would be able and ready to embark on one of the newly built escort-carriers which, we knew, were now coming out of the US yards in ever increasing number. The pilots practised ADDLs (aerodrome dummy deck landings), ALTs (air launching of torpedoes), dive-bombing attacks, catapult launches (not to be recommended after a heavy session at "The Inn by the Sea"!) and air to air firing. Early in May the observers went north to RNAS Arbroath for a week's training on how to use our new air-to-surface-vessel radar.

This radar was the key to our battle with the U-boats. To quote a recently published book, *The Arctic Convoys, 1941–45* by Richard Woodman: "Once airborne radar made it impossible for U-boats to surface in safety, the game (for them) was up." I therefore make no apology for explaining how our radar worked in some detail.

A transmitter was positioned in the belly of the Swordfish. This emitted impulses which were reflected back from any solid object on the surface of the sea within a radius of about forty miles. The reflected impulses were picked up by receiving aerials positioned on the struts of the Swordfish's wings, and thence transmitted to a screen in the observer's cockpit. The observer looked into the screen, protected by a rubber visor, and saw the reflected impulses as a "blip". The centre of the screen was where the aircraft was; the top of the screen was dead ahead, the bottom dead astern. It was therefore easy for the observer to tell the pilot immediately what course to steer to home on to the "blip", which would hopefully turn out to be a surfaced U-boat. A further and, from our point of view, equally important use of radar was that it also picked up the ships of the convoy which the Swordfish was protecting, and this enabled the observer to know what course to steer to get back to the carrier. In 1944 a refinement known as BABS (Blind Approach Beacon System) was fitted to our radar sets. This brought a short range (10 mile) homing scale into operation. A central line, graduated in miles, bisected the screen and, by keeping the "blip" of the carrier dead-centre on this line, the aircraft could be homed almost literally onto the flight-deck.

The faithful old Swordfish accommodated this new equipment without complaint, just as she accommodated depth-charges, rocket-projectiles, additional passengers, luggage strapped to her fuselage and bicycles festooned from her wings, though it has to be admitted that as more and more weaponry was loaded into her, she put on weight, lost her performance, and became in silhouette more and more like an aerial clothesline.

With observers and pilots again reunited at Lee-on-Solent, our working up continued with only the occasional burst of excitement. On 2 June Bob Selley and I carried out tests with an experimental petrol bomb. This was being developed to counter the threat of a German invasion, which in the summer of 1942 was still considered possible if not probable. A couple of days later Bob and Jack Teesdale located a British submarine which was in difficulties in the Channel and shepherded it safely to Portsmouth. A couple of days after that there *was* an invasion: not of course the real thing, but one of those exercises "designed to keep our boys on their toes". Bob Selley recounts his role in it.

"It was close on midnight when a naval officer, resplendent in oilskins and gaiters, burst into the wardroom and called for volunteers to 'repel borders'. I gathered together a somewhat reluctant band of our maintenance personnel, and we set out to locate the 'enemy'. More by luck than judgement, we found two or three dozen of them asleep in a barn. The barn had a roof of corrugated iron. I got my men to collect a whole lot of small rocks, and at a given signal we lobbed them on to the corrugated iron roof. It must have been a rude awakening. An extremely irate major, wearing an umpire's armband, came rushing up to me.

"'What the hell do you think you're doing?'

"'Everyone in the barn is dead,' I told him. 'We've lobbed hand-grenades into them.'

"This obviously didn't fit in with preconceived plans for the 'invasion'. 'I'm the umpire,' he spluttered. 'I'll decide who's dead. You lot are eliminated!'

"I asked him if this meant that we could go back to bed; and, obviously eager to get rid of us, he agreed."

At the end of a pleasant if not particularly exciting month at Lee-on-Solent we were ordered to proceed to RNAS Hatston, in the Orkneys.

Hatston was adjacent to the anchorage of the Home Fleet in Scapa Flow, and, in our innocence, we thought of it as a staging post to a carrier and thence to the Atlantic.

As usual one half of the squadron made the move by land and the other half by air. Jack Teesdale and I were in charge of the land party, and we travelled first by train to London, then by the "Jellicoe Special" through the magnificent scenery of the Scottish Highlands to Thurso, then by ferry to Kirkwall, the capital of the Orkneys, and finally by RN transport to Hatston. John Lang then led our six Swordfish to the same destination via RAF Catterick and RNAS Arbroath, to be greeted on his arrival by the able and delightful but somewhat eccentric Commander of Hatston, "Loopy" Luard, resplendent in full dress uniform.

*   *   *

The Islands of Orkney straddle the 59th parallel. In winter they can be pretty depressing, great waves from the North Atlantic bludgeoning the shore, chill winds from the Arctic scouring the braes; you are lucky to get five hours of daylight. However, in summer there are times when the Islands can be unbelievably beautiful: seals asleep on the beaches, lapwing calling, the rocks at sunrise and sunset looking as though they had been bathed in fire, and over everything the sort of stillness and peace that people who live in cities can't even dream of. We were lucky to be there in summer.

Our working up continued. We did dive-bombing practice on Sule Skerry, much to the annoyance of the rock's hundreds of thousands of gulls, shags, skuas and tern. We carried out dummy torpedo attacks on ships exercising from Scapa Flow and dummy depth-charge attacks on towed targets from the Woodwick Range. We practised air-to-air firing, navigation, homing on ASV contacts and beacons and aerial photography. And ADDLs *ad infinitum*. There were even one or two "real life" reconnaissances. On 14 June, for example, several of our aircraft searched for a U-boat which had unsuccessfully attacked HMS *Nigeria*. Taffy Jones and I sighted and reported a large patch of oil, but the fate of the U-boat was never proven.

We embarked on a keep-fit campaign, and, as Squadron Sports Officer, I organized training runs and soccer, rugger, cricket and hockey matches. Sometimes we played officers v other ranks, sometimes other squadrons. The latter games were especially enjoyable and helped to create an excellent *esprit de corps* within the squadron. I remember that Harry Housser and I did battle at 0700 each morning on the squash court and that, since it didn't get dark until after midnight, golf usually started at 2215 hours as soon as the wardroom bar closed. The fact that we had played the 19th hole before the 1st, plus the fact that many of us were testing our golfing skills for the first time, led to a high mortality rate among our golf balls, many of which failed to survive the short 4th hole where a deep and sullen tarn divided green from tee.

Another diversion were the station dances. 835 decided that we would like to host one, and I was given the job of organizing this. It proved easier said than done, for young ladies were in short supply in the Orkneys, and one had first to apply for a date for the dance, then hope that the "dancing girls" – the station Wrens – could fit it into their busy social programme. We were lucky. The girls turned out in force and our dance was a great success, so great a success in fact that, instead of ending it as arranged at midnight, I let it go on until 1 am.

Next day I received an ominous invitation to take afternoon tea with the Chief Wren, First Officer Rumbelow-Pearce, generally and disrespectfully known as "Up-Spirits"!

Anticipating a well-deserved reprimand, I presented myself for tea with some trepidation. However, the afternoon could hardly have passed more pleasantly. We talked about just about everything *except* the dance and I told myself I was in luck. It was only as I was about to leave that First Officer Rumbelow-Pearce looked at me very straight and said quietly, "You won't keep my young ladies out so late again, will you?"

It was the perfect reproach – courteous, brief and to the point, and I shall always remember that lady with respect and affection. Sadly she lost both her husband and son in the war. They were one of those families who gave everything to the Service to which they dedicated their lives.

A less happy incident occurred towards the end of our stay at Hatston. By mid-August we had been working up for the better part of four months and were getting bored. We reckoned it was high time we were posted to an aircraft carrier. On one particularly wet and unpleasant day, when flying had been cancelled, we found ourselves in the Ready Room with time on our hands. By mid-afternoon we had run out of meaningful tasks to set ourselves and Jack Cramp (a New Zealand pilot who had recently joined the squadron after a spell of distinguished service in Malta) produced a pack of cards and started a poker school. All went well until the CO happened to look in. He summoned me to his office and said that the poker game should stop immediately. He also said that, since the aircrew apparently had nothing better to do, they should each write an essay on one of the subjects he proceeded to enumerate. I passed on this somewhat curious order to my colleagues. There was a lot of muttering, but in the end everyone got down to his essay: everyone, that is, except Jack Cramp, who with typical Kiwi independence said the whole thing was "bloody silly", and started playing patience. The subject I chose for my essay was *The Atlantic Air Ferry* and I wrote a short but vitriolic article, advocating that the Americans would be well advised to get on with ferrying their aircraft across the Atlantic by themselves, since although the British had aircrew fully trained and eager to fly, all they could think of using them for was to write pointless essays. Our literary efforts were then duly presented to "Blinkie". After a while he again called me to his office. My essay was on the desk in front of him.

"I could have you court-martialled," he said, "for this."

I decided the best form of defence was attack: "I would welcome that, sir."

"You would?"

"Yes, sir. To bring to the attention of higher authorities how good aircrew are being wasted."

I remained rigidly at attention. My eyes never left his. In a battle of eyes I obviously had an unfair advantage over the unfortunate "Blinkie", and the interview ended with his saying inconclusively, "We shall have to discuss this later." But we never did.

Jack Cramp was right. The whole thing was bloody silly, and it is hard to say who was right and who was wrong. John Lang was obviously right according to the letter of the law, because gambling was prohibited in the Navy, except in the wardroom. I was probably right in thinking he might have been a bit more flexible in enforcing this rule and that telling us to write essays was ill-advised because it smacked of a headmaster disciplining his wayward pupils. And if you wonder why, after fifty years, I have dredged up such a trivial incident, the reason is that it brings home the fact that the squadron was about to enter a difficult period in its history, a period of increasing frustration when morale was none too high.

As summer gave way to autumn, rumours began to circulate that the Squadron would soon be on the move.

We had now been at Hatston for more than three months and had achieved a high standard of flying – over a thousand hours in the air, many of them at night and in poor weather, without incurring the slightest damage to any of our planes or the slightest injury to any of our personnel. (These times in the air may be small compared with the hours flown by many RAF aircrew. However, it should be remembered that flying the Fleet Air Arm involved flights of short duration. A hundred hours flying with Coastal Command would probably mean no more than a dozen take-offs and landings; a hundred hours flying with the Navy would probably mean a hundred take-offs and landings – the times when accidents are most likely to happen. Indeed, glancing through the Squadron's Fair Flying Log, quite a few entries read "ADDLs: 20 mts;" and in those twenty minutes a pilot might take-off and land anything up to half-a-dozen times.)

After all this working up we had high hopes that we might be posted to HMS *Activity*, the first of the British-built escort carriers to come into service. We knew that *Activity* had been doing sterling work in the Atlantic, and word had got round that her squadron needed a rest and that we would replace them. However, on 20 September we were ordered to report to RNAS Stretton, an unprepossessing airfield on the border of Cheshire and Lancashire.

This was the start of a succession of seemingly pointless moves which can be explained only with the knowledge of hindsight. At the time we found it, to say the least, depressing to be forever shunted from pillar to post; and, to prevent the reader becoming as bored and depressed as we were, I shall limit myself to writing no more than a paragraph about each of the airfields which, in the course of the next year, offered us accommodation but never a home.

We were at Stretton from 22 September to 28 October, 1942. This was one of our less memorable ports of call. Accommodation was poor – cold and uncomfortable Nissen huts – and our work unexciting. Our pilots found themselves undergoing a course in instrument-flying, and each morning, complete with sandwich lunches, they would report to the nearby aerodrome at Ollerton, where RAF instructors in ancient Oxford aircraft would wax eloquent on the need to trust one's artificial-horizon and homing-beacon. In the evening the pilots returned to Stretton and, after a meal in the wardroom, most of us found our way to the local pub, the Appleton Thorn, where we soon became regular and most welcome patrons. It was in this fine old inn that we celebrated the award to Jack Cramp of the Distinguished Service Cross for his work with 830 Squadron in Malta. His citation read: "During a critical stage in a convoy in June, 1942, he led four Albacores on a strike against two Italian cruisers and five destroyers, and hit and stopped one cruiser." I have only two other memories of Stretton. Each Sunday morning we attended Matins at the local church. Rather to our embarrassment, we found that the front three rows of pews were invariably reserved for us. And to our even greater embarrassment as we filed in all the local parishioners stood up, and repeated the performance as we filed out! My other, and most pleasurable, recollection is of how the station's excessively "pusser" first lieutenant got his comeuppance. This gentleman was forever reprimanding the more carefree officers of the squadron for unseemly behaviour. However, in his self-appointed role as the upholder of Naval good order and tradition, he fell resoundingly from grace when, at a formal mess dinner, he rose in magnificent solitude for the Loyal Toast. (Ever since Charles II hit his head on a beam in one of his warships when rising to the Loyal Toast, it has been a tradition in the Navy that all should remain seated when the King's or Queen's health is drunk.) For this *faux pas* the First Lieutenant subsequently suffered the unceremonious removal of his trousers – and it was, I remember, some time before he got them back! For the rest of our stay he kept a low profile, and was doubtless much relieved when, after five weeks, we were posted to RNAS Machrihanish.

We were at Machrihanish from 30 October to 12 November, 1942. Machrihanish was a typical Fleet Air Arm aerodrome. When, in 1918, the Navy handed over to the Air Force 126 of its airfields, it didn't envisage that Naval flying would ever require the use of large aerodromes. Most of the Royal Naval Air Stations which were retained were therefore small in size, and, from the point of view of flying, poorly sited. Machrihanish, for example, nestles in a hollow, surrounded by hills, at a spot on the Scottish coast where rainfall is heavy and cloud prevalent. It would be hard to imagine a more idyllic spot scenically, but for aircrew operating at night and in poor visibility it is a death-trap. Yet this was probably the most-used Naval airfield in the war. For, since it was situated near the tip of the Mull of Kintyre, it guarded the approaches to both Liverpool and the Clyde. Liverpool was a major terminus for Atlantic convoys and the Clyde was a naval base, an assembly point for convoys and a training-ground for

Fleet Air Arm aircrew. (It was in these waters that virtually every pilot in the Air Arm made his first deck-landings, more likely than not on the ancient aircraft-carrier *Angus* which spent the greater part of the war steaming up and down the Clyde between Ardrossan and Ailsa Craig.) Machrihanish was therefore in constant use for both operational flying and training. It was also used as a staging post for aircrew about to embark on a carrier. A squadron would fly in and wait, maybe a couple of days, maybe a couple of weeks, for its carrier to appear in the Clyde; it would then fly aboard and its place in Machrihanish would be taken by another squadron awaiting another carrier. No wonder the station became known as "Clapham Junction". For the hundreds of aircrew who passed through it, it had obvious disadvantages; it was remote, isolated and devoid of night life. But it also had much to offer: heather-covered hills, magnificent sunsets, white beaches backed with grassy sand-dunes, and the peace and beauty of a landscape that can have changed little through the millennia. On long walks you could find plovers' eggs, or, if you were lucky, see an eagle. And when the sun was shining and little clouds were forming, bowling along and then dissolving above the shore, there are few coastlines in the world more attractive to fly over than the Mull of Kintyre.

On 11 November we received a most welcome signal. The Squadron was to embark in HMS *Activity*. We remained aboard this carrier from 13 November to 27 November, 1942.

*Activity* was the first British-built escort carrier to come into service. Converted from a 10,000 ton merchantman, the SS *Telemachus*, she was a small but well-built and seaworthy vessel. She had only one lift for moving her aircraft between hangar and flight-deck, and the flight-deck itself was only 60 feet wide – since the wingspan of a Swordfish was 45 feet, 6 inches, there was obviously going to be little margin for error when we took-off and landed. Accommodation was spartan, with the officers' cabins like matchboxes and the mess decks cramped. However, this didn't worry us. We were delighted to be on a carrier at last. *Activity*'s captain, Guy Willoughby, welcomed us aboard and said he looked forward to a long and happy association with us, and we immediately began an intensive working up programme, consisting mostly of deck-landings and low level depth-charge attacks on a towed target. A glance at the Squadron Fair Flying Log confirms that all the deck-landings were accomplished successfully. Likewise all the depth-charge attacks. Yet, to our chagrin and disbelief, on 27 November the Squadron were ordered to disembark and return to Machrihanish. At the time we were never told why and some of us had a sneaking (but quite unjustified) suspicion that John Lang hadn't pushed as hard as he might have for us to go on operations with the *Activity*.

It has since become clear that there was a totally different reason for our being asked to leave the ship. The powers-that-be had decided to transfer *Activity* to training! This was in spite of the fact that she had only recently been commissioned and that the Battle of the Atlantic was going badly, with convoys crying out for air cover. In one month alone in the autumn of 1942 U-boats in the North Atlantic sank 122 merchant ships totalling 615,570 tons. With this background one wonders how such an order can have been contemplated, let alone promulgated.

Our second visit to Machrihanish lasted from 28 November to 18 December, 1942, and included a week's leave. We were then moved again, this time to RAF Kirkiston. We remained at Kirkiston from 18 December, 1942, to 29 January, 1943.

Travelling to our new base was no problem. The Swordfish made the journey in less than an hour, while the ground crew, together with all the Squadron's baggage, mobile equipment and stores, were flown there in the maw of a huge Harrow transport. Kirkiston was a satellite of the much larger RAF Ballyhalbert, which lay close to the mouth of Strangford Loch, a few miles south of Belfast. Nobody seemed to know why we had been sent to this disused airfield, but we could only assume that the Admiralty was running out of accommodation on its own airfields and had decided to farm us out to the RAF. By this time we were finding it hard to maintain our enthusiasm for training, and working up continued in a somewhat desultory fashion, not helped by Kirkiston's superabundance of seagulls. They were a menace to planes taking-off, and Johnny Hunt and I had a narrow escape when we had to turn back and make an emergency landing after running into a flock of them. As sports officer I did my best to keep up morale by encouraging a keep-fit programme and arranging soccer matches. But even the latter seemed to be jinxed. One afternoon during a practice-game we could see two of Ballyhalbert's Spitfires high above us in a cloudless sky indulging in mock combat. There was a muffled explosion, a high-pitched whine, and looking up we saw to our horror they had collided, and one of them, minus its tail plane, was plummeting vertically out of the sky. It crashed only a couple of fields away. But worse was to come, for in its wake fell its pilot, his unopened and obviously damaged parachute streaming out behind him like a shroud. We could only hope he had lost consciousness before he too smashed into the field. This was the start of a period in the Squadron's history when one or two of us began drinking "not wisely but too well". There didn't seem a great deal else to do and we were helped by Northern Ireland's excessively liberal licensing laws. Draught Guinness was in copious supply and available almost twenty-four hours a day. In our local pub in Kirkcubbin the landlord might dutifully call "time" at

2200 hours, but, a few minutes later, invited guests, including as often as not several members of 835 and the local policeman, would assemble in his kitchen and stay there drinking until the small hours. Nor was the wardroom bar poorly attended. And one evening early in January it was, I remember, particularly *well* attended. There were at Ballyhalbert a large number of WAAFs, some of whom became friendly with 835 Squadron officers ("It must," an RAF pilot was heard to remark testily, "be their uniform!") The WAAFs had put on a Christmas pantomime at Ballyhalbert and they suggested they should enliven our New Year by giving a repeat performance at Kirkiston, an offer we accepted with alacrity. On the night of the performance the pantomime party arrived in good time, dressed, for reasons of etiquette, in civilian clothes, and we thought it might be helpful to the young ladies if we limbered them up with a few drinks in the wardroom bar. As a result the pantomime was an absolute riot, with characters entering when they should have exited and vice versa, and the prompter much in demand. The *pièce de résistance* was a Cossack dance, with the girls ending up in a giggling heap on the floor. As ill luck would have it, the Group Captain from Ballyhalbert chose this inopportune moment to visit his satellite station. He was not amused, and rumour had it that a signal was sent to the Admiralty demanding the removal of the delinquent squadron. There are two ways of looking at this affair of the pantomime, and they sum up the difference between the RNVR way of thinking and the RN way. "No harm was done," wrote Jack Cramp, "and a good time was had by all." "It is not to the credit of the squadron officers," wrote John Lang, "that they allowed their young WAAF guests to become intoxicated."

Anyhow, whatever the rights and wrongs, and for whatever reason, we found ourselves back in Machrihanish.

Our third visit to "Clapham Junction" lasted from 29 January to 8 April, 1943.

More ADDLs, more night attacks with flares, more long walks along the sand-dunes. Then, on the afternoon of 9 February, at a time when it seemed as though nothing exciting was ever going to happen, the squadron had its first serious accident, though this was hardly of our making. We had been briefed to carry out dummy torpedo attacks on HMS *Cardiff*, and three of our Swordfish were queueing up at the end of the runway, waiting to take-off. Hank Housser and I, together with our telegraphist air gunner Alec Thompson, were in the leading aircraft. However, instead of being cleared for take-off by the expected green flash from an Aldis lamp, we were given an ominous red. And we soon saw why. A Blackburn Skua which had just taken off in front of us had got into difficulties and, instead of making an emergency landing dead ahead with his wheels up, the pilot decided to try and get back to the airfield and land with his wheels down. Red Very lights started shooting up from all directions as the Skua came hurtling back downwind, out of control and straight towards us. Hank tried to swing our Swordfish out of its path. But about 50 yards short of us the Skua tipped on to its nose. Its engine was torn clean away and went sailing over our heads; and the rest of the plane, with a terrible screeching of metal and fabric, slithered along the runway and smashed straight into us. If its engine had still been in place that would have been the end of us all. As it was, the fuselages of the two planes collapsed in a shattered heap, but there was no seepage of petrol, no explosion, no fire. At least not for the moment. I grabbed the Swordfish's fire-extinguisher, struggled out of the cockpit, and came face to face with the pilot of the Skua, dangling upsidedown but by some miracle not seriously injured. I was wondering how to free him so that he didn't drop headfirst on to the runway, when the crash-tender and ambulance came screaming to a halt beside us, and within seconds we were extricated, all more or less intact, and helped to a safe distance from the shattered planes. At least we could no longer complain that nothing exciting ever happened!

The only other incidents that seem worth recording during this visit to Machrihanish are our success in cross-country running and our somewhat pointless introduction to the decompression chamber. The fierce and balding Commander Sears, who was in charge of flying-personnel at Machrihanish, considered with some justification that his aircrew were indulging in too much drink and too little exercise. He therefore ordered us all out of bed at 0700 each morning for compulsory physical training. Hank Housser and I, who both had a streak of obstinacy, felt disinclined to obey this order, on the grounds that we already got up each morning at 0630 and played squash. We were given special dispensation and, as evidence of our fitness, I later led 835 Squadron to victory in the station 5-mile cross country run. We had, I remember, three out of the first five home.

A few weeks later we found ourselves seated in a large sealed cylindrical tank, while the internal air pressure was gradually reduced. The idea was to demonstrate the danger of flying at high altitude without oxygen. Since Swordfish never climbed above 10,000 feet and seldom above 1,000, the exercise as far as we were concerned was somewhat academic. However, when the dial in the decompression chamber indicated we were at the equivalent of 20,000 feet, we were told to write the poem "Mary had a little lamb". The results were instructive. Although we felt more or less normal, our brains were so starved of oxygen that few of us managed to remember even the second line. Perhaps as a result of my keep-fit campaign, I was able to complete the first verse, but towards the end my writing had become completely illegible.

On 8 April we received the order that we had long been hoping for. The squadron was to embark in the US-built escort carrier HMS *Battler*.

Our first visit to *Battler* lasted from 9 April until 7 May. I found myself once again in charge of the land party, following the now familiar route from Machrihanish to Greenock, and thence by lighter to the carrier which lay at anchor in the Clyde. As we came alongside, the first thing I noticed was the smoothness of her hull. All British warships were rivetted. *Battler* was welded. It was a difference of some significance.

Looking back, I can now see that the story of 835 Squadron is very much tied up with the story of these "Woolworth carriers" or "banana boats" as the *Battler*-class vessels were nicknamed. *Their* shortcomings were the source of *our* frustration. These shortcomings, however, were not immediately apparent and our first impression of our new home was favourable.

The *Battler*-class warships were hastily-cobbled-together-hybrids, born of the Navy's need to have stop-gap carriers which could protect the Atlantic convoys until their own warships came into service. The Americans offered to provide such stop-gaps. The thinking was that in US shipbuilding yards, which were free from the threat of bombing and which had unlimited sources of labour and materials, it would be possible to turn merchant vessels into aircraft-carriers by converting their interior into a hangar and their superstructure into a flight-deck. The resulting vessels were known as CVEs (Convoy Escort Vessels), a nomenclature soon changed by their ships' companies to "Combustible, Vulnerable and Expendable"!

However, as we came aboard that April, we saw no reason to be critical. The aircrew were impressed by their spacious and comfortable cabins, and by the reassuring width (102 feet) of the flight-deck: impressed too by the plaque in the wardroom recording that a certain young lady, while working on our carrier, had won the title "Welding Queen of the Atlantic"; as evidence of her speed if not her precision a squiggly line of welding zigzagged from deck to bulkhead. The groundcrew were impressed by their folding bunks (instead of the traditional hammocks) and by the promise of hot meals from a cafeteria, and of seven different types of icecream and milkshakes from a soda fountain. The captain was impressed by his compact roman *"island"* – *Battler*'s only superstructure – from which the ship and her aircraft could be controlled; in fact the one thing at first that Captain Stephenson *wasn't* happy about was the lack of a bath; US warships go in for showers. It was only by slow degrees that *Battler*'s lack of a bath was seen to be the least of her shortcomings.

We hoped to sail right away on convoy protection duties, but we ought by this time to have known better. We were to spend the next four weeks working up in the Clyde, although it soon became apparent that this was more for the benefit of the ship than the squadron.

During the last three weeks of April and the first week of May our pilots carried out 207 deck-landings, sixty-two of them at night, without their Swordfish incurring so much as a scratch. Our observers carried out exhaustive tests on their ASV radar without ever getting lost or failing to find their target, while our telegraphist air gunners got used to their new TR 1304 radio equipment which at last replaced the old wireless transmitters with their Morse keys. There was nothing wrong with the squadron.

The same couldn't be said for the carrier. The crux of the matter was that the Woolworth carriers had been built too quickly. At the time there were conflicting views about them. The Americans felt that the British had asked for a rush job and had no reason to complain when they got what they asked for. They also pointed out that the US Navy was managing to operate several of *its* Woolworth carriers quite effectively, albeit in the Caribbean and the South Atlantic where weather conditions were relatively benign. The British felt that the carriers they took delivery of were sub-standard; most had niggling defects, and because of their lightweight, open and welded construction they were ill-suited to work in the place where they were needed most, the North Atlantic. As evidence of this, the Navy pointed out that after only three months' service *Archer* repeatedly broke down and had to be retired to care and maintenance (i.e. she had "defects beyond economical repair"), while *Dasher,* on only her second convoy, first turned back with engine failure and buckled plates, then blew herself up and sank in the Clyde.

Perhaps the reaction of 835 Squadron says it all. A brief honeymoon was followed by the gradual realization that our first impressions of our new home had been through rose-tinted spectacles. It wasn't long before the plaque in the wardroom commemorating the exploits of "the Welding Queen of the Atlantic" mysteriously disappeared. A few days later it was found welded upsidedown to a bulkhead in the officers' "heads" (lavatories)!

While working up with *Battler* there were quite a few changes to squadron personnel. We were allocated two new Swordfish, three new pilots, three new observers and three new telegraphist air gunners; so the enlarged squadron now consisted of nine aircraft and thirty-three aircrew.

We said goodbye to several old friends: Jack Cramp (who eventually found his way back to New Zealand), Taffy Jones ( who went to train the large number of RNVR pilots now joining the Air Arm) and Jackie

Parker (who volunteered to join a night fighter squadron and was tragically killed only a few months later).

We welcomed five new pilots and three new observers. The pilots were W.E.F. Elliott who, in spite of his impressive initials, was known as Teddy and soon became one of the most popular and dependable members of the Squadron; John Cridland and Joe Supple, firm friends who had gone through flying training together and now found themselves appointed on the same day to the same carrier. John and Joe were reserved but reliable and resilient characters who felt their way with caution in the wardroom of their first carrier. The last of our new pilots, Tony Costello, had no such inhibitions. A most elegant product of Harrow, he got gloriously drunk on his first night with the Squadron and was found on the flight-deck a little after midnight flinging £1 notes into the Clyde with cries of "filthy lucre!" Tony was one of those gifted characters who lived life to the full and who won the respect and affection of all who got to know him. Among his more tangible assets was a superb collection of jazz records. I can never hear Glen Miller or Harry James without remembering the evenings we spent in his cabin listening to what were then the great modern exponents of jazz.

Our new observers were Lt Bill Buckie, who was both older than me and senior in rank, but had completed his training at a much later date; it says much for his diffidence and good nature that he didn't demur when John Lang confirmed my position as the Squadron Senior Observer. The other observers were Sub-Lt Stan Smith, a small and cheerful cockney who looked (and acted) a bit like Charlie Chaplin and was not a great favourite of our Commanding Officer; Jack Dalton, an ebullient, belligerent and somewhat overconfident Lancastrian, and finally Sub-Lt MacCormick, who (for reasons best not gone into) was christened by his fellow Scott Jimmy Urquhart as "Micknormac".

On 7 May we left *Battler* and returned to Machrihanish. This, we were told, was a case of adieu rather than goodbye, an interlude in which our long-suffering pilots were to undergo yet more training, this time a rocket projectile course. Rocket projectiles in 1943 were the up-and-coming weapons. Two racks were slung beneath the Swordfish's lower mainplane, each containing four rockets with solid metal warheads. The Stringbag, being remarkably stable in flight, proved an ideal launching-platform. She was put into a shallow dive of about 25°, aimed at her target, and all her pilot had to do was press a button to fire salvoes of two, four or eight rockets. In mock attacks in the Clyde we accounted for an impressive number of "enemy" submarines. On the way back from one of these exercises there was an incident which *could* have been fatal. Bob Selley had a sudden and complete engine failure. The Mull of Kintyre is not a good spot in which to have to make a forced landing, but Bob spotted a postage-stamp of a field and managed to glide safely into it and brake to a halt literally inches from a ditch. To give some idea of how small the field was, although the Swordfish was undamaged and was subsequently stripped of every possible piece of extraneous equipment to reduce its weight, it was three weeks before there was sufficient wind for it to be flown out. Bob's observer that day happened to be the CO, and Blinkie was so impressed with his pilot's skill that he gave him a well-deserved "Green Ink Recommend" in his log book "for an instance of exceptional flying skill".

We returned to *Battler* on 14 May, and a couple of days later were on the move again for yet another training course. This involved a second visit to Northern Ireland, first to RAF Ballykelly, then to RNAS Eglinton.

From 15 May until 4 June we played what would now be called "War Games", with models of U-boats, merchantmen and corvettes, the idea being to bring us up to date on recent developments and tactics in the battle of the Atlantic. This was a well-run and instructive course. It brought home to us how complex and technical the war at sea was becoming and how every move of every ship, plane and U-boat was monitored by Western Approaches Command from its headquarters in Liverpool. It also brought home a fact which is widely recognized today, but which, at the time, not everyone had taken aboard: the fact that sea power and air power had, by the 1940s, become inextricably intertwined, and that the Navy couldn't hope to maintain mastery of the sea unless it recognized that ruling the waves was now dependent on also ruling the air. The *Punch* cartoon (over page) says it all.

After a week at Ballykelly and a week at Eglinton, the Squadron suddenly found itself divided into two parts. A sub-flight of three Swordfish, under the command of Lieutenant Shirley-Smith, remained at Eglinton. The other six Swordfish, under the command of John Lang, were flown to the airfield at Sydenham (near Belfast), taxied down to the docks and hurriedly hoisted aboard *Battler*.

We had, the CO told us, been ordered to join Convoy OS49, bound for Gibraltar.

At long last we had caught up with the Battle of the Atlantic.

★　　★　　★

Convoy OS49, from the United Kingdom to Gibraltar, must surely have been one of the least eventful of the war! It was a small convoy, no more than three dozen merchantmen and a dozen warships, its objective being to take aircraft and military equipment to the Mediterranean as part of the

## ELEMENTARY.

Britannia (*in holiday mood*). "'WHAT ARE THE WILD WAVES SAYING?'"

Mr. Punch. "WELL, IF YOU ASK ME, MA'AM, THEY'RE SAYING THAT, IF YOU WANT TO GO ON RULING 'EM, YOU'VE GOT TO RULE THE AIR TOO."

build-up to the Allied invasion of Italy. *Battler* was as much a store-ship as a fighting ship. As evidence of this, there were in our hangar twenty-one Spitfires. These, with their fixed wings, took up a lot of space. And it was because of this lack of space that *Battler*'s operational strength had been reduced to six Swordfish from 835 Squadron to provide anti-submarine patrols, and four Seafires from 808 Squadron to provide fighter cover.

We rendezvoused with our merchantmen a few miles from Rathlin Island off the tip of Northern Ireland, and almost at once began anti-submarine patrols. Harry Housser and I flew the first, taking-off at dawn on 6 July in difficult conditions, with a lot of low cloud and drizzle. Once airborne, visibility was so bad it was impossible to see all the ships in the convoy at the same time. However, we soon realized that one of our charges was belching smoke and lagging behind. (We later learned that the *Maxeffell* was unable to maintain more than five knots and almost at once gave up the unequal struggle and returned to Oban.) Conditions were still bad when we returned to land-on at the end of our three-hour patrol and, much to his mortification, Harry missed all the arrester wires and ended up in the barrier. In view of our dearth of Swordfish, it was lucky the plane was no more than slightly damaged.

The rest of the day's patrols were uneventful, with the convoy maintaining a steady nine knots and the ships keeping station with precision. Moving a whole lot of ships from one port to another in convoy isn't as easy as it sounds, especially in wartime.

In the early years of the war convoys usually consisted of forty to fifty merchantmen, with anything up to a dozen warships to guard them. The merchantmen sailed in parallel columns, six or seven ships one behind the other. The warships guarded their flanks. In charge of the merchantmen was a Commodore, usually a Royal Naval Reserve officer of flag rank. The debt that the country owes to these tough, knowledgeable, responsible, overworked men has seldom been properly acknowledged. It was they, every bit as much as the pilots who flew in the Battle of Britain, who helped win the war. Sailing from Liverpool alone, over twenty Commodores were lost on Atlantic convoys: the official records tell us how:-

"Captain H.C. Birnie, *Bonneville*, Convoy SC121, torpedoed by U-405; sank in 20 minutes, in rough seas and snow squalls . . . Vice-Admiral H.J.S. Brownrigg, *Ville de Tamatave*, Convoy ONS 160; capsized in storm-force winds; all hands lost . . . Captain R.H. Garstin, *Stentor*; Convoy SL125; torpedoed by U-509; blinded, last seen telling the doctor tending him to take to the boats . . . Captain E. Rees, *Empire Howard*, Convoy PQ14; torpedoed by U-403; last seen in the water clutching a plank of wood and smoking a cigar; his ship sank in less than one minute."

In charge of warships was a Senior Naval Officer, flying his flag in the most powerful of the escort vessels, usually a cruiser or aircraft-carrier. Although one might have thought such a system of divided command would cause problems, in fact it worked well, for both men were experts in their field and were in frequent consultation; also, most importantly, they were on the spot. It is significant that the most disastrous convoys of the war – "Vigorous" to Malta and PQ17 to Russia – were *not* controlled by the Commodore and SNO on the spot, but took their orders from a shore-based headquarters (in Alexandria or London) a thousand miles from the scene of action.

In the case of OS49 our Commodore's task was easy. His ships could all maintain 9 knots, the sea was calm, the enemy conspicuous by his absence.

Over the next few days our Swordfish provided more or less continuous anti-submarine patrols, circling the convoy at a range of 20 or 25 miles. About the only moment of excitement was when Bob Selley and Jack Teesdale found they had a well-defined "blip" on their radar screen. It was evening, and visibility was none too good, with nine-tenths low cloud and mist. The "blip" seemed to be moving very slowly towards the convoy – just as a U-boat might be expected to move – and they homed on it hopefully. Emerging from cloud, Bob spotted an ill-defined grey object on the surface. He was about to dive into the attack, when his "target" suddenly spouted a fountain of water and stale air. They had been stalking a cachalot, one of the great whales hunted by the fishermen of the Azores.

The first few days of our run to Gibraltar were almost devoid of incident. The weather was far from ideal for flying, with poor visibility, virtually no wind and a great deal of haze. Nonetheless it was a benign introduction to operations for our less experienced aircrew. One of them, John Cridland, recalls taking off on his first patrol a few days before his 21st birthday:-

"I remember the walk along the flight-deck to our plane which was parked near the stern of the carrier. My parachute was slung over my shoulder. My observer beside me was carrying his green canvas chart-case and the other tools of his trade; knowing it was my first patrol, he was probably as nervous as I was! We had to be careful not to trip over the arrester-wires, even though they weren't raised; and it seemed a very long way to the plane. However, once in the cockpit, the ritual of starting up was all I had time to think about: the rigger or fitter turning the inertia starting-handle, while

10. A Skua collides with Hank Housser's and Barry Barringer's Swordfish at Machrihanish, 9 February, 1943.

11. A Beaufighter taking Sam Mearnes and 'Chiefie' Banham to Casablanca crashes into the cemetery, Gibraltar, 7 September, 1944.

Some of the
aircrew:

12. L. to R.:
George Sadler
(pilot), Stan
Thomas
(observer), L/A
Defraine
(telegraphist air
gunner).

13. L. to R.:
P.O. Armstrong
(telegraphist air
gunner), Jimmy
Urquhart (pilot),
Barry Barringer
(observer).

14. L. to R.:
Dave Newberry
(observer), Bob
Selley (pilot),
P.O. Lang
(telegraphist air
gunner).

15. L. to R.:
Derek Ravenhill
(observer), P.O.
Wise
(telegraphist air
gunner), Ted
Pitts (pilot).

16. L. to R.:
P.O. Sheldrake
(telegraphist air
gunner), Joe
Supple (pilot),
Johnny Lloyd
(observer).

17. L. to R.:
P.O. Tidman
(telegraphist air
gunner), Bill
Buckie (observer),
Teddie Elliott
(pilot).

I checked the fuel level and the magnetos. I remember the sweet, warm smell of oil as the engine fired and gradually warmed up . . . I remember too, when I was flying the dawn patrol a few days later, being much impressed by the beauty of the sunrise. When we took off at 0640 the sea below us was still dark as ink, but the sky above us was pale and filled with irregular rows of fluffy little cumulus clouds. As we climbed towards these clouds, I noticed their undersurface was turning a brilliant pink as one by one they caught the first rays of the rising sun. It came to me that we were seeing the sort of bird's-eye-view of the sunrise that one never gets from ground level, and I remember thinking it a pity that we in our aircraft were the only people able to appreciate it."

Ironically the first suspicion of enemy action turned out to be a false alarm, yet led to tragedy. The convoy was coming up to the Cape Saint Vincent when an unidentified aircraft was picked up on *Battler*'s radar. Two Seafires from 808 Squadron were scrambled to investigate. The first took off safely. But the second, three-quarters of the way down the flight-deck, started drifting to port. The tip of its wing caught one of the for'd ack-ack guns. The Seafire cartwheeled over the side and crashed into the sea. No trace of the pilot was ever found.

What made the accident doubly tragic was that the unidentified aircraft turned out to be not an Axis shadower but an allied plane which had forgotten to switch on its IFF (Identification, Friend or Foe).

Next day, as we approached Gibraltar, the 808 pilots began flying off the Spitfires which had been in our hangar. Since there were twenty-one of these Spitfires and only three 808 pilots to fly them, there obviously had to be a good deal of to-ing and fro-ing, with Johnny Hunt, Jimmy Urquhart and Tony Costello in their Swordfish shuttling the Spitfire pilots backwards and forwards between the carrier and Gibraltar's North Front airfield.

That evening (14 July), all the Spitfires having been safely delivered, *Battler* made fast alongside the mole in the outer harbour.

We were all looking forward to shore leave, but were told that no one could disembark until a staff officer from naval headquarters had come to brief us on what we could and couldn't do on the Rock. That evening, to mark the successful completion of our first operation in *Battler*, there was a mild celebration in the wardroom, and in the small hours Hank Housser and Jimmy Urquhart decided to go for a swim. They lowered a jack-ladder over the side, stripped off and plunged gaily into the water. It could well all too literally have been their final plunge. For almost at once they were spotlit by searchlights and launches with guns and depth-charges at the ready bore down on them from all directions. What they didn't know was that Italian frogmen, operating from the nearby and supposedly neutral Bay of Algeciras, had recently sunk or damaged nearly a dozen allied vessels in Gibraltar; naval launches were therefore on patrol each night, itching to shoot up and depth-charge anything or anybody seen in the water. We heard afterwards that there was an Admiralty enquiry into the incident, and that the staff officer who ought to have briefed us was given an official reprimand for not having come aboard as soon as *Battler* secured to the mole.

There followed a week in the sun, in a very different atmosphere to that of wartime England. Gibraltar is an almost sheer outcrop of limestone, rising to over 1,390 feet from a promontory overlooking the entrance to the Mediterranean. It is a natural fortress of obvious strategic importance, and ever since the days of the ancient Greeks it has been subjected to endless invasions and sieges. It became a British colony in 1713 and was turned into a naval base which, in spite of its land border with Spain, was reckoned to be impregnable.

It was a strange sensation, in wartime, to be able to walk quite openly into a neutral country. It is true one needed a permit to do this, but Jack Teesdale and I had no difficulty getting one, and crossing the Bay of Algeciras by ferry we lunched magnificently at the Hotel Cristina. Some of the finest sherry in the world, I remember, was 4/6d a bottle. Others in the squadron made their way through the Rock's impressive labyrinth of tunnels, and emerged at East Beach, one of the few places where swimming *was* permitted, while yet others paid a visit to a bullfight, and caused consternation among the locals by cheering the bull instead of the matador!

We were just getting used to *la dolce vita* when shore leave was cancelled, and on 22 June *Battler* and her escorting warships weighed anchor and stood west into the Atlantic. Our orders, John Lang told us, were to escort a homeward-bound convoy KMS16/XK9

Once again we had an uneventful passage. Looking back, I think a lot of the credit for this must go to 808 Squadron. The convoy had barely assembled and got under way when our radar picked up an enemy aircraft which was obviously trying to shadow us. Two Seafires, piloted by Lt Constable and Sub-Lt Penny took off and managed to make an interception. The enemy aircraft, a four-engined Focke Wulf Condor, was shot down and the two Seafires, returning to *Battler*, succeeded in landing-on safely in spite of the fact that the sun had set and it was almost dark. So the U-boats remained unaware of our convoy's course, composition and speed.

Another factor to thwart them was that, from Gibraltar to the Clyde, our Swordfish kept up near-continuous anti-submarine patrols, taking-off as early as 0545 and landing-on as late as 2245. There were U-boats about. During the six days that the convoy was at sea Coastal Command sighted several in the Bay of Biscay and the cryptographers decoding their radio transmissions confirmed that up to half-a-dozen were, at different times, in a position to cause us trouble, but none came near us. One reason undoubtedly was that, as soon as they surfaced, they picked up our patrolling Swordfish on their sea-to-air-radar-type-detectors and were forced to submerge. So the convoy sailed along peacefully, day after uneventful day.

It is possible to attribute our safe passage to several factors. We could, quite simply, have been lucky. It could be that the U-boats had other fish to fry and didn't consider our relatively small convoy worth bothering over. It could be that our passage coincided with a lull in Dönitz's offensive and he was regrouping his forces. However, it is, I think, significant that only a few weeks later another convoy which followed much the same route but was *without* the protection of an escort carrier suffered crippling losses; out of its thirteen merchantmen seven were torpedoed and sunk. On 28 June we dropped anchor in the Clyde.

Our first tour of duty in *Battler* had been uneventful but by no means unsuccessful. We had flown fifty-eight anti-submarine patrols without serious mishap, and not one of the merchantmen we were guarding had been attacked, damaged or sunk. In spite of her teething troubles *Battler* struck us as being a relaxed and efficiently-run carrier; we got on well with her ship's officers, and it seemed reasonable to hope we were on the threshold of a permanent association with her.

The Admiralty, however, had other ideas. On rejoining our sub-flight at Eglinton, we discovered that we had become a composite (combined fighter and TBR) squadron. For there, waiting to join us, were not only our three Swordfish but six Hurricane IIcs and five fighter pilots.

The idea of a composite squadron had much to commend it. Intelligence reports indicated that U-boats in the Atlantic were changing their tactics. Their new orders were that, when attacked, instead of trying to escape by diving, they should stay on the surface and fight it out. With this in mind, their anti-aircraft weaponry had been upgraded and updated, and a slow and vulnerable Swordfish lumbering in to the attack was now liable to find it had bitten off more than it could chew. The idea of a composite squadron was that Swordfish and Hurricanes should work in tandem, with the fighter going in first to silence the U-boat's ack-ack and the Swordfish following up with an unopposed and hopefully accurate attack with depth-charges or rocket-projectiles. One obvious difficulty was that Hurricanes and Swordfish flew at very different speeds – the former at well over 200 mph, the latter at well under 100 – so practice would be needed to achieve the necessary co-ordination. A further and obvious advantage of having fighters in the squadron was that they could provide a convoy with defence against enemy aircraft, being able to drive off both shadowing Condors and attacking Junkers.

However, it was something of a letdown for our newly appointed fighter pilots to find themselves nursemaids to a gaggle of antediluvian Swordfish. They had come from 804, an élite squadron with a fine war record, a high profile and high morale. As well as accounting for an impressive number of enemy aircraft, 804 had the distinction of providing pilots for the CAM (Catapult Armed Merchant) ships. (The once-only flights of these catafighters were, to say the least, hazardous; for most of their flying was done far from land in the lonely reaches of the Atlantic, and once a pilot had been catapulted-off he had no hope of ever being able to land; on completing his mission he had either to ditch in the sea or bail out.)

In the summer of 1943 804 Squadron had been told that they were going to convert to Hellcats, the latest, well-liked and high-performance fighters to arrive from America. Indeed the pilots had actually done a fortnight's engine-handling course to familiarize them with their new aircrafts' 2,000 hp Pratt and Whitney Double Wasp power-plant. However, at the end of this course the CO and most of the senior pilots had unexpectedly been given shore appointments and the rump of the squadron had been ordered to Eglinton, where, instead of the hoped-for and modern Hellcats, they found waiting for them half-a-dozen somewhat ancient Hurricanes and a dozen even more ancient Swordfish. It didn't help their morale when they were told that their new section-leader, who had not yet arrived, was going to be a Lieutenant RN ex-Walrus pilot who had only recently completed his fighter-training course!

It says much for their good nature and adaptability that they buckled to without complaint to learn the new tactics that an unfamiliar type of flying would call for.

Among these recently-joined pilots were three who were to become long-serving stalwarts of the squadron: Sam Mearns, an imposing figure with a piratical manner, a refreshing disdain for formality and a great desire to get on with the war; and two New Zealanders: Pete Picot, popular, even-tempered and an outstanding pilot; and Al Burgham, slightly-built and with a dry sense of humour, who was soon to lead his fighter-section with quiet efficiency on some of the most amazing feats of flying in the war.

The fighter pilots had just started to get to grips with thinking in terms of air-to-ground combat rather than air-to-air, when their new section-commander arrived to take over. Lieutenant Wilfred Waller, RN, turned out to be a modest and most approachable person, with an engaging grin emerging at frequent intervals out of a huge black beard. The latter earned him the nickname "Abo", though I suspect his resemblance to an Australian Aborigine was more fanciful than factual. In spite of his unpretentious qualifications – Walrus are, if possible, even easier to fly than Swordfish – Wilf Waller was to prove a thoroughly competent pilot and a born leader. He quickly won the respect and affection of his fighter pilots, not least because he was aware of his limitations. Although senior in rank to both Al Burgham and Sam Mearns, he realized that they were more experienced than he was; he therefore left much of the day-to-day running of the fighter section to them.

At about this time there were more changes among the Swordfish personnel. We lost one stalwart and gained two. Harry Housser left us to join another squadron which was being equipped with Grumman Avengers. His replacement was Eric McEwan, a handsome and soft-spoken young Scot who had started his career at sea in the Merchant Navy. Eric was one of those people who find it a great deal easier to make friends than enemies – indeed I reckon he was about the only member of the squadron that nobody *ever* had a cross word with! He teamed up with a new observer, Paddy Hall, an Ulsterman who quickly settled into the ways of the squadron.

After a couple of weeks at Eglinton we rejoined *Battler*. We were, rumour had it, about to provide air cover for another convoy.

There followed the usual spell of working up in the Clyde, with the Hurricanes perfecting their deck-landing by day and the Swordfish by night. In a fortnight of decidedly hectic flying there was only one incident worth recording and this involved our gallant aircrews' efforts to come aboard *Battler* by means other than landing on the flightdeck.

The carrier had dropped anchor off the Tail O' the Bank; twenty-four hours leave had been granted and "liberty boats" were busy ferrying the off-duty watch between ship and shore. Jack Teesdale, Teddy Elliott and I paid a visit to Glasgow and, returning that night to the quay at Greenock a little after 2230 found to our chagrin that we had missed the last of the liberty boats. Loth to spend the night ashore – which five of us had done once before, sleeping top to toe in a not very salubrious boardinghouse – we managed to get a "distress" signal to *Battler*'s officer of the watch, and, much to our relief, he agreed to send a jollyboat to pick us up. A jollyboat is a diminutive clinker-built cutter, able to carry five or at the most six people: not the sort of craft to be out in at night in bad weather. And unfortunately for us the weather now began to deteriorate – rapidly. By the time we had been picked up from the quay and had made our way to the carrier, the waves were so high and the wind so strong that we found it quite impossible to come alongside the gangway. With more valour than discretion, we asked to be hoisted aboard. This involved lowering the falls, hooking-up the jollyboat fore and aft (with its occupants of course still in it) and having it raised by a derrick on to the quarterdeck. Jack and I managed to hook-up successfully, and all seemed to be going well until we were almost halfway up the ship's side. Then the shortcomings of "the Welding Queen of the Atlantic" came home to roost. A joint in the derrick snapped, and the jollyboat fell with an almighty crash into the water.

Jack Teesdale and the only other occupant of the boat, its coxswain, managed to grab hold of and cling to one of the falls; they clambered aboard the carrier, shaken but safe. Teddy Elliott and I were thrown into the sea. I struck out for the gangway. It was less than a dozen yards away. But I was wearing my greatcoat. Made of doeskin, it was heavy dry and even heavier wet. For a few terrible seconds I thought I wasn't going to make it. Then my hand closed over the bottom step of the landing-ladder and I was dragged aboard, panting and gagging.

The three of us were put under a hot shower and, with the help of several tots of brandy prescribed by the ship's doctor, made a rapid recovery. But what had happened to Teddy? Nobody seemed to know, and, as time passed and nothing was heard of him, we began to fear the worst. Then, in the small hours of the morning, he miraculously reappeared. He told us that his first reaction on surfacing had been to grab hold of anything that was solid. The nearest solid object was the jollyboat, which was drifting away full of water but the right way up. He caught hold of it, hauled himself into it, and found he was being swept seaward by a combination of wind and an ebb tide. It was a wild night, and with the howl of the wind and the roar of the sea he reckoned his shouts for help might not be heard.

"I was lucky," he told us. "In one of the lockers in the jollyboat I found a ship's bell. I rang it for all I was worth."

The bell was heard by a vigilant officer of the watch in HMS *Nelson*. The battleship lowered a longboat and Teddy was rescued and towed back, ignominiously but safely, to the *Battler* – an escape which called for yet more tots of brandy!

A couple of days later something more vital than a derrick gave way in our accident-prone carrier. We were doing high-speed trials when the upper part of our mast broke off and came crashing down on the flight-deck, narrowly missing those on the bridge.

And a couple of days after that, there occurred what was for us an even more shattering event. We were once again disembarked, this time to the RAF aerodrome at Ayr, while "our" carrier sailed without us, in her hangar not a squadron of Swordfish to protect merchantmen in convoy but a squadron of Seafires to protect troops in Italy. Looking back, it made sense. But at the time, to say that we felt unwanted would be an understatement.

The next few months were not a happy time for the squadron; for once again we were shunted every few weeks from pillar to post for no apparent reason. We remained at Ayr from 30 July until 9 September. The aerodrome was large, bleak, bespattered with Nissen huts and shared between the Navy and the RAF. It would not have been much fun in winter, but in the height of summer it had quite a lot going for it, not least the Tam O'Shanter, the famous old Inn once frequented by Robbie Burns, and now frequented with equal enthusiasm by most of 835.

Only a few days after our arrival we came within a hair's breadth of suffering our first fatality. Eric McEwan describes an incident that was as sudden and unexpected as it was tragic:-

"I was flying back one evening from Machrihanish to Ayr, with a Lieutenant Wilkinson, RN (senior pilot from another squadron) as passenger. The weather was bad, with low cloud and poor visibility, so we were flying at no more than 500 feet. Suddenly the engine cut, stone dead. There wasn't a hope of reaching land, but I managed to ditch safely some miles to the south of the Isle of Arran. The Swordfish sank almost at once, though not before we had managed to free the inflatable dinghy from her wing. To our dismay it was useless, punctured by splinters from the shattered wing. No one appeared to have seen what had happened to us except a farmer and his family living on Arran, who lit a bonfire on the shore to guide us towards land. However, the shore was a very long way away.

"It was getting dark, and the sea was rough and extremely cold, as Wilkinson and I struck out towards the light of the fire. Unfortunately, in the heavy seas we soon became separated. It took me over three hours to reach the shore, by which time I was at the end of my tether and suffering from hypothermia. The farmer and his children dragged me up over the rocks and carried me to their farmhouse, where I was first plunged into a hot shower and then put to bed covered by an enormous number of blankets – in spite of which I couldn't stop shivering. A few hours later a Naval doctor, complete with ambulance, arrived from Lamlash. His first thought was to get me, as fast as possible, to a Naval Sick Bay. However, the farmer, Peter Craig, and his wife reckoned I would be better off with them, and to this the doctor eventually agreed. He departed, leaving behind instructions and a bottle of 'medicinal' brandy.

"The family, meanwhile, had been searching the shore in the hope of finding Wilkinson. But sadly he was drowned; his body was washed up on the coast of Arran in the small hours of the morning.

"By the following afternoon I had stopped shivering and was well enough to be transferred by ambulance to the Sick Bay at Lamlash. I think I must have been their only patient, because I was given VIP treatment. Each of the nurses, I seem to remember, visited me at least once during the night with a cup of cocoa! I also remember, on my return to Ayr, being greeted on my first night at dinner by a WRAF steward's astonished: 'I thocht youse wis deid!' It was the same girl, incidentally, who complained that one of our officers kept winking at her – poor Blinkie. So often misunderstood!"

On 9 September the squadron was again moved and again split up. Most of the Hurricanes embarked in HMS *Ravager* for yet more deck-landing training, while most of the Swordfish embarked in HMS *Argus* to carry out tests on a new type of buoyancy bomb.

*Argus* was unbelievably old. She was already old in 1918 when, as the passenger-liner *Conte Rosso*, she was purchased from the Italians and converted into an aircraft-carrier. Every trace of her superstructure was removed and, instead of discharging smoke through a funnel, she discharged it through vents in her stern. It was this which led to her being described during inter-war naval manoeuvres as "a small hulk, on fire aft . . . floating bottom up"! But for all the rude things said about her, *Argus* did valuable work in the war as a deck-landing-training carrier, and she now continued with these duties while 835, supervised by three boffins from Whitehall, tested the Allies' Latest Top Secret Weapon: the buoyancy bomb.

The thinking behind this new device was that it could be used to dive bomb vessels at sea. The theory was that the attacking aircraft should go into a dive and release its bomb well ahead of its target. The bomb would then perform a parabola underwater, and, because of its buoyancy, would come up to the surface and explode against the keel of its target – the keel usually being a vessel's weakest spot. The CO put me in charge of the tests, and throughout the latter half of September our Swordfish carried out dummy dive-bombing attacks with these new weapons. We carried out sixty-six attacks in all, each time dropping our bomb almost exactly where we had been told to, then landing back safely on the *Argus*. As far as we could tell, the attacks were successful. However, at the end of a fortnight the three boffins went back to Whitehall without saying a word to anyone and nobody ever heard of the buoyancy bomb again!

Instead of returning to Greenock at the end of each week's flying, *Argus* would sometimes drop anchor in Lamlash Bay off the coast of Arran. Twenty-four hours' shore leave was usually given and one Sunday afternoon several of the squadron set off to walk along the coast to Whiting Bay. Here we found a hotel. Knowing that Scotland was "dry" on a Sunday, we went in and asked for tea – a request which obviously surprised the hotel's elderly retainer.

"Haven't you walked from Lamlash?" he asked us.

When we confirmed that we had, he said, "As you've come more than three miles, you're *bona fide* travellers. So long as you sign the register, you can drink what you like."

The register was promptly signed and the orders for tea superseded by orders for something stronger. In the weeks that followed we more than once took advantage of this loophole in the otherwise strict Scottish licensing laws, some of us going to the lengths of keeping old bus or train tickets to prove we had indeed been travelling.

At this somewhat chaotic moment in our history, with some of us at Ayr, some aboard *Argus* and some aboard *Ravager*, John Lang left us to take up a new appointment. He had had the misfortune to command us during a difficult and frustrating period, and, looking back, I think we may have blamed him unfairly for some of our trials and tribulations. I have since learned that he did in fact try very hard to get us assigned to operational duties, even suggesting to the Admiralty that if no carrier was available we should be given the job of minelaying. It was sad that, because the Squadron was so fragmented, he left without the usual farewell party and without ever meeting his successor, Wilf Waller.

On 6 November we moved again, this time to HMS *Chaser*, one of the many "Woolworth" carriers now swarming into the Clyde like bees to a hive. If only they had been as reliable as they were numerous!

We were welcomed aboard by *Chaser*'s commanding officer, Captain McClintock, who said he appreciated that we had been badly messed about. But all that, he told us, was in the past. From now on 835 was *his* squadron, *Chaser* was *our* ship, and we could expect a good long spell of operational duty together.

Three weeks later, after the usual working up in the Clyde, we were again disembarked, this time with such haste that it was apparently impossible for the carrier to put to sea to enable us to fly off. Our aircraft had to be immediately lowered into lighters, ferried ashore and taxied to the nearby airfield at Abbotsinch. *Chaser*, we gathered, had been earmarked for an urgent overhaul, followed by duties other than convoy protection.

It seemed a strange decision. For that month (December, 1943), in the Atlantic alone, the Allies lost some thirty merchant ships, totalling well over 150,000 tons. It seemed to us that convoy protection was needed and doubtless the large number of merchant seamen who died in the ships that were lost would have agreed.

Our disembarkation had its lighter moments. First to be offloaded were the Sea Hurricanes, and our CO told Al Burgham to rig up a derrick to swing the aircraft over the side. Al had never seen anything remotely resembling a derrick aboard the carrier and was somewhat disconcerted to be shown what appeared to be a heap of rusty lengths of scrap-iron, with the duty watch standing round it and looking at him hopefully for instructions. Kiwis are renowned for their practical skill and ingenuity, but Al hadn't the slightest idea where to start. He was much relieved when Wilf Waller himself appeared on the scene: "And in no time flat [according to Al] the heap of scrap iron was transformed into a derrick with a Hurricane dangling from the top of it. My opinion of our CO, already high, rose even higher."

One by one our seventeen aircraft, with their pilots sitting somewhat apprehensively in the cockpits, were lowered over the side of the carrier and into a lighter, ferried to the landing-stage, swung ashore, and taxied through the docks to RNAS Abbotsinch. So, by the end of an extremely busy day, we found ourselves once again dumped on to an unfamiliar airfield, with nobody knowing why we had been sent there or what we were meant to be doing.

Abbotsinch in winter was not a good place to be dumped in. It was bitterly cold that December, and everything within a dozen miles of Glasgow and its airfields was shrouded in near-perpetual and near-freezing smog. The so-called "coal" with which we were expected to warm our Nissen-hut-cabins consisted of dull-grey and unburnable slate; icicles hung from the hot water pipes. We were thankful to learn that this was not to be our permanent home, but that, as soon as the weather cleared, the Squadron would reassemble at Eglinton in Northern Ireland.

It was a week before the smog lifted, but on 16 December a patch of clear blue sky appeared in the west, and the meteorologists' forecast was favourable. Hoar frost was scraped off the wings of our Hurricanes and Swordfish; engines were started up and the squadron prepared, in several sub-flights, to head for Eglinton.

First to get airborne were a pair of Hurricanes, piloted by Al Burgham and a relative newcomer to the Squadron, Bill Armitage. Visibility when they took off was poor, but once they had climbed through the smog they found themselves in bright sunlight and a cloudless sky. Although they couldn't see the ground, they had their compasses to rely on and settled down to what promised to be a pleasant flight. After a while Al was surprised to get a call from his fellow pilot who was in formation beside him:

"Leader! Is the sun in the right place?"

Al suddenly realized that the sun, which should have been to his left, was to his right. He was steering a reciprocal to his intended course i.e. he was heading due east instead of due west! Once this little error had been rectified, the rest of the flight was uneventful, and in due course the whole squadron arrived safely at Eglinton.

In the last few days of 1943 there were yet more changes to our personnel. In particular we acquired a new chief telegraphist-air-gunner and a new commanding officer.

Petty Officer (Air) J.W. Armstrong, DSM, probably had a more distinguished war record than anyone else in the Squadron. For it was his ingeniously transmitted signal which set in motion the sequence of events which led to the sinking of the *Bismarck*. The German battleship was of course sunk before 835 Squadron was even formed, but, to my mind, Armstrong's role in this not unimportant event is worth recording because it says something about the standard of airmanship in the Fleet Air Arm.

Towards the middle of May, 1941, the *Bismarck* and the *Prinz Eugen* moved into a position among the Norwegian fjords from which they could at any moment break out into the Atlantic. This, for the Navy, was a nightmare scenario. German U-boats were already sinking our merchantmen at the rate of half-a-million tons (some 150 ships) a month, and if the most powerful battleship in the world had broken out into the Atlantic and caused further carnage among our convoys this would have had a serious effect on the course of the war. So the Navy, that spring, had one objective only: to sink the *Bismarck*. To this end they stripped the convoys of escorts and assembled warships not only from both sides of the Atlantic but from the Mediterranean. However, to sink the great battleship they had first to locate her; and to do this it was essential that they knew exactly when she left Norway and headed into the Atlantic. On 20 May reports were received from the Norwegian Resistance that *Bismarck* was heading north up the Skagerrak, and the following afternoon she was sighted by a reconnaissance aircraft of Coastal Command in Kars Fjord to the south of Bergen. Coastal Command was given the job of keeping her under surveillance. However, on the morning of 22 May the weather took a turn for the worse. A low front came to rest in the middle of the North Sea, and Coastal Command aircraft found that they couldn't get through to Kars Fjord. Every plane that tried was forced to turn back, unable to penetrate the curtain of mist and low cloud that shrouded the Norwegian coast. By mid-afternoon Coastal

Command was grounded. The Admiralty were in despair. And it looked as though they were about to pay a high price for their neglect of their Air Arm, for the Navy had no long-range reconnaissance aircraft capable of reaching the Norwegian coast and returning to the British Isles. It was now that Captain Fancourt, commander of RNAS Hatston in the Orkneys, came up with a suggestion. Among his aircrew was a Commander Rotherham whose reputation as an observer was second to none; also a Lt-Commander Goddard with the same sort of reputation as a pilot. He asked them if they thought that *they* could get through where Coastal Command had failed. They agreed to "have a go", flying one of the unarmed and obsolescent Maryland bombers used at Hatston for target-towing, but they pointed out they would need a telegraphist-air-gunner to operate the radio. "Willy" Armstrong volunteered.

The flight that followed was a minor epic in the history of aerial warfare, for it demanded pinpoint navigation and flying of exceptional skill. Rotherham decided to adopt the old trick of making a landfall some miles to the right or left of his true objective; this way if he hit the coast at a point he didn't recognize, he would know which way to turn. The landfall he chose was Marsten Island, about a dozen miles south of Bergen. The weather in the Orkneys was fine and clear as they took off and headed for Norway, but it wasn't long before visibility deteriorated and halfway across the North Sea they saw ahead of them a vast bank of cloud and mist rising like a solid wall out of the water. The cloud extended from horizon to horizon without a break; it was high and its base was right down on the sea. At 100 feet the Maryland was flying blind. Even at fifty feet it was passing through eddies of mist-cum-drizzle-cum-cumulus. It would be hard to imagine anything more taxing than flying through a low, ill-defined tunnel between cloud and sea, with drifting fragments of cloud rushing at one out of the murk like puffs of gunfire. Yet after they had been airborne for roughly an hour and a quarter, and had made two fractional alterations of course to allow for a changing wind, Rotherham said, "A couple of minutes and Marsten ought to be one mile dead ahead." And at the end of a couple of minutes the cloud, as by a miracle, fractionally lifted and fine on their starboard bow a mile ahead they saw the low cliffs of Marsten Island.

It was not too difficult now to find their way to Kars Fjord, a forbidding corridor of water, hemmed in by high hills and low cloud, but mercifully free of mist. They made a thorough reconnaissance of the fjord, but there was no sign of the *Bismarck*. Nor was there any sign of her in the nearby Hjelke Fjord. There was, however, one other place she might be: sheltering from the bad weather in Bergen. They knew that Bergen would be heavily defended, but they knew too that their mission wouldn't be conclusive until they had reconnoitred it. Inevitably, as they approached the harbour they were spotted. Ack-ack burst around them, shattering the pilot's cockpit-canopy and destroying the intercom-system by which the crew kept in touch with each other. Goddard took the Maryland down to sea level, weaving in and out of the ships and skimming low over the roof-tops; then, having satisfied themselves the *Bismarck* wasn't in harbour, they were heading for the safety of cloud. As the swirling canopy of white enfolded them, they set course for the open sea, and Hatston.

They had one more job to do. In case they were shot down by enemy fighters on their way home, it was essential they at once signalled to the C-in-C the news that the *Bismarck* and *Prinz Eugen* had sailed. But here there was a problem. A Maryland is so constructed that pilot, observer and wireless-operator are in separate cockpits, cut off from one another, and, since their intercom was inoperative, Goddard, Rotherham and Armstrong had no way of communicating. Rotherham therefore wrote on a piece of paper: "Signal C-in-C 'the battleship and cruiser have left'," and pushed the message through a hole in the cockpit-bulkhead to Willy Armstrong. But now came another and more serious problem. Willy tried again and again to call Coastal Command to whose frequency he was tuned, but he couldn't get a reply. Realizing there must be a maladjustment on that wavelength, he hit on the idea of tuning in to the frequency used by Maryland training aircraft at Hatston. Target-towing over the Orkneys was in full swing that evening when the telegraphist-air-gunners, to their amazement, suddenly picked up a most urgent operational signal: "Signal C-in-C 'the battleship and cruiser have left'." Within minutes Rotherham's message had reached the Commander-in-Chief of the Home Fleet.

So in the sinking of the *Bismarck* the Fleet Air Arm was in at the beginning and in at the end, for it was of course Swordfish from the *Ark Royal* which finally crippled the great battleship. How different the story might have been without the efforts of our newly-appointed chief telegraphist-air-gunner!

Our newly-appointed CO, Lt-Cdr(A) T.T. Miller, RN, had been a flying instructor at RNAS Arbroath and it was his misfortune to take over the squadron in difficult circumstances. His predecessor, Wilf Waller, had been our Commanding Officer for only a few months, but in that short time he had earned the respect and affection of both the wardroom and the lower deck, not least because of his iconoclastic disregard for the more pompous aspects of naval tradition; he was given a memorable send-off, and my last and abiding memory of him is seeing him with his lighter carefully setting fire to all the Admiralty Orders on a notice-board in the wardroom. This was a hard act to follow. It was also unlucky for Miller that he took over at the very moment our period of enforced idleness came to an end and our period of demanding operations began. So, whereas the rest of the squadron had had months of working up in which to perfect their carrier-based skills, the unfortunate Miller was pitchforked straight from flying-training into the turmoil of the battle of the Atlantic.

On 23 December all aircrew were given Christmas leave. On 29 December all aircrew were recalled: "Urgent. Report forthwith to RNAS Eglinton." The moment we arrived at Eglinton we were told to embark immediately in HMS *Nairana*. On 31 December *Nairana* sailed, the last of her aircrew being hoisted aboard from Belfast docks almost literally at the last minute. We had been promised action before and been disillusioned. This turned out to be the real thing.

# 4

# *MATURITY*

War has been described as "long periods of boredom punctuated by brief moments of excitement". This was not the way we found it.

835 Squadron had enjoyed an eventful, if not a particularly hazardous, first few months. This was followed by a year-and-a-half of increasing boredom and frustration, with the squadron fully trained and eager for action, but kept waiting in the wings at a time when the Battle of the Atlantic was going badly and we were needed. Then came fifteen months of near-continuous operational flying, with the squadron employed on convoy protection duties in the North Atlantic and the Arctic Ocean. During these fifteen months we were driven to the very limit of our endurance in an unremitting battle against the enemy and the elements. Altogether we helped to escort and protect nineteen convoys, and it is a measure of our effectiveness that, from all the convoys we escorted, only one merchantman (and that a straggler) was lost.

For these last fifteen months we operated from HMS *Nairana*. After a while the squadron and the carrier became one, interdependent and indivisible. This was a bonding which had its moments of discord, but which resulted nonetheless in a hugely effective fighting unit.

So what sort of ship was the *Nairana*? She was laid down in March, 1942, at John Brown's shipbuilding yards on the Clyde, not as a warship but as a "cargo liner". In June, 1942, by which time her hull had been partially constructed, she was taken over by the Navy for conversion into an escort aircraft-carrier. At much the same time two other vessels were taken over for similar conversion; these were eventually commissioned as HMS *Vindex* and HMS *Campania*. The three vessels had the same basic design, here and there a keen eye could spot minor differences, for each bore the individual hallmark of the yard in which it was converted. The John

Brown conversion was commissioned as HMS *Nairana* on 26 November, 1943, her specification being:-

## HMS *Nairana: technical data*

| | |
|---|---|
| Displacement: | 13,825 tons (standard) |
| Length: | 524'0" (extreme) |
| Beam: | 68'0" |
| Draught: | 25'6" forward, 25'9" aft |
| Machinery: | John Brown diesels, 2 shafts |
| Speed: | 16 1/2 knots (designated) |
| Armament: | 2 ×4" guns |
| | 4 ×2pdr pompoms (later increased to |
| | 16 ×2 pdr pompoms in quad. mounting.) |
| | 8 Oerlikons (later increased to 16 ×20mm |
| | Oerlikons in twin mountings.) |
| | 21 ×18" Mk XII-XV torpedoes |
| | 270 Mk XI depth charges for aircraft |
| Aircraft: | 6 Hurricane IIcs and 12 Swordfish IIs |
| | (later increased to 6 Wildcat VIs and |
| | 15 Swordfish IIIs.) |

It is interesting to compare her to the American-built "Woolworth" carriers. *Nairana*'s flight-deck was 495 feet long and 60 feet wide; the American carriers' flight-deck was 450 feet long and 102 feet wide. *Nairana* had only one lift (aft); the American carriers had two lifts (one for'ard, one aft.) *Nairana* had no accelerator for launching her aircraft; the American carriers had a powerful accelerator for'ard of the barrier. From the point of view of handling and operating aircraft, the American carriers were undoubtedly superior. Their wider flight-deck made take-off and landing a great deal safer; their two lifts made it easier to move aircraft between flight-deck and hangar (even while flying was in progress), while their accelerator enabled their planes to get airborne even in conditions of dead calm. The American carriers also had a slight edge over their British counterparts in what might be called "working conditions". Their cabins were more spacious and better appointed; their messdecks, equipped with folding bunks, were more comfortable; their cafeteria system provided better food than the traditional British galley; their ancillary services – like the sick-bay, photographic darkroom and laundry – were better equipped.

The British carriers, however, had one great plus point. They were less prone to accident or breakdown, and, being of sturdier construction, they were able to operate in far worse weather conditions. They were more seaworthy.

For centuries the Navy had taken it for granted that their warships would, above all else, be good sea ships. This was a tradition dating back to the wars against France and Spain, when British frigates had had to spend year after year at sea, often in foul weather, blockading continental ports. Judged by the Navy's traditional standards, the "Woolworth" carriers were unseaworthy. They were felt to be too lightweight. *Nairana* and *Battler* were much the same size but the former weighed 14,000 tons, the latter only 9,000. They were welded rather than riveted; this meant that in bad weather their plates were liable to buckle or even disintegrate (which is what happened to *Dasher* in the middle of the North Atlantic). And their design was thought to be too open – whereas *Nairana*'s hangar was completely enclosed, *Battler*'s was in places open to the sea and in bad weather she shipped it green into her innards.

The Navy therefore spent a considerable time tinkering with the "Woolworth" carriers, trying to get them up to the required standard. This was the basic reason why 835 Squadron was formed in the first month of 1942, but didn't get a carrier to operate from until the last month of 1943.

Although this was frustrating at the time, in retrospect I'm extremely glad that the Squadron didn't set off on its voyages to Murmansk in a "Woolworth" carrier!

One of the first people to be appointed to HMS *Nairana* was her gunnery officer, Sam Hollings. This was in early October. Sam had never heard of the *Nairana*, and, arriving in Glasgow, was somewhat disconcerted to be told that no such ship existed! However, he eventually located his quarry, surrounded by a web of scaffolding, in John Brown's yard, and was told to "stand by daily until completion". In the weeks that followed Sam had little to do and plenty of time to think, and one of the things he thought about was his new ship's unusual name. He discovered that a nairana was a rare type of Tasmanian eagle; he also discovered that a crest had already been designed for the carrier with the motto "She Swoops to Conquer". Sam pointed out that eagles don't in fact "swoop", they "stoop"; and, in deference to his erudition, the ship's motto was altered to "She Stoops to Conquer", the title of the Oliver Goldsmith play.

The next few weeks saw the contractors putting the finishing touches to their conversion, and the ship's officers arriving one by one to take up their new appointments.

Our Commanding Officer was Captain R.M.T. Taylor, RN. Like many officers of staff rank who found themselves in charge of a carrier in the Second World War, Captain Taylor was neither a pilot nor an observer, and had no first-hand experience of flying. Inevitably, when it came to operating *Nairana*'s aircraft, he made mistakes because he didn't realize what his aircrew could and couldn't do. However, he had the good sense to listen to the views of his Commander Flying, with the result that by and large *Nairana* under his command was not only a well-run ship but a happy one.

Our Commander Flying was Lt-Cdr(A) Edgar Bibby, DSO, RNVR, whose job was to supervise the day-by-day operating of the carrer's aircraft. Edgar Bibby was one of those decisive and dedicated men who drive themselves to the limit of their endurance to achieve the best possible results. The trouble was that his tasks aboard *Nairana* were on a par with the labours of Hercules. For during carrierborne operations a Commander Flying was expected to be on the bridge whenever aircraft were taking-off or landing; he was also ultimately responsible for handling aircraft on the flight-deck and briefing the aircrew. Yet we were now about to take part in operations during which *Nairana*'s planes were not only flying every day but for twenty-four hours every day. This meant that, for week after week, Edgar Bibby never got more than a cat-nap of about an hour or at the very most an hour-and-a-half, and was never able to get out of his uniform.

> "I did four trips with *Nairana*," he writes, "and at the end of the fourth I had to see the ship's doctor. I told him I wanted desperately to sleep and sleep and go on sleeping, but couldn't because of my back.
>
> "'What's wrong with your back?' he asked me.
>
> "I told him it wouldn't stop itching.
>
> "He asked me when I'd last taken my clothes off, and I said about three weeks ago.
>
> "'Well, you can take them off now,' he told me. 'I want to see your back.'
>
> "He took one look: 'Good God,' he said, 'you've got scabies!'
>
> "I wasn't sure what scabies was. I'd always thought of it as something that disappeared with sailing ships and the Victorian

Poor House. Anyhow, I can't recommend it. I was taken to hospital and given a course of sulphur baths and scrubbing – treatment which went on for so long that by the time I was fit and had reported back to *Nairana* the carrier had sailed for Murmansk without me and with a new Commander Flying."

Among the rest of our ship's officers were several I can recall clearly even after fifty years. Most senior was Commander Healey, RN, known to millions as the "Uncle Mac" of the BBC's Children's Hour. Recalled to the Navy after years of retirement in South Africa, he brought with him a parrot, a wretched bird which delighted in pecking sub-lieutenants' ears and had been taught by Healey's steward to come up with startling pronouncements like "Ten days Number Eleven, you bastard!" (Number Eleven was one of the set punishments meted out to defaulters.) Our Chief Engineer, Commander Edwardson, and our Chief Electrical Officer, Lt-Cdr Bruce, were Royal Naval Reserve officers; both were bottle-a-day men who fraternized with us more readily than did many of our more formal RN colleagues. One of my happiest memories of *Nairana* is of the interest they took in our flying and of the long evenings we spent together discussing not only practical problems like deck-landing-and-lighting, but esoteric matters like what was the maximum length to which it was possible to build a carrier without it breaking its back in heavy seas.

There were also a number of specialist officers on whom our lives depended. Among these were the Batsman, the Fighter Direction Officer, the Meteorological Officer and the Operations Officer.

The Batsman's job was to help our aircraft land safely. To do this he had a pair of "bats" (a bit like big-headed squash rackets) with which he signalled his instructions to the pilot as he came in to land. These "bats" were illuminated at night and when visibility was poor. When an aircraft was ready to land the Batsman would take up his position on a small platform on the carrier's port quarter. From here he would watch the plane as it approached the flight-deck, and assist the pilot by giving him the following signals:-

*You are too high:*
*lose height*

*You are too low:*
*gain height*

*You are too fast:*
*reduce speed*

*You are too slow:*
*increase speed*

*You are right-wing*
*low: straighten up*

*You are left-wing*
*low: straighten up*

*You are doing fine:*
*keep coming as*
*you are*

*Cut your engine:*
*and touch down*

*Don't land:*
*Go round and*
*try again*

It was essential for pilots to trust the Batsman. This was particularly the case in heavy seas at night, when the stern of a carrier might be rising and falling thirty or even forty feet, and all a pilot could see was two lines of landing-lights dimly outlining a heaving flight deck. In such conditions a Batsman was often better able than a pilot to judge whether or not an approach was likely to result in a safe landing.

The Batsman's job was both demanding and dangerous; demanding partly because each time a plane came in to land the lives of the aircrew were in his hands, and partly because (like a Commander Flying) he had to be on call twenty-four hours a day, and, with planes on continuous round-the-clock patrols, he got little sleep. Dangerous because there is clearly a high-risk risk in standing in the path of a plane that is hurtling towards you at almost 100 mph. This risk was accentuated aboard the *Nairana* by our unusually narrow flight-deck. This was only 60 feet wide. The wingspan of a Swordfish was 45 feet, which meant that, even if the plane landed exactly dead-centre, there would be a gap of no more than 7½ feet between the wing tip of the plane as it landed and the Batsman's head. (60 feet minus 45 feet = 15 feet, and half of 15 feet = 7½feet.) Landing dead-centre on a wild night, with poor visibility, a buffeting wind and the stern of the carrier corkscrewing this way and that, was not easy; many a Batsman had to dive into his safety-net to avoid being decapitated as a plane landed almost on top of him. Some left their dive too late.

We were lucky on the *Nairana* to have two exceptionally skilled Batsmen: initially Lt(A) Bill Cameron, RNVR, and subsequently Lt(A) Bob Mathé, RNVR. Bob in particular, who was with us on our convoys to Russia, performed what can only be called a succession of miracles in getting our Swordfish and Wildcats safely on to the flight-deck in about the most difficult conditions it would be possible to imagine: wind 70 knots gusting to over 100, waves 40 feet high, and the cold so numbing some of our aircrew were literally frozen into their cockpits. If ever a man earned his awards – a DSC and bar – it was Bob Mathé.

The work of our Fighter Direction Officers was almost as important, if less spectacular. In the words of the naval historian Captain Roskill: "It is no exaggeration to say that in radar development Britain led the world," and it is now generally recognized that radar was one of the factors which helped us win the war. It helped the RAF win the Battle of Britain and it helped the Navy win the Battle of the Atlantic; for warships equipped with radar were able to spot the presence, not only of other surface vessels, but of approaching aircraft. A Fighter Direction Officer's job was to detect these approaching enemy aircraft and help our fighters to intercept them. In the early years of the war only *Illustrious*-class carriers were equipped with radar. *Ark Royal*, for example, had to receive radar reports in morse from other warships and then pass these on, again in morse, to her aircraft. No wonder that, with the lengthy time lag this involved, few interceptions were made! However, by 1942 all carriers which were being built and/or converted had, as part of their standard layout, a well-equipped Fighter Direction room in their island. A training school for Fighter Direction Officers was set up first at RNAS Yeovilton and subsequently at nearby Speckington Manor. By the time we joined *Nairana* the business of detecting enemy aircraft and homing our fighters on to them had become an exact (and exacting) science.

*Nairana* had three Fighter Direction Officers; and one of them, Alan Kerry, writes:

"With the help of our equipment, we were able to build up an 'Air Scene'. Radar enabled us to determine the bearing and distance of any aircraft that approached us, and this information was at once recorded by plotters in the F.D. Office and transcribed on to a vertical perspex screen; this screen had a spider's web superimposed on it, the carrier being in the centre of the web.

Our problem was that the position of the aircraft on the screen was never its real position; because of the time lag, it had always moved on. However, with the help of judgement and experience, a good FDO could estimate the probable position of an approaching aircraft; and his job was then to help the carrier's fighters, which usually operated in pairs, to make an interception. It was important to make this interception as far away from the ship as possible, and in advantageous circumstances: i.e. from a greater height, from up-sun or from cloud-cover etc. The secret was never to direct one's fighters straight at their target; one had always to 'aim off'; and each interception had its own problems, its own timing and its own particular feel. It helped the atmosphere in the F.D. room if the fighter's RT could be broadcast 'live' so that we could hear the pilot; and an ecstatic 'tally ho!' was a wonderful moment for us."

Our Swordfish too were to some extent controlled from the carrier. Each patrol was meticulously plotted and transcribed on to the "Air Scene", and if a plane got into difficulties or became lost, our FDOs, at least in theory, could always give it a bearing to find its way back to *Nairana*.

All this was not only responsible work, but work that broke new ground. As Kerry puts it:

"The Royal Navy had been used to the Captain conning and fighting his ship from the bridge; but the Captain now had to come to terms with the fact that operations were controlled from elsewhere. More than once Surtees [*Nairana*'s captain in the last few months of the war] came storming into our Fighter Direction Room: 'Where are my aircraft?' I remember his hands digging into my shoulders so fiercely that the bruises were there for days . . . He may have known little about flying. But don't tell me he didn't care."

Another key job was that of our Meteorological Officer, Mike Arrowsmith. Met Officers were usually graduates, who were given six weeks' basic training, commissioned as sub-lieutenants, then sent on an intensive three-month course at the Royal Naval College, Greenwich. Here they learned how to use the various instruments which were the tools of their trade, and how to put together weather-charts and forecasts from whatever information was available. The trouble was that on a carrier not a lot of information *was* available, and a met officer was very much on his own.

"Some information," writes Arrowsmith, "came to us in coded broadcasts received every twelve hours from the Met Office at the Admiralty; but I found that my own observations of wind, sea, temperature, pressure and so on tended to be of greater use . . . . I soon discovered that my reputation didn't depend on the accuracy of my forecasts. If the weather was good I was thought to be a good met officer; if it was bad I was thought to be a bad one! However, I remember one occasion when a bad forecast brought me unexpected kudos.

"We were escorting a west-bound convoy through the mid-Atlantic gap. It was winter and we were a fair way north. U-boats were thought to be about, and the captain was anxious to keep our Swordfish airborne and circling the convoy. The trouble was that I felt certain the weather was about to close in and that conditions for flying would soon be impossible.

"'How long do you reckon it's safe to keep the Swordfish up?' the captain asked me.

"'1315 is the deadline, sir,' I told him. 'If you go on flying after that I can't be responsible.'

"It was lucky he listened to me. At 1300 hours, although the weather didn't look too bad, the patrolling Swordfish was recalled. At 1310 it landed-on. At exactly 1315 a huge wall of cloud came rushing towards us, and within seconds the island and the barrier had disappeared from sight as *Nairana* was engulfed in a violent snow storm that lasted the rest of the day!"

Continually compiling weather charts is not the sort of job that catches the eye, but there were times when our lives depended on the accuracy of Mike Arrowsmith's forecasts.

Equally unspectacular and equally important were the duties of our Operations Officer. His task was to ensure that our routine flying programme (anti-submarine patrols and fighter interceptions) was carried out with maximum efficiency, and that special operations (like our anti-shipping strikes among the Norwegian fjords) were carefully planned and executed.

*Nairana*'s Operations Officer from March, 1944, until March, 1945, was Lt-Cdr(A) Dick Mallett, RNVR, a well-balanced and sensible man who, at the ripe old age of 24, was regarded by our aircrew as a sort of father figure.

Dick was closely involved with our flying. Yet he was a ship's officer, not a squadron officer, which meant that he could perhaps take a more impartial view of things than some of our pilots and observers. This makes his recollections particularly interesting:-

> "When you got in touch after all these years," he wrote to me in 1990, "I couldn't sleep for nights. I was so haunted by memories of what we had all been through . . . . You ask for my impressions of those days. Well, my impression is that for more than a year 835 was almost continually flying in the most appalling conditions, and close to the limit of possibility. There was a tremendous *esprit de corps* in the Squadron; but towards the end everyone became operationally fatigued. Not round the bend; just totally bloody exhausted. Surtees knew very well that he was driving us to the limit of our endurance – and beyond. However, on the Russian convoys our function was to keep the enemy at bay, no matter what the cost, and it could be that his policy was justified" – a view to which not everyone in the Squadron would subscribe!

One other person had our lives in his hands: Chief Air Artificer Banham, who was in charge of the maintenance of our aircraft. The Squadron's Sea Hurricanes were old, and with their fixed wings were ill-suited to operate from a carrier, while the Swordfish were soon to be flown without respite for month after month in the North Atlantic and the Arctic. Under these taxing conditions Banham was expected to keep aircraft serviceable without being able to draw on any of the spare parts which, on an airfield, could be obtained by lifting a telephone. He managed it with the help of our Stores Officer, Jack Teesdale, and his own ingenuity.

When I became CO of the Squadron, which turned out to be a great deal sooner than I expected, I had a long chat with Jack Teesdale about how we could help Banham in his efforts to keep our planes flying. The key was spare parts. Our mobile equipment, which we had carried round with us over the last eighteen months as we moved from place to place, consisted largely of things like chocks, drip-trays, jacks and a plethora of repair tools. This is not what was needed in the middle of the Atlantic. What we needed, above all else, was replacement items like tyres, undercarriage oleo-legs, tail wheels, engine and radio parts, new radar valves etc. But alas, even after four years of war, the Admiralty seemed blissfully unaware that operational squadrons simply had to have such spares. According to KR and AI (King's Regulations and Admiralty Instructions), new parts could only be obtained by a laborious procedure which involved requisitioning each individual item as it became needed; nothing new would be provided unless the part that was damaged or unserviceable was returned. Faced with this unrealistic embargo, Jack and I were determined to build up a reserve of spare parts, and we hit on the idea of salvaging what we could from crashed aircraft.

During our first spell of operations in *Nairana*, we both noticed that planes which had crashed on landing and were badly damaged were sometimes pushed over the side. The reason for this was that, since *Nairana* had only one lift, there were usually some of our aircraft parked for'ard of the barrier; this meant that, if the landing-area had to be cleared quickly, the only way to get rid of a crashed plane was to tip it into the sea. Our idea was to train a team of squadron "scavengers" who could quickly strip a plane of its most valuable component parts before it was jettisoned.

And the operative word had to be "quickly", for the whole object of pushing a plane overboard was to clear the flight-deck fast. However, no aircraft could be so disposed of without the Captain's approval and the signing of Admiralty Form A25. This involved Commander Flying having a quick word with the Captain and getting his authorization; and in the two or three minutes this usually took, our "scavengers" sprang into action. Organized by Banham and led by Leading Air Mechanics Bert Timms and Alf Gibbons, our maintenance crews soon perfected the art of stripping and in next to no time the most useful items – tyres, oleo-legs, tail-wheels, compasses etc. – were extracted from the shattered plane; on one occasion we even managed to salvage a complete Pegasus engine! These valuable spares enabled our aircraft to be repaired and kept serviceable in spite of the parsimony of the Admiralty.

Another example of the sort of improvisation which kept us flying was Banham's ingenious use of roller-skates. When our fighter pilots saw that *Nairana* had only one lift and that this was barely wide enough to take one of their Hurricanes, whose wings couldn't be folded, they realized that moving their aircraft quickly between hangar and flight-deck was going to be a problem, a problem that would be accentuated by the difficulty of manoeuvring planes with such a large wingspan round a small and crowded hangar. Banham, however, hit on the idea of building a number of small trolleys which could be placed beneath the Hurricanes' wheels. To the underside of these trolleys were fixed pairs of coupled roller-skates, and this enabled the aircraft to be moved this way and that on the proverbial sixpence. It would be difficult to overestimate the amount of time and labour saved by this ingenious device – and time, when there were enemy planes or U-boats about, could be of the essence.

By the end of November most of *Nairana*'s ship's company of 800 had reported aboard and, on 12 December, the carrier was officially commissioned. Next day she moved downriver to the Tail O' the Bank.

The first member of 835 to come aboard was Jack Teesdale who, in his capacity as Stores Officer, had the job of loading and storing our mobile equipment. He arrived on Boxing Day to find a riotous party going on in the wardroom. The Captain was scrambling about among the vents of the air-conditioning, and one of the deck-officers, "Tug" Wilson, suddenly appeared in the companionway, dripping wet. He had, he explained, "walked over the side"! All of which, Jack felt, augured well for a good relationship between ship and squadron officers!

A couple of days later our Sea Hurricanes and Swordfish were flown aboard and, on the last day of 1943, *Nairana* weighed anchor from the Tail O' the Bank and stood into the estuary of the Clyde to begin the inevitable spell of working up.

You might have thought that by now we had had our fill of working up, but this time it was different. This time, right from the start, we had the feeling we were on the threshold of something important.

For one thing there were changes to our aircraft and to our tactics which were obviously being made with a specific job in mind. For example, the camouflage of our Sea Hurricanes was altered. They were painted white.

The camouflage of naval aircraft had been standardized between the wars, both fighters and torpedo-bomber-reconnaissance planes being painted green, with the idea of their merging into the colour of the sea. However, experience in the Atlantic had shown that green was clearly visible against a backdrop of cloud, and it is cloudy most of the time in the Atlantic; also that our planes' conventional camouflage made them stand out against the sea, which was more often grey than green. With the support of our fighter pilots, Edgar Bibby suggested that the Sea Hurricanes were painted off-white. Captain Taylor had his doubts and said that we needed Admiralty approval for such a change. Bibby, however, had the courage of his convictions. One day the Hurricanes were green, the next day they were white, and their subsequent successes undoubtedly owed much to their camouflage, for on more than one occasion they were able to close right in on their target without being seen.

Our working-up that January was unusually demanding. By day the Hurricanes concentrated on air-to-air and air-to-ground firing, and on interceptions controlled by Alan Kerry; this involved 93 hours' flying, and 88 deck-landings. By night the Swordfish concentrated on homing by radar on to towed targets which were then attacked with live depth-charges or rockets; this involved 302 hours flying and 22 deck-landings. On more than one occasion, even in the Clyde, we were glad of *Nairana*'s radar beacon to home on; this spelt out the carrier's identification letters on the observer's ASV screens.

On 21 January we had a VIP visitor: Rear Admiral Lumley Lyster (Flag Officer Carrier Training). It was Lyster who had masterminded the attack on Taranto, when a handful of Swordfish had sunk or crippled almost half the Italian fleet; and we would have liked to turn on a display to convince him that the standard of flying in the Fleet Air Arm was as high in 1944 as it had been in 1940. It was not to be. We planned a dummy night torpedo attack and the CO and I, together with Urquhart and Buckie and McEwan and Hall, duly took off a little after seven o'clock. Then the weather closed in and the CO decided that conditions were too dangerous for flying and headed for the safety of the RAF aerodrome at Turnberry. The other two pilots found their way back to the carrier and landed safely. Lumley said nothing, but he could hardly have been impressed.

There was, I remember, some discussion next day among the fighter pilots about what had happened and one of them, Norman Sargent, remarked that the CO seemed permanently worried, "as though he has something on his mind" – an observation both shrewd and prophetic.

A couple of days later *Nairana* was put under forty-eight hours' notice to sail and the moment this deadline expired we weighed anchor and, together with the *Activity*, headed for the mouth of the Clyde.

Here we joined the 2nd Escort Group: HM Ships *Starling, Wild Goose, Wren, Woodpecker, Magpie* and *Kite*. This was the famous hunter-killer team, led by Captain Walker, which had already accounted for seven U-boats and was about to account for a good many more.

We were now on the threshold of fifteen months of continuous operational flying, so this seems an appropriate place for an update on our aircraft and aircrew.

The squadron now consisted of six Sea Hurricane IIcs and nine Swordfish IIs. Several long-serving aircrew had left, most of them to take up training duties ashore, and in the previous few months we had been joined by four new Hurricane pilots – Sub-Lt(A) C. Allen, RNZVR, Sub-Lt(A) O.K. Armitage, RNZVR, Sub-Lt(A) C. Richardson RNVR, and Sub-Lt(A) N. Sargent, RNVR; by three new Swordfish pilots – Sub-Lt(A) R.G. McLaughlin, RNZVR, Sub-Lt(A) K. Wilmot, RNVR and Sub-Lt(A) H.R.D. Wilson, RNVR, and by four new Swordfish observers – Sub-Lt(A) G. Arber, RNVR, Sub-Lt(A) W. Cairns, RNVR, Sub-Lt(A) A.R.J. Lloyd, RNVR and Sub-Lt(A) G. Strong, RNVR.

It was these aircrew, together with "old timers" like myself, Bob Selley, Johnny Hunt and Jack Teesdale, who formed the experienced core of the squadron in the hazardous times ahead.

Captain John Walker, to quote Admiralty records, "probably did more to free the Atlantic of the U-boat menace than any other single officer." In the late 1930s he had been passed over for promotion, largely because he was impatient of the "big ship" mentality that was prevalent between the wars. He was a "little ship" man, one of the few with the sense to realize that, if it came to a battle against the U-boats, it would not be battleships and cruisers that would give the Navy control of the Atlantic, but sloops, destroyers and corvettes. In 1943 his exploits proved his point. However, Walker had little experience of working with aircraft-carriers, and, before sailing in January in command of the 2nd Escort Group, he had remarked in confidence to his officers that "the flat-tops should be good bait to tempt the U-boats to attack us". It was as well for the morale of *Nairana*'s ship's company that we were unaware of the role for which we had been cast!

The Group headed into the Atlantic in its usual hunting formation, the six sloops a mile apart and in line abreast. The two carriers, positioned centrally, were stationed roughly a mile astern.

In spite of bad weather, A/S patrols were maintained throughout 31 January, and these patrols were continued on 1 February. A little before midday *Nairana* had just turned into wind to fly off two Swordfish and land-on the two which were returning from patrol, when *Wild Goose* flashed us an urgent signal: "U-boat about to attack you". Captain Taylor took violent evasive action and the two carriers withdrew at high speed, screened by *Kite*, *Wren* and *Woodpecker*. *Wild Goose* meanwhile dropped depth-charges in the spot where the periscope had been sighted and the U-boat, which had shown great skill and courage in penetrating so close to *Nairana*, now found itself hunted to death. In a creeping, aptly named "plaster" attack, the sloops *Starling* and *Wild Goose* dropped more than sixty depth-charges, set to detonate at 700 feet at five-second intervals. To quote Walker's biography:

> "Cease Fire was ordered and both ships stood by to wait for evidence of a sinking. It was not long in coming. Oil, clothing, planks of wood, pulped life jackets and the mangled remains of bodies provided all the proof that was needed of death and destruction."

German records confirm that U502, Kapitänleutnant Jeschke, was sunk in position 50°29'N, 17°29'W. There were no survivors.

Next day saw more excitement – for the squadron if not for the Escort Group. McLaughlin, Cairns and Hamilton took off in mid-morning on a routine patrol. They should have returned after three hours, yet at the end of three-and-a-half hours there was still no sign of them. For some time I had had my doubts about Will Cairns' ability as a navigator and only the day before I had said to his pilot that, if he ever found himself lost, his best bet would be to climb as high as he could, switch his IFF to distress and hope to be picked up and homed back to the carrier. After nearly four hours Alan Kerry reported a "friendly" blip on our radar screen. An experienced aircrew (Elliott, Winstanley and Defraine) were flown off and vectored towards the aircraft, which did indeed turn out to be our missing Stringbag heading in quite the wrong direction. It was guided back to the carrier. As McLaughlin came in to land, we all knew that he had been airborne for over four and a half hours and that four and a half hours was the maximum time a Swordfish could stay airborne before it ran out of fuel. An anxious "Bats" gave the signal to cut and land, but the irrepressible McLaughlin wasn't happy with his approach and decided to go round again. We were all at praying stations as the Swordfish circled the carrier a second time before coming in to make a perfect landing. As the plane taxied for'ard of the barrier, its engine spluttered, coughed and cut stone dead. Not a drop of fuel was left in its tanks.

What happened next will always trouble me. There were two possible reasons for the Swordfish getting lost: faulty compasses or navigational error. I had never been entirely happy with the compasses in Swordfish YNE989, the plane which McLaughlin and Cairns had been flying. This aircraft had already played an unusual role in our squadron story: smuggling aboard personnel. As I mentioned earlier, our departure from the Clyde had been precipitate, and several people who had been on thirty-six hours' leave only just got back to the ship before she sailed. Jack Dalton, in fact, *didn't* get back; he had been on a romantic escapade in Manchester, cut things too fine and the ship sailed without him. This could have landed him in very serious trouble indeed. I therefore left a message with the RTO (Rail Transport Officer) at Greenock to tell Dalton that the moment he turned up he should make *post haste* for the nearby airfield at Renfrew, where we were due that afternoon to pick up a replacement aircraft. In the afternoon George Sadler, Eric McEwan and I duly arrived at Renfrew. I checked the replacement aircraft, YNE989 and noted with some concern that its compasses had not been swung recently. However, it was the only Swordfish available, so I signed for it and we settled down to wait for Dalton. We were about to take off without him when he turned up, jaunty as ever. I told him he was a bloody fool and advised him to hide in the rear cockpit and stay there until the plane had landed and been struck down into the hangar. Thus was he smuggled back aboard.

At the time I thought I had done him a favour, but this was not the way things worked out. After Cairns' and McLaughlin's narrow escape, I asked another aircrew to go through a complicated manoeuvre with Swordfish YNE989, a manoeuvre which involved flying over the carrier at a precise time and taking compass bearings of the sun on north, south, east and west headings; these bearings were then compared with those taken at the same moment by the ship's navigating officer. The results seemed to indicate that the Swordfish compasses were OK. I therefore decided that Will Cairns' dead reckoning must have been at fault. In view of what happened next, I shall always wonder if I was right.

During the next couple of days, in spite of bad weather, we flew a large number of A/S patrols and a smaller number of fighter patrols. However, neither U-boats nor enemy aircraft were sighted. Early on 5 February two aircraft took off as usual a little before dawn: Selley, Newbery and Long in Swordfish HJ665; Costello, Dalton and Nield in Swordfish YNE989. The latter were never seen nor heard of again. They simply disappeared. No signals or distress calls were picked up. No wreckage was found. After four hours we started to search for them, using every available aircraft. The entries in our Fair Flying Log are repetitive: "search for lost aircraft", "search for lost aircraft", "search for lost aircraft". The CO searched. I searched. Even Edgar Bibby, our Commander Flying, searched. But Costello, Dalton and Nield had vanished as though they had never been. I shall always think of those compasses and wonder if there was anything more I could have done.

It was a sad little group who gathered that night in Tony Costello's cabin to play some of his favourite records on the gramophone which he had always said would belong to the Squadron if anything should happen to him. To say he was missed would be an understatement.

Next day, 6 February, we were ordered to go to the help of the huge homeward-bound convoy SL147 – eighty-one merchantmen and warships – which was being shadowed in mid-Atlantic by enemy aircraft and was under threat of attack by a pack of more than twenty U-boats.

Our first job was to get rid of the shadowing aircraft, and as we approached the convoy first Mearns and Sargent, then Armitage and Gordon, were flown off in their Sea Hurricanes. The weather was fine but cloudy and hazy, with eight-tenths cumulus coming down in places to no more than 1,000 feet – better weather for shadowing than for making an interception. The enemy aircraft were never engaged. They were, however, driven away. Their "blips" disappeared from our radar screen and never returned. But they had done their job. The U-boats had been homed on to the convoy and were all around us. *Nairana* and *Activity* moved into an open "box" inside the convoy. Here they were screened from the U-boats and able to turn into wind to operate their aircraft without disrupting the orderly lines of merchantmen. Captain Walker ordered all ships to action stations, anticipating that as soon as it was dark the convoy would come under attack.

He was right. His biographer sets the scene:

"As dusk turned to darkness . . . a heavy, damp mist covered ships and men in a white frostlike dew. Sea and sky merged into a haze of midnight-blue, so that the horizon was blotted out, and the vessels seemed to be flying through a layer of whispy low-lying cloud. As darkness closed in a hush settled over both sea and ships . . . . It was a game of patience, Walker and his officers waiting to see from which quarter the enemy would make his first lunge. The Merchant Navy captains waiting to see whose number would come up first: which of them would be the first to explode in flames."

It would be idle to pretend that the Squadron played a major role in the battle that followed. On 7 and 8 February we flew more than thirty patrols, nearly all of them in poor visibility, and without doubt this helped to keep the U-boats submerged and at bay and prevented them from getting into favourable positions to attack the convoy. But this was the hour of Walker and his diminutive sloops. In the course of fifteen eventful hours they sank three U-boats – and it is worth remembering that Churchill reckoned that every U-boat sunk had an effect on the course of the war equivalent to a thousand-bomber raid on Berlin.

*Wild Goose* was first to make contact. Her lookouts spotted a U-boat trimmed down on the surface with only her conning tower visible; she was trying, engines idling, to creep undetected through the screen of warships. *Wild Goose* first attempted to ram her, then, in concert with *Woodpecker*, carried out a creeping attack. Depth-charges rained down on the hapless *U762*, which, German records confirm, went down with all hands in position 49°02'N, 16°58'W.

Less than an hour later another U-boat (*U734*) was picked up on the opposite side of the convoy by *Starling*'s Asdic. Three sloops carried out a concerted attack on her. The last to attack, *Woodpecker*, dropped a pattern of twenty-six charges set to explode at maximum depth. As the sound of the last charge died away there was a moment of silence. Then came the most terrible roar as the submarine disintegrated. Once again the sea frothed and bubbled as oil, buckled plates and broken bodies came churning to the surface.

In the early hours of the morning *Kite* picked up an Asdic contact some miles ahead of the convoy, but this turned out to be no easy kill and, after making several attacks without success, the sloop came within a hair's breadth of being hit by a torpedo. *Magpie* then made a "creeping" twenty-six-charge attack, but the submarine (*U238*), constantly altering its course, depth and speed, avoided them all. "This chap knows his job," Walker was heard to remark. "It's almost a pity we have to kill him." Three hours and 150 depth-charges later, *Magpie*'s "Hedgehog" (a multi-barrelled bomb-thrower which flung depth-charges *ahead* of the sloop rather than rolling them off its stern) scored a direct hit, and that was the end of a brave and resourceful adversary. "*U238*", the German Admiralty confirms, "Kapitän Hepp, was lost with all hands in position 49°44'N, 16°07'W."

As well as making these confirmed "kills", Walker and his sloops were so effective in keeping the U-boats' heads down that not a single torpedo was launched against the convoy. The sloops themselves, on the other hand, came under frequent attack. Several acoustic torpedoes were fired at them, and on one occasion *Starling* only escaped destruction by exploding the torpedo speeding towards her by throwing her depth-charges into its path.

By midday on 9 February it was clear that Convoy SL147 had been saved. There wasn't a U-boat within 100 miles of it. Walker and his sloops were therefore ordered to head west to protect another homewardbound convoy, while *Nairana* and *Activity* remained with the Sierra Leone (SL) merchantmen for the rest of their passage home. As Walker headed deeper into the Atlantic, where he was to sink another two U-boats, he sent us a signal which went a long way towards assuaging the disappointment we felt at still not having a U-boat to our credit: "Well done, *Nairana*. Your pilots have performed miracles."

The rest of the voyage home may not have made the headlines, but, as far as the squadron were concerned, it was by no means lacking in incident. Almost as soon as Walker left us an enemy aircraft appeared on our radar, and Burgham and Richardson were flown off to attempt an interception. The plane, a four-engined Focke Wulf "Condor", was sighted, but once again there was a great deal of cloud about, the enemy aircraft took refuge in a belt of cumulus and our Hurricanes were never able to get it in their sights. It seemed to Captain Taylor that the 'Condor' had probably been trying to home more U-boats on to us; he was therefore determined to keep A/S patrols circling the convoy by both day and night. Two Swordfish, the first flown by our CO, Lt-Cdr Miller, with me as his observer and Willie Armstrong as his telegraphist-air-gunner, and the second flown by Bob Selley, took off in the late afternoon. There

18. 'Dusty' Miller leaning against his Sea Hurricane at Gibraltar in the summer of 1944. He was killed in action off Murmansk, 12 December, 1944.

19. Some of the Squadron's telegraphist air gunners:
Back Row, L. to R.: L/A Defraine, P.O. Armstrong, L/A Brown, P.O. Long.
Front Row, L. to R.: L/A Sellings, P.O. Sheldrake.

20.

21.

22.

These three photographs, taken from the cockpit of a Swordfish, show a pilot's view of what it was like coming in to land on the escort carrier HMS *Nairana*. No. 20 shows the plane at the start of its approach, coming in at an angle so that the engine-cowling doesn't obstruct the pilot's view. (Note that the Swordfish on the flight-deck of the carrier, for'ard of the barrier, has its wings spread.) No. 21 shows the plane, still at a slight angle, approaching the round-down. No. 22 shows the plane a couple of seconds before touchdown. It is too high. The batsman (arrowed) is giving the pilot the signal to 'come lower'. If he doesn't react quickly he will end up in the barrier! Note too that the Swordfish for'ard of the barrier now has its wings folded.

23. Barry Barringer's speech at the dinner to celebrate his promotion to C.O. — February, 1944.

24. Wilf Waller's party, Cabin 12, HMS *Chaser*.
Back Row, L. to R.: John Winstanley, Jack Teesdale, Wilf Waller, Barry Barringer, Sam Mearns.
Front Row, L. to R.: Bob Selley, three ship's officers, Dave Newbery.

was little wind, a lot of mist, and visibility was poor. All the same, it seemed to Willie and me that conditions for flying were not too bad and that our CO was making unnecessarily heavy weather out of what ought to have been a fairly routine patrol. It was as though he had something on his mind. After we had been airborne for the better part of our allotted two hours I got a message from *Nairana* ordering us to continue patrolling for a further hour. When I passed this message on to the CO, he seemed to be rather concerned. And we soon discovered why. It had not escaped our notice that Lt-Cdr Miller didn't care for night flying. Not once since we left the Clyde had his name appeared on the duty rota for a night patrol, whereas some pilots like Johnny Hunt and Bob Selley, had flown half-a-dozen. And it was a not very confident pilot who now muttered that he had expected to be back before dark, that he hadn't done any night flying lately, and that landing with so little wind was going to be difficult. Knowing how he felt didn't do much for our peace of mind, and the rest of the patrol passed in a somewhat strained silence.

By the time we got back to the carrier there was not a glimmer of daylight. Miller's first approach was too high and he was waved round again. His second approach was no better. Nor was his third. Sensing trouble, I told Willie Armstrong to secure his "G-string" (the wire which was supposed to ensure that, in the event of a crash, aircrew weren't catapulted out of their cockpit). Although poor Miller's fourth approach was far from perfect, "Bats" gave him the signal to cut. It was obligatory to obey this. Miller, however, was obviously afraid that this approach too was not good enough to ensure a safe touch down. He rammed open the throttle and tried to go round yet again. It was not to be. The heavily-laden Swordfish, weighed down with depth-charges and with little wind to give it lift, couldn't gain height sufficiently quickly. As it tried to claw its way skyward, its landing hook caught the top of the barrier. It was a scenario for disaster. The Stringbag, its engine at full throttle, came crashing down on top of one of the Hurricanes parked on the for'ard part of the flight-deck. Sitting in the cockpit of the Hurricane, only seconds earlier, had been our senior fighter pilot Al Burgham, who is not sure to this day what instinct made him leap to safety as the Swordfish came lumbering out of the night. We slithered across the flight-deck and would have gone over the side if the Swordfish hadn't still been attached, like a hooked fish, to the barrier. We came to rest in the catwalk. Looking down, the CO, Willy Armstrong and I could see the sea below us and the flight-deck somewhere above us. Wondering by what miracle we were still alive and uninjured, we extricated ourselves from the remains of our aircraft.

The unfortunate Miller was summoned to the bridge and placed under cabin arrest. Willy and I, our knees still knocking, watched our shattered Swordfish being hoisted back on to the flight-deck. And suddenly there was another shock. One of the armourers reported that the depth-charges were still primed. If the Swordfish had fallen into the sea, its depth-charges (which detonated on contact with water) would have exploded and that would certainly have been the end of us, and quite likely the end of *Nairana* too.

While all this was going on, Bob Selley had been circling the carrier, waiting to land. He couldn't, of course, see what was happening but he knew by the long delay that Miller must have crashed. He knew too that, with a heavy load and no wind, landing wasn't going to be easy. He asked permission to jettison his depth-charges. This, however, was curtly refused. After about fifteen minutes, by which time the flight-deck had been cleared, Bob came in and managed at the first attempt to make a perfect landing. When he reported to the bridge, he asked Edgar Bibby why he hadn't been allowed to jettison his depth-charges. The answer was brief and to the point: "I wanted you to land with them on," Bibby told him, "just to show it could be done. To keep up morale."

As soon as we saw that Bob had landed safely, Al Burgham and I made our way to the wardroom for a much-needed drink. We had barely sat down when I was called to the bridge.

"I want you," Captain Taylor said, "to take over the Squadron."

I pointed out that, although I might have been the most experienced officer in the Squadron, I was not the most senior.

But Captain Taylor cut me short: "Just get on with it, Barringer," he said.

I didn't have much option. Indeed I didn't have *any* option. So I called the Squadron together, told them what Captain Taylor had said and asked them to give me all the help they could. This, throughout the eventful months to come, they unfailingly did. And I certainly needed their help. For I was barely twenty-three; I had less than a year's seniority as a lieutenant, and I hadn't been given any sort of training to fit me to take command of a squadron.

The rest of our passage home was lacking in incident, and on 12 February we delivered our seventy-odd merchantmen into the safe waters of the Clyde.

For the Squadron it had been an eventful and somewhat costly initiation to the battle of the Atlantic. We had carried out almost 100 patrols, searches and interceptions, many of them in difficult weather; this had involved over 220 hours' flying. On the debit side, one Swordfish and its crew had been lost and four Swordfish and two Sea Hurricanes had been damaged; and we had, alas, sunk no U-boats and shot down no enemy planes. On the credit side, not one of the merchantmen we were guarding had been attacked, let alone damaged or lost. This was a pattern to be repeated on more than one occasion during our operations in the Atlantic.

When we berthed at Greenock one of the first people to slip quietly ashore was Lt-Cdr Miller. I felt sorry for him. It was hardly his fault that he had been asked to do a job that was clearly beyond his capabilities, and it seemed to me that the sad little story of what happened to him proved two points. It proved firstly that, even in this comparatively late stage of the war, the Navy was still having to pay for the way it had neglected its Air Arm; for there was now a serious shortage of aircrew with both operational experience *and* the required seniority of rank to be given command of a squadron. It also proved the value of our working up. In the last year we had worked up *ad nauseum*. We were heartily sick of it. But there can be no denying that all our trial deck-landings, navigation exercises and dummy attacks had honed our flying skill to the point at which we could (to quote our Operations Officer) "fly almost continually in the most appalling conditions and close to the limit of possibility". Miller had done no working up. He was more senior than any of us. He had more flying hours in his log book than any of us. But he had not flown operationally for a long time, and he had lost the flying skill that the job demanded. And he knew it.

At the time my appointment as CO came as a considerable shock; but looking back I suppose I was better prepared than poor Miller.

The few days we spent at Greenock were a busy time for me. My first priority was to get replacements for the aircraft that had been lost or damaged beyond repair. In this, my right hand man was Jack Teesdale, who flew from airfield to airfield, meticulously testing and checking the aircraft that were available. The last thing we wanted was more suspect compasses. As a result of his efforts, our strength was soon restored to ten Swordfish and six Sea Hurricanes. No sooner were the aircraft aboard than we set off on another assignment – escorting a convoy to Gibraltar. We got to know Gibraltar pretty well in the next few months, for we escorted no fewer than four outward bound convoys *to* the Rock, and four homeward bound convoys *from* the Rock and back to the United Kingdom.

The Gibraltar convoys were neither the most important in the war nor the most hazardous. However, without them the Allied landings in North Africa, Italy and the South of France would not have been possible, and they did have their own particular problems. At the approaches to the Bay of Biscay (which the convoys had to cross) the seas were nearly always high, while the weather tended to alternate between calms with sea mist, and storms with high winds – not the best conditions for flying. Also the Bay of Biscay was the route by which large numbers of German submarines, from their pens on the west coast of France, moved into and out of the Atlantic; the enemy were never far away.

The official file on *Nairana*, compiled by the Historical Branch of the Admiralty, reads:

"On 24 February 1944 HMS *Nairana*, with HMS *Activity* sailed from the Tail O' the Bank to provide air protection for Convoy OS69/KMS43 to Gibraltar. No enemy air attacks were intercepted, no U-boats were encountered, and the convoy arrived safely at Gibraltar on 6 March."

However, from the point of view of the squadron there was more to it than that.

Our first problem was that somebody at the Admiralty had come up with the not very bright idea that we should carry Fulmars which could be used as night fighters. We were therefore saddled with three of these antiquated aircraft from 787 Squadron. The Fulmars took up much-needed space in our already overcrowded hangar and in the event they did no night flying at all, and only six daylight patrols during which they managed to write off two out of their three aircraft. It was all a bit of a fiasco.

In fairness to the pilots from 787 Squadron it has to be said that flying conditions were difficult. For much of the trip our Hurricanes were confined to the hangar, while our Swordfish were only kept flying by the skill of their pilots. Throughout the first part of the voyage the swell was not only heavy but was at right angles to the direction of the wind. This meant that whenever *Nairana* turned into wind to enable her planes to land-on, the carrier was rolling and corkscrewing. This in turn meant that, as a plane neared the flight-deck, the stern of the carrier would suddenly disappear from sight into the trough of a swell and roll away from the approaching plane. Again and again "Bats" had to wave the Swordfish away. Sometimes as many as ten approaches had to be made before a plane got down safely. Landing in these conditions was particularly difficult at night, when several pilots reported that the deck-landing lights appeared to go on and off as the ship pitched into the swell. On the night of 29 February Lou Wilmot crashed on landing. However, the crew were unhurt, and at least there were pickings for Banham and his scavengers!

A couple of days later there was another near-disaster, this time with one of the Sea Hurricanes. An enemy aircraft had been picked up on *Nairana*'s radar and, although conditions for flying were not good, Al

Burgham and Charles Richardson took off to attempt an interception. There was, however, too much cloud about for them to catch sight of their quarry. When they returned, they found *Nairana* pitching wildly, and Al had one of his rare crashes. There was nothing wrong with his approach, but, just as "Bats" gave him the signal to cut, the stern of the carrier suddenly reared up some thirty feet. The main wheels of the Hurricane landed squarely on the flight-deck, but its tail wheel just caught the end of the roundown. The impact broke the plane's back. It flipped on to its nose, skidded along the deck and became enmeshed in the arrester wires. So Al joined the exclusive group of pilots who have managed to land by picking up the first arrester-wire not with their tail-hook but their propeller!

A couple of days after this, on the evening of 4 March, we suffered not a near-disaster but an all too real one. There was a heavy swell and a gusting wind and, although Lou Wilmot, "Albert" Arber and their telegraphist-air-gunner, George Ferguson, took off in daylight, it was dark by the time they got back. Their Swordfish missed the arrester-wires, smashed into the island and fell broken-backed into the sea. Wilmot and Ferguson were drowned. Arber survived, but his lungs were so affected by fumes from the flares and smoke-floats triggered off in the sinking plane that he spent the rest of the voyage in *Nairana*'s sick bay and never flew with the Squadron again.

Next morning we paraded on the flight deck. Wilmot and Ferguson weren't the first of our aircrew to die, but they were the first to be buried at sea. It was a moving ceremony: the vastness of the sky, the moan of the wind and the sound of waves breaking against our keel as our friends were committed to the deep. And I shall never forget the moment of silence. For, as the bodies slid over the side, every ship in the convoy stopped its engines. There were perhaps twenty seconds of absolute silence, absolute stillness. Then engines picked up, propellers again churned up the water, and the convoy and the Battle of the Atlantic went on.

Years later Johnny Cridland added a postscript to this. It seems that he and Wilmot had been particularly close friends, and only a few hours before the accident Wilmot had admitted to Johnny that he had doubts about his ability to land in the dark in bad weather. Johnny had suggested that his friend should have a talk with me, to see if I would excuse him from flying that night, but Lou Wilmot had said this wouldn't be fair, because it would mean that someone else in the Squadron would have to face the danger of extra night flying. His selflessness cost him and George Ferguson their lives.

On 6 March the convoy arrived in Gibraltar after a passage not as lacking in incident as the Admiralty report might lead one to suppose. For many of us this was our second call at Gibraltar, and we lost no time in revisiting old haunts and old acquaintances – the Hotel Cristina amid the orange trees of Algeciras, the voluptuous Juanita and her all female band. Some of us joined the bull-fighting aficionados at La Linea. Most of us bought silk stockings and perfume (which were of course unobtainable at home). And all of us enjoyed the bright lights which, after dark, gave the Rock an aura of gaiety and excitement – a welcome change from the austerity of blacked-out Britain.

It was good while it lasted. However, after only forty-eight hours we were back at sea, guarding the homeward-bound convoy MK529, which consisted of twenty merchantmen, many of them troopships. Among the escorts was the veteran battleship *Warspite*. She had been damaged during the allied landings at Salerno and now left behind her a telltale trail of oil, which McEwan and Hall found extremely helpful one evening when they were lost; they simply followed the oilslick back to the convoy.

"The passage home," records the Admiralty file on *Nairana*, 'was uneventful, and on 15 March the carrier parted with the convoy and arrived at the Tail O' the Bank." And there is indeed not much else to say about Convoy MK529, except for the all-important fact that it enjoyed a safe passage, with no U-boat getting near enough to make an attack. This was largely because the convoy followed a route unusually close to the shore and for much of the time was guarded by land-based aircraft of Coastal Command. All the same, between 9 and 15 March the squadron flew more than twenty-five A/S patrols, a fair number of them at night. There were known to be U-boats in the Bay, and it seems reasonable to suppose that our efforts kept their heads down. Not spectacular work, but I dare say that the thousands of men in the troopships were glad to hear the throb of Pegasus engines as, for hour after hour, our Swordfish circled the convoy.

We wouldn't have minded a spot of leave, but no sooner had we dropped anchor in the Clyde than we were put on forty-eight hours readiness to sail and a couple of days later we were back in the Atlantic, providing air cover for the slow southbound convoy OS72/KMS46. Once again our destination was Gibraltar.

You could say that this was another "uneventful" passage, for, although there were U-boats and enemy aircraft in the vicinity, none got close enough to launch an attack. Because the convoy was unusually slow and took a full ten days to cover the 1800-odd miles to Gibraltar, we had a good deal of flying to do. The squadron carried out fifty-two anti-submarine patrols and searches, which involved more than 150 hours flying. The Hurricanes carried out fifteen patrols and interceptions, involving some twenty hours flying. Many of the Swordfish patrols were made at night and in bad weather, while, on two of the Hurricane interceptions, conditions for flying were difficult in the extreme. It says much for our pilots' skill and concentration that there were only three accidents, none of them serious – two Swordfish and one Sea Hurricane ending up in the barrier.

The convoy arrived safely at the Rock on 5 April and it was during the ensuing spell of shore leave that a longstanding and niggling antipathy came to a head. It would be silly to make too much of this, but the relationship between some of the Squadron and some of *Nairana*'s T124X officers and stewards was not always as good as it might have been. In the early days of the war a number of Merchant Navy officers, in particular engineering, electrical and supply officers, chose to serve in warships rather than merchant vessels; they were therefore given what was known as a T124X contract and Royal Naval Reserve rankings. In the Merchant Navy these men had been used to certain standards of pay, certain privileges and certain codes of conduct, and these they expected to maintain – as they were perfectly entitled to – aboard the *Nairana*. To give an example: if a T124X officer carried out a duty watch at night, he expected to be allowed to spend the next morning asleep in his bunk – a practice unheard of in the Royal Navy. Another bone of contention was pay. Some of the T124X stewards were earning considerably more than the squadron's pilots and observers, which, when one considers the relative importance of their duties, seems not as it should have been. (When Tony Costello offered his steward £2 a week to do his laundry, he was considerably put out when the steward replied that he would pay Tony £3 a week to do his!)

Matters came to a head over the running of the wardroom bar. This was in the hands of Surgeon-Commander Dodds, a much-respected and well-liked doctor, but not the best of administrators. As a result of his somewhat lax control, our T124X stewards were able to siphon off large quantities of liquor to their companions below deck. Commander Healey, who was the man ultimately responsible for discipline aboard the *Nairana*, transferred the running of the bar into the capable hands of Jack Teesdale, who at once went to the heart of the problem. He relieved the bar stewards of their keys to the liquor store and initiated a régime whereby supplies had to be brought to the wardroom daily, under supervision, entered into a stock book and signed for. The result was an efficient, well-run bar.

However, the cutting off of their illegal supplies didn't please the T124X people. There were attempts to steal the keys, attempts to fake a burglary, and many heated arguments. In one of the latter, Bill Armitage, with typical Kiwi forthrightness, flattened an aggressive T124X Sub Lt(E) with a crunching short left. Those who saw the blow swear it travelled less than six inches, but the news of it travelled a good deal further, and from then on squadron aircrew were treated with wary respect!

However, you might say that the ex-Merchant Navy officers had the last laugh. During one of our many visits to Gibraltar some of the fighter pilots and some of the engineer officers went wining and dining one evening at the Bristol Hotel. On their way back to the ship they spotted a party going on at the exclusive Gibraltar Yacht Club. This they proceeded to gatecrash. They then blotted their copybooks by chatting up the more attractive ladies and telling their RN escorts that they ought to learn to fly. In the eyes of the Commodore of the Yacht Club such behaviour put them beyond the pale, and a formal complaint was made to Captain Taylor. Next morning all officers were summoned to *Nairana*'s wardroom and our captain asked those who had been at the Yacht Club to stand up. Our delinquent fighter pilots got reluctantly to their feet and were given harbour duties, watch on watch off, for the rest of our stay in Gibraltar – "not," as Norman Sargent put it, "an experience to be recommended!" The delinquent T124X officers, who marched to the beat of a different drum, remained seated and escaped punishment.

Much to the relief of Sargent and his colleagues our stay in Gibraltar was a brief one. On 10 April we joined the slow, homeward-bound convoy SL154/MKS43.

The evening before we sailed an intriguing notice appeared in the wardroom, confirming rumours that a German U-boat had been sunk off the Rock and that we were taking its crew back to the United Kingdom for internment.

> "As you may be aware," Commander Healey wrote, "we have some German prisoners on board. It is unlikely that you will come into contact with them, but if you do please treat them as you yourself would wish to be treated if you were a prisoner of war."

In fact we *did* have contact with them, because, towards the end of the voyage, they were invited to a concert in the hangar and, with the help of George Gordon (who spoke fluent German), they joined in the singing. Later, when we had dropped anchor in the Clyde and the Germans were on their way to internment, they all stood up in the launch that was taking them ashore and waved us goodbye.

The Battle of the Atlantic was one of the most terrible ever fought. Allied seamen were burned to death in patches of blazing oil and frozen to death in ice-cold waters; they died of starvation clinging to rafts and were trapped alive in sinking ships. German submariners, caught in the beam of our Asdic, were hunted to death with depth-charges; they were suffocated by carbon monoxide poisoning and blown, degutted, to the surface. Yet, as far as we were concerned, it was a battle fought without hatred and without rancour. Of course we would have sent a U-boat to the bottom if we had had the chance. But more than one member of the Squadron has since admitted to me privately that he was thankful to get through the war "without blood on my hands". For of all the deaths that man in his inhumanity has invented for man, few are as terrible as the death facing a submariner.

Convoy SL154/MKS43 was another so-called "uneventful" one, although, since we again provided almost continuous air cover, a more descriptive adjective from the squadron's point of view would be "demanding".

The Hurricane pilots may have flown less than a dozen sorties, but they spent goodness knows how many hours strapped into their planes which were ranged on the flight-deck at instant readiness for take-off. Two interceptions were attempted. On the first, the enemy plane disappeared into cloud and was never seen again. On the second, the aircraft they intercepted turned out to be an American "Flying Fortress" being ferried to the United Kingdom. When Al Burgham and Charles Richardson appeared out of the murk in their Sea Hurricanes and took up station on either wing tip, the US aircrew obviously thought their last moment had come; they started flashing the code letters of the day at our fighters so fast that neither Al nor Charles could read them! As Al remarked, "It was good, for once, to scare somebody other than myself!"

The Swordfish aircrew flew fifty-eight patrols, many of them at night and in bad weather. All went well until we were approaching the British Isles in particularly unpleasant conditions – gale force winds and a heavy swell coming in on our beam. We then had one mini and one major disaster. Teddy Elliott bounced over all the arrester-wires and went into the barrier; fortunately the wind was so strong his aircraft had virtually come to rest before he hit it. On the same day, taking off in the dark, Eric McEwan was halfway down the flight deck when *Nairana* corkscrewed violently. The Swordfish was flung sideways and its wing tip smashed into the island. The plane slid over the side and started to sink.

Eric remembered that, as the Swordfish went down, it seemed to take him a very long time to struggle out of the shattered cockpit. This, as it turned out, was just as well, because, as he came up towards the surface, he heard the beat of the ship's propellers getting louder and louder as they passed directly overhead. He surfaced in the *Nairana*'s wake. He could see no sign at first of his observer and telegraphist-air-gunner; then, as he was lifted up on the crest of a wave, he spotted them, hauling themselves into the aircraft's dinghy. (He learned afterwards that, as soon as the

Swordfish started to sink, its rubber dinghy stowed in the wing had automatically inflated and broken clear of the plane.) Luckily the corvette HMS *Clover*, which as rescue ship had been positioned on the carrier's port quarter, was on the *qui vive*. She saw what had happened, stopped engines and lowered a cutter. The cutter made straight for the dinghy, and finding the two aircrew in it safe and uninjured, started searching for the third. "They found me in next to no time," recorded the imperturbable McEwan, "and the three of us were taken aboard the corvette and put to bed, none the worse for our ducking."

Thirty-six hours later we were at anchor in the Clyde. We were given eight days' shore leave, or, in the case of one of our ship's company, indefinite sick leave. Over the last few months Edgar Bibby had worked himself to exhaustion on behalf of the squadron. It was typical of him that, instead of going straight to hospital, he insisted on flying to Liverpool to supervise the making, by his family firm, of the improved lights and screens which he had designed to help with our deck-landings. Captain Taylor was not too enthusiastic about these lights, and the Admiralty were never asked to approve them (it would, Bibby knew, have been impossible to get the go ahead quickly); nevertheless they were built and installed before the start of our next operation. Like most innovations they had teething problems, but there was no doubt about their usefulness, and their basic design – with a green light indicating a good approach, a white light a too high approach, and a red light a too low approach – has been the basis of all night deck-landing systems from that day to this. Edgar Bibby was everything a Commander Flying should be: knowledgeable, committed and able to establish a *modus operandi* between what the captain wanted to do and what the aircrew were able to do.

His successor arrived a few days before we sailed. Lt-Cdr(A) Nigel Ball, DSC, RN, turned out to be a competent, pleasant and easy-going man who, as an ex-Swordfish pilot, had the right qualifications for the job. Rumour had it that he had won his DSC in the early days of the war by shooting down a Messerschmitt 109 (then Germany's ace fighter) with his single antiquated front machine-gun: for which improbable feat of marksmanship he became known as "One gun Ball".

It was during this spell of leave that I was promoted to Lt-Cdr and confirmed as Squadron CO. Together with a couple of other aircrew and a fair number of ship's officers I was spending my leave aboard the *Nairana*, for I had discovered there was a great deal more to running a squadron than flying. That evening we had a celebratory dinner in the wardroom. It made me think. Here I was only twenty-three years old and commanding a squadron which consisted entirely of RNVR and RNZVR aircrew who had joined up since the start of the war – evidence of the scarcity of experienced personnel in the Air Arm capable of filling even moderately senior positions.

13 May saw us again heading into the Atlantic, this time as part of the 15th Escort Group. Our orders were both flexible and complex. We were to provide air cover for a succession of convoys in the mid-Atlantic gap, and in between times to join a "hunter-killer" flotilla to search for U-boats.

*Nairana* had now been at sea almost continuously for six months, and her engines, like some of her aircraft and aircrew, were beginning to feel the strain. During her commissioning trials she had achieved a maximum speed of seventeen knots; now she could barely make fifteen. This reduction may not sound very serious, but, because it reduced the wind speed over our flight deck, it made take-off and landing in calm conditions particularly difficult. The heavily laden Swordfish now needed every inch of the flight deck to get airborne, while the Sea Hurricane came into land like the proverbial bats out of hell.

On 16 May we went to the assistance of the inward-bound convoy SL157/MKS48. They were being shadowed by long-range German reconnaissance planes, which were acting as beacons and homing the U-boats on to them. The weather was bad, with low cloud, blustering winds and driving rain. Nonetheless our Hurricanes took off and succeeded in driving away the shadowers. The convoy altered course and, as soon as it was clear that both planes and U-boats had been shaken off, we moved to help another group of vessels that were under threat: SL158/MKS49.

The protection of this large, slow and vulnerable convoy was our most demanding and eventful operation to date. The weather was bad: strong winds, heavy seas and low cloud, which meant that flying (and particularly flying at night) was never easy. Yet from the moment we joined the convoy on 19 May until the moment we left it on 28 May our Swordfish maintained almost continuous A/S patrols. There were plenty of U-boats about. Several times our observers picked up contacts on their ASV screens, but each time the plane was vectored towards the target it disappeared; it seemed that the submarines were picking up the emissions from our elderly ASV Mark II on their Metox detectors and were diving to safety as the Swordfish closed in. So once again we made no kills. We did, however, keep the U-boats under pressure and under water, with the result that not one of them got close enough to the convoy to make an attack. In view of the weather, this was no small achievement.

How often do I find myself remembering the weather. It would be true to say that, in our operations in the North Atlantic and Arctic Oceans, we had two adversaries: the Germans and the elements, and it was the elements which were the more dangerous. We lost more aircrew through incidents caused by bad weather than through enemy action.

Flying from an aircraft-carrier always involves a certain element of risk, and this risk is increased when the weather makes flying difficult. In absolute calm, planes taking-off tend to topple over the end of the flight-deck before they can build up sufficient airspeed to get airborne, while planes coming in to land tend to approach so fast that they float or bounce over the arrester-wires and end up in the barrier. In very high winds navigation is difficult and this is especially true if the wind is variable. Rain clouds and snow squalls make the images on the observers' ASV screens difficult to interpret; more than one of our Swordfish spent its night patrol circling not the convoy but a patch of particularly dense cloud! Poor visibility makes the carrier difficult for observers to find and the batsman difficult for pilots to see. Heavy seas will cause the carrier to pitch and roll, which means that, even if an aircraft makes the perfect approach, it is liable to find its touch-down area suddenly rising up, falling away or slewing sideways. These problems seemed to loom particularly large at night!

We all accepted the need to fly in bad weather when the safety of a convoy was at stake. What we found difficult to accept was that we were sometimes asked to fly in the most appalling conditions and put our lives in jeopardy, without justification, at the command of someone who knew little about flying. What happened to George Sadler is a case in point.

George, it should be remembered, was a matter of fact and down-to-earth Lancastrian, not the sort to gild the lily. So you can take it that his account of what happened a few days after we joined Convoy SL158/MKS49 is the truth, the whole truth and nothing but the truth.

"It was 22 May, 1944," he writes, "*Nairana* and *Campania* were operating in mid-Atlantic protecting a slow-moving convoy. It had been agreed that one carrier should fly routine patrols, while the other stood by. The weather was foul – mountainous seas, gale-force winds, low cloud and minimal visibility – and *Campania* had very sensibly decided that conditions were too bad for flying and had cancelled her patrols.

"Aboard *Nairana* my air-gunner, my observer Stan Thomas and I were standing by. We had taken a look at the tactical plot and seen that no U-boats were about; it seemed obvious there would be no flying because of the weather, and we were about to get our heads down when Captain Taylor came into the air control room.

" 'Fine night,' he said, 'to catch a sub on the surface. *Campania* not flying? I'll fly.'

"We thought he had to be joking. But he wasn't. And when he said 'I'll fly', that didn't of course mean him. It meant us. We went to collect our flying gear. When we got back we found a heated argument in progress. Our Met Officer, Mike Arrowsmith, was telling the captain that flying was out of the question, and the captain wasn't liking what he was being told. Arrowsmith was trying to explain that we were in an occluded front, that pressure was falling, that the speed and direction of the wind was changing, and that conditions were likely to get worse rather than better. The captain, however, was determined to have us airborne. What made the prospect particularly daunting from our point of view was that radio silence was in force and we could therefore expect no homing aids from the carrier; our patrol would have to be made entirely by DR navigation. I remember Arrowsmith's last anguished plea to us: 'For God's sake keep checking the wind.' Then we were fighting our way down the flight-deck to our plane. The diminutive Stan, hampered by his chart-board and gear, was almost blown over the side.

"Take-off was no problem. The wind was so strong we were barely a third of the way down the flight-deck when we became airborne.

"It was a terrible night, black as the Styx. We tried to find the strength and direction of the wind by dropping a flame float. From a thousand feet the flames were invisible. We tried from five-hundred feet, but the aircraft was being so buffeted about that straight and level flying was impossible; so too was taking bearings, because for most of the time the flame-float couldn't be seen. We did the best we could and began our designated patrol, more concerned with survival than submarines.

"After a little more than half-an-hour there was merciful relief. Someone – we learned later that it was our Commander Flying – realized we had been sent on a mission impossible and insisted we were brought back. Even though it meant breaking radio silence he insisted we were recalled.

"However, finding the carrier and landing-on was to prove a great deal easier said than done. Our patrol had taken us astern of the escort group and downwind; so we now had to head back into the teeth of a 50-knot gale. Stan's navigation was spot-on and after what seemed like a very long time his relieved voice told me he had picked up the *Nairana* on our ASV. He gave me a course to steer. At a range of two miles he gave me a slight correction. He kept asking me if I could see the carrier, but even when the range was down to one mile I could see nothing. I came down to 200 feet on my altimeter, but could still see nothing. With our eyes popping out like organ stops we peered into the driving rain. We were within an ace of flying slap into her. Suddenly her island loomed out of the murk about half a wingspan to port and *above* the level at which we were flying. (Before take-off I had as usual set my altimeter to zero, which should have given us a clearance of forty-six feet – the freeboard of the carrier – above the sea; however, the atmospheric pressure had dropped so sharply that the altimeter was now wildly inaccurate. I quickly reset it.) Stan had done his bit by getting us back. Now it was up to me to land-on. Since I couldn't even see the carrier, this clearly was not going to be easy!

"I guessed that she had probably turned into wind, set my gyro-compass accordingly and began what I hoped was a trial landing circuit. Flying at 200 feet in vile weather in pitch darkness and trying to land by instruments on an invisible carrier is not an experience to be recommended. Coming round into wind and approaching what I hoped was her stern, I at last spotted her deck-lights. These, however, could only be seen through a very restricted arc, and kept disappearing as the carrier pitched and rolled. I made no fewer than eleven approaches, but each time the batsman reckoned landing was impossible and waved me away. Then came near disaster. My gyro-compass must have precessed (i.e. toppled out of control through 180 degrees) because I suddenly found myself trying to come in to land downwind and over the bow. I swung aside just in time to avoid the island and almost decapitated poor "Bats" as he dived into his safety net. Enough, everyone agreed, was enough. I was told to gain height, circle the carrier until dawn, then try again.

"The hours passed slowly. I knew that I would soon be running out of fuel. 'Visibility 50 yds,' Stan later wrote in his logbook. 'Could not land on. Stayed airborne until dawn. Not a very pleasant experience!!!'

"Dawn brought a sickly grey light, but no improvement in the weather. However, at least I could now see the carrier. *Nairana* turned into wind.

"In the heavy seas she was pitching heavily, and her roundown must have been rising and falling a good thirty feet. I knew that trying to pick up the first or second arrester wire would, in such conditions, be dangerous. I therefore decided to try and land farther for'ard, as close as possible to the pivotal point of the deck. I came half-sideslipping in, in a steeper than usual descent. Bats gave me the signal to cut, and I managed to pick up the third arrester wire and was jerked to a stop. I've never known so many members of the flight-deck handling party rush out to grab hold of a plane to prevent it being blown over the side.

"Captain Taylor called it a 'good show'. However, to my mind he was guilty of a grave error of judgement in risking three lives and an aircraft to no material advantage. This sort of thing was inevitable when naval officers who had little knowledge of flying requirements were given command of aircraft carriers.

"Looking back, I'm sure Stan Thomas helped me to get down that morning. He was a deeply religious man – never swore, never complained – and I knew that he had absolute trust in me. I felt it was up to me to see that his trust was justified and he came to no harm, and in my concern for him, my fear for myself seemed to disappear."

For a couple of days the weather was so bad that both merchantmen and U-boats were too preoccupied with survival to think of combat. However, on 25 May conditions improved; stragglers which had become separated from the convoy were rounded up, and this was as well because it wasn't long before both long-range reconnaissance aircraft and submarines were probing at our defences.

That afternoon two Hurricane pilots, Sammy Mearns and George Gordon, were on patrol ahead of the convoy when they sighted a pair of U-boats, close together, at periscope depth. The Hurricanes, lacking the fire-power to sink a U-boat themselves, called up for Swordfish reinforcements, and George Sadler and Johnny Hunt, who had been at readiness, were flown off. George (who as one of our more senior pilots knew what he was talking about) asked to be armed with "Oscar", the Navy's experimental acoustic torpedo; this, when dropped in the vicinity of a U-boat, was designed to home-in on the sound-vibrations of its target's propellers. Captain Taylor, however, insisted that the Swordfish were armed with depth-charges and rocket projectiles. The result was that the U-boats picked up our approaching planes on their Metox and dived to safety before an attack could be pressed home. Depth-charges *were* dropped, but more in hope than expectation, and German intelligence reports have since confirmed that neither U-boat was damaged. They were, however, given a very considerable fright and dissuaded from returning to periscope depth; this meant that they failed to spot the convoy's alteration of course and never got into position to launch an attack.

SL158/MKS49 may have moved on unmolested, but from the point of view of the Squadron this was a frustrating incident, and George Sadler remains convinced to this day that if he had been armed with "Oscar" he would have achieved a kill. For the acoustic torpedo could have been dropped at long range at a comparatively early stage in the aircraft's approach; it would then have homed on to the sound of the diving U-boats, and that for one of them would have been that.

A couple of days later, if it hadn't been for a quite remarkable piece of luck, I would have been stretched out dead on *Nairana's* island. A little after 2100 hours our radar picked up an enemy aircraft approaching the convoy. The summer evening was drawing to its close and, although there was still just enough light for our Hurricanes to take-off, by the time they had made an interception and returned to the carrier it would almost certainly be pitch dark. In spite of the risk, Al Burgham and Charles Richardson were flown off.

They spotted the enemy plane, a Ju 290, and both managed to get in a burst of cannon-fire before it escaped into cloud. It disappeared from our radar screen, though whether this was because it was shot down or because it ran for home will never be known. After almost exactly half-an-hour our Hurricanes returned, eager to get down while there was still a faint glimmer of light.

Nigel Ball and I were standing close together in our usual position on the island, watching anxiously, and Nigel asked me to do something that I don't think I had ever done before. He suggested that I go down to the flight-deck, stand on the centre-line for'ard of the barrier, and watch the approaching aircraft so that I could warn him if anything looked like going wrong.

Al Burgham came in first. As it happened, he was flying not his usual Sea Hurricane, but Bill Armitage's, and Bill had warned him that on his last patrol he had had trouble lowering his flaps. And now, in the darkness, Al couldn't read the indicators which in normal conditions would have warned him if the flaps were not fully down. He therefore decided, very sensibly, to come in a shade faster than usual in case the flaps were not giving him as much lift as they ought to. He made the perfect approach, but, because his airspeed was about five knots too fast, he bounced over the arrester-wires and crashed into the barrier. He had, of course, set his gun-button to "safe", but after his attack on the Ju 290 one of his cannon still had a shell in its breech, and, as he hit the barrier, the force of the impact triggered it off. There was a staccato crack, and a cannon-shell smashed into the island, missing Nigel by a couple of feet, but sending a shower of ricochet splinters into his arm.

Nigel was given first aid and turned out to be quite badly but not seriously wounded. Al's damaged aircraft was dragged for'ard of the barrier. Then it was Charles Richardson's turn. To everyone's very considerable relief, he made a perfect approach and touch-down, one of the first night deck-landings ever made in a Hurricane.

When I found time to visit the island, I had a good look at the hole made by the cannon-shell. And there was no doubt about it. If I had been in my usual position, where I had been standing only a few minutes earlier, it would have gone straight through me – at heart level.

"You're like a cat with nine lives," Nigel said when I went to see him in the Sick Bay.

That gave me something to think about. Because, when I started to add together all the "near-misses" I had had since joining *Eagle* way back in 1940, I realized I had now used up eight out of my allotted feline quota. And before I dossed down that evening, Captain Taylor gave me something else to think about.

"I want you," he said, "to take over as Commander Flying."

Next day, 26 May, turned out to be even more eventful. It was the day we shot down our first aircraft – though at a terrible price.

Soon after sunrise the shadowers were back. It says much for Burgham's and Richardson's resilience that, in spite of the drama of the night before, at 0730 they were strapped into their Hurricanes ranged on the flight deck, waiting to take off. There was not much cloud that morning and the German aircraft came in low, hoping to avoid our Radar. Low, but not low enough, because *Nairana*'s Fighter Direction team picked him up, and Burgham and Richardson were scrambled to intercept. After only a few minutes there was an excited "Tally Ho!"

> "A four-engined Ju 290," writes Al Burgham, "was approaching at sea level on the starboard beam of the convoy. This was the sort of interception that Charles and I had practised and dreamed of. We climbed above him and took up position on either side, so that as soon as he committed himself to turn, one or the other of us would be in the ideal position to attack. As soon as he saw us, he went down even closer to the sea and turned to starboard. This gave Charles the opportunity to make a diving attack. The Junkers tried to take evasive action by turning towards him, which put *me* in the ideal position. As I closed in, I could see that Charles was almost on his tail. No one will ever know what happened next. It could be that Charles was caught in the German plane's slipstream; it

could be that he was hit by fire from its rear-turret 29 mm cannon. Whatever the reason his Hurricane's wingtip touched the sea and the plane flicked over and exploded in a sheet of flame and a cloud of spray. I pressed home my own attack, hitting the Junkers repeatedly at close range. It crashed into the sea and exploded. I went back to look for Charles. I saw what might have been his Mae West, but there was no sign of life. All that remained of the Junkers was an oil slick and a few floating pieces of débris. It all happened unbelievably quickly."

Three Swordfish were flown off to search for survivors. They found the wreckage of two planes and one body. After a while the Swordfish were joined by the destroyer *Highlander*, which recovered the body; it was that of Charles Richardson. There was no trace of the German airmen, and after about an hour the search was called off.

In the afternoon, there were more shadowers, and another interception. By now there was a great deal of cloud about and a little before 1600 hours two aircraft were detected coming in from the east at 5,000 feet. Sam Mearns and Frank Wallis, who were strapped into their Hurricanes at instant readiness, were flown off and vectored towards the approaching planes.

Alan Kerry remembers this as the perfect interception. Our Hurricanes were manoeuvred into the ideal position: about a thousand feet above the enemy aircraft – which were identified as a pair of Ju 290s – and up sun. Mearns and Wallis then carried out a diving attack on the leading Junkers, which saw them coming, opened fire with tracer and tried to get down to sea level. (The idea of this was that at sea level it couldn't be attacked from below.) However, it had neither the manoeuvrability nor the defensive armament to escape. Opening fire at a range of 250 yards with high explosive incendiaries, our Hurricanes brought a lethal weight of fire to bear on the German plane which was quickly shot down, though the pilot, with no little skill, managed to ditch his shattered aircraft before it exploded. Mearns and Wallis then turned their attention to the second Junkers. It, however, very prudently first sought refuge in the clouds, then made for home.

Returning to the first aircraft, Mearns and Wallis saw that some of the German airmen had survived the crash and were struggling to get into their dinghy. They must have thought their last moment had come when Sam came diving down on them. However, he had no intention of shooting them up; all he wanted was proof of his "kill" on his wing camera. Our two Hurricanes then headed back for the *Nairana*.

As they disappeared into the path of the sinking sun, one imagines that the German airmen can't have fancied their chances of survival. However, as I've said, as far as the Squadron were concerned the Battle of the Atlantic was fought without rancour and a Swordfish, with Joe Supple as pilot and Johnny Lloyd as observer, was flown off to locate the survivors and keep them company. Joe and Johnny found them, a tiny speck in a vast sea, and stayed circling them, waving encouragement, until they were picked up by one of the escorting corvettes.

Next morning *Highlander* took station close on our starboard beam. Once again the squadron lined up on the flight-deck. Once again there was a moment of absolute silence while every ship in convoy, its flag at half-mast, stopped its engines as the body of Charles Richardson slid into the grey waters of the Atlantic.

The Commodore sent us a message of sympathy. He had, he told us, arranged for a collection to be made aboard each of his ships. The response was quite overwhelming, and the very considerable sum of money that was raised was passed first to Captain Taylor, then to Charles Richardson's family. It was used to fund a bed in his memory in the hospital close to his home town.

Life for the rest of us went on. We had a job to do. And we did it. And that was that. But I don't think I was the only one to do some calculations that summer. In the last four months we had lost seven pilots, observers and telegraphist air gunners, and come within a hair's breadth of losing a great many more. We were a small squadron and if we kept up this sort of mortality rate you didn't need to be Einstein to work out that by the end of the year there wouldn't be many of us left.

A few days later we were joined by another carrier, HMS *Emperor*, and fighter patrols and interceptions were shared with her. Our Swordfish, however, continued to provide air cover against the U-boats unaided, first for Convoy SL158/MKS49, then briefly for a southbound convoy and finally for the 15th Escort Group. On 30 May Bob Selley made the Squadron's thousandth deck-landing on the *Nairana*, and a couple of days after that we were back in the Clyde.

*Nairana* had been at sea for twenty eventful days. Our fighters had flown forty-five sorties and destroyed two enemy planes. Our Swordfish had flown eighty-two sorties, and although no U-boats had been destroyed, several had been attacked and once again our patrols had been so effective that not a single ship in any of the convoys or escort groups that we were guarding had been attacked.

The safe passage of these vulnerable and near-defenceless ships made the risks that we had taken and the sacrifices that we had made worthwhile.

We wouldn't have minded a few weeks' leave. We were given forty-eight hours. Then, after a brief stay in the Clyde during which we took aboard new aircraft and new aircrew, we were back again in the Atlantic, our destination, for the third time, Gibraltar.

The passage of Convoy KMF32 was remarkable only for the weather. It was midsummer. Yet for the whole of our six-day voyage the wind was an almost perpetual gale, rain fell without respite out of a lead grey sky and great rollers came surging endlessly in on our beam. Our Swordfish flew only a dozen patrols. Our Hurricanes never got off the deck. And this was because the U-boats and Junkers obviously found conditions as impossible as we did. For during the whole of our passage not a blip was seen on our Radar screen, nor a ping heard from our Asdic.

Our return passage, escorting the troop convoy MKF32 to the United Kingdom, was almost equally uneventful, although two of our recently joined Hurricane pilots, Ken Atkinson and Dusty Miller, had a somewhat novel experience. Al Burgham decided that his "new boys" could do with as much deck-landing practice as they could get, yet he was reluctant to risk practising on our unusually narrow flight-deck. It so happened that sailing with the convoy was HMS *Ravager*, an aircraft carrier which had just taken a squadron of Spitfires to Malta and was now returning empty to the United Kingdom. Our flight-deck was 60 feet wide, *Ravager*'s was 100. Ken and Dusty were therefore flown in a Swordfish to *Ravager*; Al Burgham took over a Hurricane and, under his fatherly eye, the two young pilots successfully completed a number of deck-landings. There can't be many pilots who can claim to have done a deck-landing training course in the middle of an Atlantic convoy!

The only other thing worth recording is our running feud with our new Commander Flying. The unfortunate "One Gun" Ball had departed on sick leave with his arm in a sling. His successor, Lt-Cdr Hugh Davenport, RN, was a little man with a rather big opinion of himself. He turned out to be a real martinet, and was forever rebuking the more high-spirited members of the squadron for "conduct unbecoming". Our fighter pilots, for example, when they returned from patrol, had on previous convoys brought pleasure to all and harm to none by flying low between the columns of ships and waving to the servicemen (and servicewomen!) lining the rails of the troop ships. This practice was prohibited by the aptly named "Little" Hugh. Nor did the misdemeanours of our Swordfish pilots escape his critical eye. Bob Selley, about the most experienced pilot in the squadron, was taken to task like a naughty schoolboy because he too flew low over the ships in convoy while carrying "Oscar". "Little" Hugh severely reprimanded him for revealing this supposedly secret weapon to the troops. It was typical of

Davenport that, whereas all squadron officers and most ships' officers wore the comfortable and practical battledress, he was invariably dressed in a formal reefer jacket, with the traditional 1½" of white shirtcuff below the jacket sleeves. How delighted we were, at the start of our next operation, to welcome back Nigel Ball!

About the only moment of excitement during our passage home occurred as the convoy was nearing the British Isles. It was a beautiful night with a full moon and a quiet sea, and the fifty-odd ships in their parallel columns were keeping station with guardsmanlike precision. Sam Hollings was our officer of the watch and was surveying the peaceful scene from *Nairana*'s bridge when the moment came for all ships to make a 10° turn to port. (Convoys in wartime nearly always zigzagged; this was to make it difficult for the U-boats to predict their course.) At the given moment every vessel made the turn correctly, every vessel, that is, except the *Dominion Monarch*, which was on our port beam. She turned not 10° to port, but 10° to starboard. This put her on collision course with the carrier. Sam ordered *Nairana* to swing away, but once helm has been applied in one direction, it is quite a while before a ship is able to alter course on to another direction. For a moment it looked odds on on a collision, but in the end the two vessels, their propellers churning frantically, passed within a dozen yards of one another, throwing Sam's stomach and the centre of the convoy into great confusion. The signal sent by our Commodore to the *Dominion Monarch* doesn't bear repeating!

On 3 July we were back in the Clyde, having successfully completed what was to prove my last tour of operations with the squadron. We reckoned we were overdue for leave, but it was not to be. On 4 July we received a signal to report to RNAS Burscough. Here, we were told, the Squadron would convert to Swordfish Mk IIIs, which were equipped with the latest 3cm ASVX air-to-ground Radar.

Burscough was a not unpleasant but somewhat undistinguished airfield west of Bolton. Here we settled into our inevitable Nissen hut cabins and became acquainted with our "new" aircraft.

We found that our poor old Swordfish had been transformed into what had become little more than a vehicle for carrying the new and highly sophisticated ASVX. Externally, this equipment was housed in a bulky transmitter/receiver scanner which was slung under the belly of the fuselage; this gave the aircraft a decidedly pregnant look and reduced its performance. Internally, the equipment was so complex that it took up the whole of what had once been the observer's cockpit; this meant that the observer now had to move into the telegraphist-air-gunner's cockpit, while the unfortunate TAGs (since there was no room for them) became redundant. From the pilots' point of view, although the Swordfish Mk III remained reliable, robust, forgiving and easy to fly, the sheer weight of the equipment now loaded into it and the extent to which this equipment cluttered up its aerodynamic profile, meant that the plane became ponderous. Its top speed – never its best feature! – decreased; its stalling speed was increased; and it needed a longer take-off run – indeed it was so overweight that it often required RATOG (rocket accelerated take-off gear) to lift it clear of the flight-deck. From the observers' point of view, the new sets were a great improvement technically. They could pick up the U-boats at a greater range; the U-boats had difficulty detecting their emissions; and their screens gave a clearer and more easily understood picture. However, there were drawbacks. The equipment was temperamental and needed careful maintenance by specially trained radar mechanics. And it was bulky. As one observer put it:

> "We now found ourselves crammed into the much smaller and more exposed air-gunner's cockpit. Here we had to face for'ard to watch the ASVX screen; while every now and then we needed to perform contortions to reach backwards to tune the radio, read the compasses or work out our DR plot."

From the point of view of our telegraphist-air-gunners the Swordfish Mk III was a disaster. It did them out of a job. Willie Armstrong and his colleagues now found themselves surplus to requirements and were obliged to leave the Squadron. This was sad. And since fewer and fewer Fleet Air Arm planes now needed air-gunners, many of these brave, skilled and air-minded men had to be assigned to other and less worthwhile duties. Although this may have been the inevitable price of progress, one can't say that the TAGs got a particularly good deal out of the Navy.

All in all, although the Squadron accepted the need for change and recognized the value of our improved ASVX, our feelings were summed up as we sang *The Pregnant Swordfish*, to the tune of "She was Poor but she was Honest".

> "Oh, I used to think my Swordfish
>  Was as slow as she was tame,
> But I'm sorry to inform you
>  She has lost her maiden name.
>
> For she's going to have a baby;
>  You can see that by her shape.
> You can tell from her performance
>  She's been sub-jected to rape!

See that bloody great protusion?
    You can spot it from afar.
If you ask me what's inside it –
    It's a bastard like its ma!

Once my thoroughbred old Swordfish
    Was my pride and my delight;
But now that she is preggers
    I'll go fly some other kite."

For the Squadron our time at Burscough was, above all else, a time of change. Not only did we acquire new aircraft, we acquired new aircrew and a new commanding officer, while *Nairana* acquired a new captain.

Our fighter strength remained the same – six Hurricanes and eight pilots – but our TBR strength was now increased to twelve Swordfish and fourteen pilots and observers. As well as meeting this increase in number we had to find replacements for our aircrew who had been killed and for those "old timers" who now left the Squadron to take up appointments ashore. Among the latter was Jack Teesdale. I was not too happy, at this time of reconstruction in the Squadron, to face the prospect of losing not only a personal friend but the most efficient Stores Officer; so (with Jack's approval) I asked if his appointment could be deferred. Our request, however, was turned down. And it was this, among other things, that now made me consider my own position.

I was glad to have Nigel Ball to talk things over with. On 2 August he arrived unexpectedly at Burscough. His arm, he told me, was no longer a problem and he had been reappointed as *Nairana*'s Commander Flying. I explained to him that I was a bit concerned at the whittling away of our more experienced personnel, and we had a long discussion about the Squadron aircrew. It came up in the course of conversation that I had been serving continuously in front-line squadrons for the last four years – as well as my two and a half years with 835, I had previously spent a year and a half with 813 on the *Eagle*. He was amazed. As I have already explained, the Navy, unlike the RAF, had no set tour of duty at the end of which aircrew were automatically rested; however, eighteen months was usually reckoned to be a fair stint. I had been in front-line squadrons almost three times as long as was usual, and Nigel put it to me that I would be well advised to request a shore appointment. I told him I'd sleep on it.

It was a hard decision to make. I had enjoyed being CO of 835 Squadron. I had enjoyed the challenge, the responsibility and the *Camaraderie*; and I think it would be fair to say that I had helped to build up an efficient and successful operational team. However, from the personal point of view there were compelling reasons for my now saying enough was enough. Of the eight original members of the squadron who had come together at Eastleigh in January, 1942, I was the only one left. During the past few weeks at Burscough I had been so preoccupied with administration that I had had to skip a lot of the ASVX course; it would, I told myself, be a recipe for disaster if the CO and Senior Observer of a TBR squadron wasn't *au fait* with his equipment. There was also the point that I was beginning to feel the strain. Of the nine lives proverbially allocated to cats, I had used up all but one, surviving eight times in situations where death had seemed not only possible but probable. And in recent months to the strain of flying had been added the strain of command. Finally, there was the Pacific War to consider; I could well be needed for service there. I told myself that for the time being I had done my bit, and that to go on might jeopardize not only my own life but that of others. So I let Nigel know that it might be best if I was given a shore appointment.

A couple of days later *Nairana*'s newly appointed captain called in at Burscough on his way north to take command of his ship. Captain Villiers Nicholas Surtees, DSO, RN, turned out to be a short and not very prepossessing man, with a florid complexion and a big red nose – hence his nickname "Strawberry". In the months to come he was to prove a difficult and demanding captain. Indeed, in scenes reminiscent of *The Caine Mutiny*, there was serious talk of having him declared unfit for command. It therefore seems to me important to try and establish what sort of a person he was.

I have talked to and corresponded with many people who knew the *Nairana*'s new captain a great deal better than I did and I believe a balanced judgement would be something like this. Surtees had many of the qualities that are needed to rise to high command in the Navy. He was a man of decision, although his decisions were not always right. He was a man of considerable courage and powers of endurance – during our convoys to Russia he hardly left the bridge. And he was a man determined to do his duty as a naval officer no matter what the cost; the Navy was the be-all and end-all of his life; he had few other interests and no other love. In the days of Nelson he would undoubtedly have made a first-rate commander of a ship of the line, ever anxious to follow his Admiral's instructions "to lay alongside and engage the enemy more closely." However, we were *not* in the days of Nelson, and as captain of an aircraft-carrier in the Second World War Surtees had two serious weaknesses. First, he found it difficult to communicate, especially with those from a different background. This may have been because he was a reserved man, a bit of a loner and a bit of a misogynist. He wasn't good with people. His second weakness was that he knew little about flying.

So why, you may very reasonably ask, was he given command of an aircraft-carrier? You might have thought that anyone would have been able to grasp the fact that an aircraft-carrier – which operates aircraft – ought to be commanded by a person with at least *some* knowledge of flying. Yet the Admiralty now saw fit to hand over one of its best escort-carriers to an ex-cruiser officer who had been brought out of retirement by the war and had never in his life served in an aircraft-carrier let alone flown an aeroplane. Perhaps there was no suitable candidate immediately available, but from their decision stemmed a whole series of problems, both for the Squadron and for Surtees.

Things now moved fast. The day after Surtees' visit to Burscough Jack Teesdale left the Squadron. The next day our new CO arrived, and *I* got ready to leave.

My successor was Lt-Cdr Val (for Valentine) Jones, RNVR. Val had been the senior observer of 811 Squadron in *Vindex*, and arrived with a good reputation. He had a quiet, mature manner and a sense of humour – the latter to be sorely tested in the months to come. He was the sort of man I was happy to hand over to.

On the morning of 13 August I led the squadron for the last time: back to *Nairana*. As soon as we had landed-on, I spent my last few hours aboard showing Val the ropes and introducing him to the ship's officers. There were a few administrative odds and ends to be tidied up, a few last drinks with friends in the wardroom. And suddenly I was on the quay, alone and staring back at the ship that had been my home for the last six months. I don't think I have ever felt so lonely in my life. I thought of all the things I had done and wished I hadn't, and all the things I hadn't done and wished I had. I had never even had a Squadron photograph taken with myself as CO sitting proudly in the middle. But it was too late now.

I was given two weeks' leave. Then I found myself appointed to RNAS Donibristle (near Edinburgh) to organize the running of a course for squadron commanders who would soon be on their way to join the British fleet in the Pacific.

For me, flying with 835 Squadron was over. For the rest of the Squadron it was about to restart in earnest, and the rest of this story is *their* story, told by *them*, though I have continued to use the first person plural.

★   ★   ★

*Nairana* with her new captain, and the squadron with its new CO, now embarked on the usual period of working up in the Clyde.

Surtees was to prove a demanding person to serve under. The ship was for ever practising emergency fire-drill, emergency this and emergency that; while the squadron was kept flying day and night, practising in particular rocket assisted take-offs and "Glow Worm" attacks with flares.

RATOG (rocket accelerated take-off gear) was now needed because the Swordfish Mk III, overladen with weaponry, was so heavy that, unless there was half-a-gale blowing, it had difficulty getting off the deck. So a pair of booster rockets was fitted beneath its wings. These were activated by the pilot as he came abreast of the bridge – not sooner, in case one rocket only fired, and the plane was blasted sideways into the island. It was, as one of our pilots put it, "a bit like being catapulted from an accelerator: as though a giant hand had thrust the plane into the sky. However, once the rocket had burned out and its impetus was lost, the poor old Stringbag was left hanging by its propeller, trying desperately to build up sufficient speed to stay airborne."

The idea of "Glow Worm" was to illuminate surfaced U-boats at night. Two rocket projectiles in the outboard racks had flares attached to their warheads. As the pilot dived onto his target, he was expected slightly to ease up the nose of his Swordfish and fire his outboard rockets first, so that the flares were lobbed over the U-boat and illuminated it; he would then continue his attack, firing the rockets from his inboard rack.

In a week of intensive flying the TBR pilots carried out eighty-three practice flights (twenty-three of them at night) and the fighter pilots twenty-nine. The old hands in the Squadron took this in their stride, but for our newly-joined aircrew it was a tough initiation; some ended up in the barrier, some ended up half-way over the side. Six Swordfish and two Sea Hurricanes were damaged.

This was the sort of thing which resulted from the diminution of our experienced aircrew. For there were now a lot of new and younger faces in the Squadron. As well as a new CO, we had a new Senior Pilot, Pat Urwin, and a new Senior Observer, Charles Legood; both had plenty of front-line experience, but not in escort-carriers. We also had two new Hurricane pilots, Pete Blanco and "Dusty" Miller; five new Swordfish pilots, Sub-Lts Brown, Defrates, Murray, Pitts and Provis; and six new Swordfish observers, Sub-Lts Beal, Bevan, Eames, McEwan, Ravenhill and Rose. Of these, only John Defrates had done much operational flying. We also had a new Batsman, Bob Mathé; he replaced Bill Cameron, who was appointed Chief Deck Landing Control Officer at Arbroath.

Inevitably it was the less experienced aircrew who had the accidents. Sub-Lt(A) Mick Murray, RNZVR, kept a Diary of his hazardous first few days aboard the *Nairana*.

"14.8.44. Night landings very shaky!! Did a ten-minute circuit, then stalled and pranged on my first landing. On advice of M.O. and Cdr "F", went up again almost at once. But on take-off the port brake jammed and I had difficulty getting off the deck. Half-toppled over the bow, but just managed to pick up airspeed before I hit the water. Was then kept circling *Nairana*, because the plane supposed to land ahead of me (flown by Ron Brown) had crashed. It took them 50 mts to clear the flight-deck. At last was given permission to come in. But on touchdown, swung to stbd and right wheel went over the side. Ended up in the catwalk. What a night!

"15.8.44. Had a full medical for flying and passed AI. Saw Cdr "F" and the Captain. They said I would be taken aboard *Ravager* to practise more deck-landings. . . . What a lovely big flight-deck compared to ours. Did a couple of afternoon landings – piece of cake. Then a couple of dusk landings followed by six night landings. All OK. Very efficient night landing system – strip bars at sides of deck, American style bats etc. These Yankee escort-carriers seem streets ahead of ours."

A couple of days later Mick Murray returned to *Nairana*, his confidence restored. And a couple of days after that the carrier joined the 4th Escort Group to provide air cover for yet another convoy to Gibraltar. This was MKF34, one of the last outward-bound Atlantic convoys of the war, and, seeing that Val Jones was now leading a squadron about a third of whom had little operational experience, it was as well his first assignment was uneventful. This is how Mick Murray recorded it in the Diary he wrote up each evening in his cabin:-

"Friday, 25 Aug. Picked up troop convoy off Eire: about 40 ships. Weather fine, with clear sky and calm sea. Our fighters took off pm in pairs to give a morale-boosting display of low flying and aerobatics over the merchantmen. Everyone impressed!

"Sat, 26 Aug. Weather deteriorating. How quickly it changes! Took off on my first operational patrol at 1200 hrs. Weather bad. By the time I got back at 1400 hrs full gale blowing. But landed OK. Pm weather got worse: v heavy seas. 1900 hrs Action Stations! Enemy aircraft approaching the convoy. Turned out to be a shadower. He closed to within 3 miles and circled round and round us. Weather too bad for us to fly off our Hurricanes, so not a lot we can do. Expect attack by subs tomorrow.

"Sun, 27 Aug. Duff weather. No sign of expected subs – I suppose the weather is too bad for them to find us. Another shadower picked us up pm. In spite of terrible conditions 2 Hurricanes flown off (George Gordon and Pete Blanco). They managed to intercept shadower, a Ju 290, but he escaped into cloud. Took off at 1700 hrs on my second patrol. What a trip! A 2½hrs search continuously in cloud. Apart from taking off and landing I hardly saw the sea. After a couple of hrs my Air Speed Indicator iced up. Coming in I had to guess my speed; but Bats got me down safely.

"Mon, 28 Aug. Weather improving, and the old hands say we should now be out of the danger area. Stood by 1200 hrs – 1600 hrs, then changed into tropical gear and sunbathed. A/S patrols continued.

"Tues, 29 Aug. More A/S patrols. Took off at 1300 hrs on search ahead of convoy. Picked up contact, range 100 miles. Reported, and went to investigate. Turned out to be the Portuguese M/V *Gaza*. Circled her and took photos, then resumed search. Picked up another "contact", but it turned out to be a rain cloud. Coming in to land caught the Jesus Christ wire (the last of the arrester-wires) and ended up only inches from the barrier.

"Wed, 30 Aug. Rumour that 15 U-boats on passage out of Bay are only just ahead of us. Never saw a trace of them! Wonder how these rumours start? Sqdn Duty Officer for day.

"Thurs, 31 Aug. Lovely day, sea v calm. We now have air cover from Gibraltar, so patrols called off. Took off to fly Lt Byrom to North Front, Gib 150 miles away. Landed North Front in 90 per cent crosswind – only one runway. Transport into town. Saw the legendary Juanita sing 'Solitude'. Back to HMS *Cormorant* for the night."

During this relatively quiet and uneventful passage, the Swordfish flew thirty-one patrols and searches (thirteen at night), and the Hurricanes eighteen patrols and interceptions. No enemy planes or U-boats were destroyed. None of our aircraft was lost or seriously damaged. No ship in the convoy was attacked.

The squadron spent nine days in Gibraltar, the fighter section taking up residence at North Front. From here they did a fair amount of "local flying", an euphemism which covered a multitude of sins. Sam Mearns was involved in two unofficial sorties, the first of which very nearly cost him his life.

He was anxious to visit Casablanca (a couple of hundred miles to the south, on the coast of Morocco). Officially, his excuse was that he wanted to see if he could collect some spare Hurricane tail wheels; unofficially he was keen to survey the local beauties and collect some fresh eggs for the wardroom. An RAF pilot offered him a lift in a Beaufighter, and since this was a plane which had a crew of three, "Chiefie" Banham was invited to go with them. Sam was told to sit in the navigator's seat behind the pilot; Banham, immaculate in his starched and ironed denims, was eased into the cramped space beneath the astrodome. After the plane had taxied to the end of the runway, Sam settled back to watch the RAF pilot's take-off with professional interest. He was not impressed! Halfway down the runway, a little before it should have become airborne, the Beaufighter started veering to port. The pilot tried to counter this by activating the boost over-ride on one of his engines. But something went decidedly wrong. Instead of straightening up, the Beaufighter swerved even farther to port; it went careering through a Spitfire parking bay – which was mercifully empty and ended up smashing into the stone wall which borders the old Trafalgar graveyard. The three men scrambled with some difficulty out of the shattered plane, to find themselves surrounded by tombstones. It was some seconds before they realized that although their time may have been near it had not yet come!

A couple of days later, nothing daunted, Sam tried again. He borrowed a Swordfish, and, accompanied by the ever-trusting Banham, set out a second time for Casablanca.

"I flew low along the beaches," he writes, "admiring the scenery, and in particular the expatriate young ladies from France improving their sun tan. What a shame, I told myself, I had to be fighting a war. We arrived safely, had a leisurely lunch, then collected a small number of tail wheels and a much larger number of eggs (the latter being a welcome change from the usual wardroom fare of ersatz egg powder). These eggs, bedded down in straw, were packed into crates, and the crates were then loaded into the rear cockpit. On the way back the slow speed of the Swordfish and the good view from the open cockpit enabled me once again to enjoy all things beautiful. However, part of my mission might well have failed. For on landing at North Front we found that the slipstream had sucked all the straw out of the crates, leaving the eggs unprotected.

We feared the worst, but on inspection found to our amazement that not one had been broken."

It must have been the smoothest-ever landing!

The Swordfish aircrew too found plenty to occupy them. John Defrates writes:

"Gibraltar was familiar ground to most of the squadron, and pilots and observers now blossomed forth in immaculate white uniforms and set out to try their luck with the all too few Wrens. The best I could manage was Khaki shorts and shirt. However, I consoled myself with the belief – confirmed by Norman Sargent – that I wouldn't have had much luck in any case because the Wrens were never known to speak to anyone below the rank of Commander! . . . I went to the obligatory bullfight. And wished I hadn't. Due to a misunderstanding we arrived at La Linea early, and spent our first hour sitting in the sun outside a tavern drinking sherry and eating salted almonds. This gave me a thirst, so as we went in to watch the bullfight I bought another bottle of sherry. If a brave bull had had a sporting chance of survival, I might have been less disgusted and less inclined to drink. As it was, I finished off the bottle, and returned to the ship with much difficulty and some assistance. Once aboard, I disgraced myself by being violently sick. It was many years before I could tolerate even the smell of sherry."

At the end of a week we reckoned from the increased activity in Gibraltar harbour that another convoy was in the offing. And sure enough on 9 September we were told to provide air cover for the fast homewardbound MKF34. Among the escorting warships were the battleship *Ramillies*, a survivor of the *First* World War, and the American aircraft-carrier *Reaper*, which had just delivered a consignment of Corsairs to Malta.

This convoy turned out to be another non-event, although the powers that be did their best to trigger off some action. For instead of heading west into the Atlantic before setting course for the British Isles, Convoy MKF34 followed a shorter but potentially far more dangerous route close inshore; for the first couple of days we could see the Portuguese coast quite clearly. Rumour had it that five German destroyers were lying in wait in one of the Biscay ports and that our new route was designed to tempt them out and give our Swordfish some practice with their rocket projectiles and "Oscar".

As though to give credence to this, as soon as we left the Rock our patrolling planes were armed not with the usual depth charges but with acoustic torpedoes.

"Oscar" weighed 850 lbs. That would have been no problem if the wretched thing could have been carried in a central position beneath the fuselage. However, the centre of the fuselage was where our new ASVX was housed; "Oscar" had therefore to be carried somewhere else and was slung beneath the starboard wing. This made the plane not only heavy but lopsided. To quote one of our pilots:

> "Whenever we carried 'Oscar' we needed RATOG to get us off the deck; and because one wing had less lift than the other, the plane on take-off tended to be flung not only upwards but sideways. Once airborne, you needed quite a lot of strength just to keep flying straight and level. One arm got stiff and tired continually pushing the control column in one direction. One foot got stiff and tired continually pushing the rudder in the other direction."

(Hence the evolution of Homo Swordfish(P): page 21.) We were all thankful when, at the end of a couple of days, it became apparent that the German destroyers were not going to be tempted out, and our Swordfish reverted to carrying depth-charges.

On 13 September, still following our easterly course, we sighted the Scilly Isles, and forty-eight hours later *Nairana* dropped anchor in the Clyde. Since leaving the Rock four days earlier we had flown fifty-two patrols, searches and interceptions, without suffering either damage to our aircraft or injury to our aircrew, and, for the thirteenth convoy in succession, not one of the ships that we were guarding was lost.

It had been a gentle initiation for Val Jones and Surtees. However, it was obvious even at this early stage that there was going to be friction between them. For they were like oil and water, totally different not only in character but in their concept of duty. Val Jones, a quiet, reflective and caring man, was determined not needlessly to risk the lives of his pilots and observers – and the key word here is "needlessly". Surtees, a thrusting man of action who was prepared to risk a lot to win a lot, was determined whenever possible to follow Nelson's dictum and "engage the enemy more closely". This was not *per se* a reprehensible objective. However, Surtees knew so little about flying that, in his thirst for action, he was for ever putting his aircrew needlessly at risk – and again the key word is "needlessly".

So the Squadron found itself tugged two ways, with its CO crying "hold back", and its Captain crying "fly off".

This dichotomy was not too much of a problem during our benign and action-free passage to Gibraltar. It was to prove a far more serious problem when our scene of operations shifted to the more dangerous and hostile passage to Murmansk.

One man who saw the storm-cones being hoisted was our Senior Operations Officer, Jasper Godden. He asked to be relieved of his duties.

However, on its return to the Clyde, the squadron was kept too busy to have time to worry about the future. For no sooner had we dropped anchor than we received a signal. Our Hurricane IIcs were to be replaced by Grumman Martlet "Wildcat" VIs: our fighter pilots were to report at once to RNAS Yeovilton for a conversion course.

Some pilots were sorry to see the Hurricanes go. As Al Burgham put it, "I always felt comfortable in a Hurricane; they were great planes to fly." And when, on 26 September, Ken Atkinson flew the Fleet Air Arm's last operational Hurricane No. 231 from *Nairana* to the Maintenance Depot at Abbotsinch, he felt he was saying goodbye to a friend. The Wildcats, however, were to prove a great deal easier to operate. They were more robust and more manoeuvrable; they had a better rate of climb and a far better endurance; and above all they had been designed to work from a carrier and had automatically folding wings. Whatever our pilots may have thought about the change, it was welcomed with enthusiasm by our groundcrew.

Al Burgham and his team were all comparatively "old hands" with considerable experience of flying from carriers. They had no difficulty converting to Wildcats. However, an incident a couple of days after their arrival at Yeovilton warned them that they needed to handle their new aircraft with care. A Wildcat coming in to land crashed in the middle of the airfield, and its pilot, to whom they had been chatting only the night before, was killed. One trait in particular they found they needed to watch out for: because of its narrow undercarriage the Wildcat had a vicious propensity to ground loop. Another lesson they quickly took to heart was that, if they *did* have a crash, it would be best not to dilly dally getting out of the plane. The pilot's seat was positioned squarely on top of the fuel tank!

While the fighter section was at Yeovilton, the TBR pilots and observers had hoped for some leave. Instead they found themselves involved in a programme of intensive flying that was every bit as arduous as most operations. For during the last ten days of September and the first ten days of October, in an unremitting round of deck-landings, Navexs and dummy Glow Worm attacks, the Swordfish flew over 200 hours and carried out over 150 deck-landings, about a third of them at night.

There were two ways of looking at this. Surtees felt that he was honing his ship's company to a peak of operational efficiency. Val Jones felt that

25. George Gordon with Al Burgham studies the film of his shooting down a Blohm and Voss 138 on 12 December, 1944.

26. Standing by in the Aircrew Ready Room on the way to Murmansk: December, 1944.
Back Row, L. to R.: Ted Pitts, Johnny Lloyd, John Cridland, Paddy Hall, Derek Ravenhill.
Front Row, L. to R.: George Gordon, Al Burgham, Pete Blanco.

27.  Lt. Cdr (A) Edgar
Bibby, DSO, RNVR.

28.  (Below left) Lt. Cdr (A)
Nigel Ball, DSC, RN; his
arm in a sling after he was
shot by cannon-fire from one
of our fighters that crashed
on landing.

29.  (Below right) Bob
Selley, the longest-serving
member of 835 Squadron
(nearly two years and nine
months) with the only female
aboard HMS *Nairana*.

30. A Swordfish landing on HMS *Nairana*.

31. A Wildcat landing on HMS *Nairana*.

32. A Seafire landing on HMS *Battler*.

33. A Sea Hurricane landing on HMS *Nairana*.

his squadron needed more rest and less flying. Whichever view one agrees with, the Squadron *had* now reached a remarkably high standard of flying. For in those 150-odd landings, the only accident was when George Sadler's arrester-hook stuck in the fuselage, and through no fault of his own he went into the barrier – his one mishap in 178 deck-landings.

And this is perhaps the place to make a point so obvious that it is easy to overlook it. Every landing (and to a lesser extent every take-off) made in our overloaded Swordfish now involved a certain degree of stress. You might of course say that any landing, any time, anywhere in any plane involves stress. Yet coming into land on an airfield is a *lot* easier and a lot less stressful than coming into land on an aircraft-carrier, and *Nairana* was a particularly difficult carrier to land on because of her narrow flight-deck: a dozen feet too far to the right or too far to the left, or half a dozen feet too high or too low, and you would very likely make the sort of nasty mess that no one walks away from. So every take-off and landing called for care and concentration. At the time we didn't think about this a great deal or talk about it at all. We simply had a job to do and we did it and that was that. However, in retrospect it seems likely that the sort of non-stop flying now expected of the Squadron was bound in the end to lead to mental and physical fatigue – and hence to deterioration.

In the small hours of 14 October *Nairana* left the Clyde and rendezvoused with the 21st Escort Group off the Mull of Kintyre. The Group then headed north. This time it was obviously not Gibraltar we were bound for and, as the warships ploughed through the heavy swell of The Minches, word got round that we were on our way to Murmansk.

Probably the least pleased member of the Squadron was John Defrates. For in the hope of impressing the Gibraltar Wrens he had just bought a full set of tropical uniform!

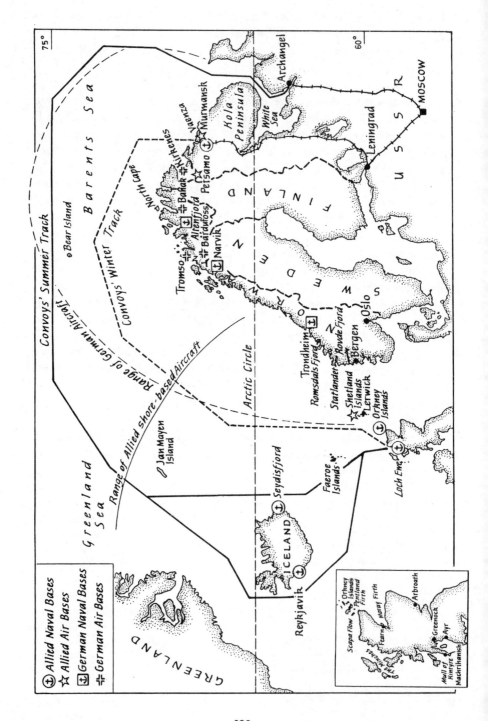

# 5

# *"THIS WAS THEIR FINEST HOUR"*

The most momentous day in the Second World War was almost certainly 22 June, 1941. This was when Germany invaded Russia and, in an instant, the USSR was transformed from a neutral to be suspected to an ally to be supported. Churchill put it very clearly: "Any state who fights against Nazidom will have our aid. It therefore follows that we shall give whatever help we can to Russia and the Russian people."

Only a few weeks after the German invasion, it was agreed at a meeting in Moscow between Stalin, Lord Beaverbrook and Averell Harriman that Great Britain and America would send as much war equipment as possible to the Russians to enable them to sustain the conflict.

There were three routes by which this equipment could be delivered: via Vladivostok in the north Pacific, via the Persian Gulf and presentday Iran or Iraq, and via the Arctic ports of Archangel and Murmansk. The Russians always favoured the last of these routes. This was largely because first-class roads and railways linked the Arctic ports with strategic centres like Leningrad and Moscow and the equipment delivered could be brought swiftly into use. So throughout the war Stalin was continually pressing for more and more convoys to be sent to north Russia.

The Royal Navy, on the other hand, was continually pressing for fewer and fewer Russian convoys. "They are a millstone round our necks," wrote Admiral of the Fleet Sir Dudley Pound, "a most unsound operation with the dice loaded against us in every direction." A glance at a map will explain his lack of enthusiasm.

Most convoys to Russia assembled off and set sail from the north of Scotland, and for virtually the whole of their 1,500 miles to Murmansk their course lay parallel to the coast of German-occupied Norway. This meant that they were under constant threat of attack by enemy surface warships, U-boats and bombers. It also meant that these German forces could sortie at will, choosing their time and place to attack, whereas the convoys had to be on guard at all times and at every stage of their passage. Another threat was the weather. Particularly in winter, huge seas and violent winds could not only scatter a convoy but could bludgeon some of the smaller vessels to destruction. More than one broke up or turned turtle with the loss of their entire ship's company. A final problem was the pack-ice. In winter this extended so far to the south that the convoys were squeezed into, and forced to sail along, a narrow corridor between the ice and the north Norwegian shore. This corridor was a happy hunting ground for U-boats. For here they could lie in wait for the passing ships unseen: unseen, because the sea mist (ever prevalent at the confluence of pack-ice and open water) made it difficult for the escorts to detect them visually, while thermal currents in the ice-cold water made it difficult for them to be detected by Asdic.

In view of these problems, the amount of equipment delivered by the Russian convoys was remarkable. Between August, 1941 and May, 1945, forty-two convoys got through to Archangel or Murmansk – an average of almost one a month – some with fewer than half-a-dozen ships, some with more than fifty. All told, they delivered 4,252,000 tons of weapons and equipment, including 5,150 tanks, 7,000 aircraft, 800,000 tons of machinery and about the same tonnage of munitions (shells, high explosives, etc). This was almost ten times the amount of weaponry that was shipped to North Africa for the much publicized campaign in the desert.

The cost of fighting through these convoys was, for the Allies, 104 merchantmen, twenty-three warships and about forty aircraft. German losses were six warships, thirty-one U-boats and about 200 aircraft.

It is perhaps worth making the obvious point that, once the ships had unloaded in Russia, they had then to return (again in convoy) to the United Kingdom, and losses on the homeward voyage were sometimes as high as on the outward. Most ships returned in ballast; although, in an effort to obtain much-needed currency, the Russians sometimes unofficially loaded the returning vessels with timber, chrome, cotton or tobacco; while every now and then a more exotic item appeared on the manifest: "17 tons of badger hair . . . 52 tons of caviar."

Initially the greatest threat to these convoys was thought to come from German surface forces, in particular the battleship *Tirpitz*. The fear that this powerful vessel might break out from some Norwegian fjord into the North Atlantic, attack a convoy and annihilate both the merchantmen and their escorts hung like a sword of Damocles over the Admiralty, and in March, 1942, the C-in-C of the Home Fleet gave a prophetic warning:

"If these convoys to Russia must, for political reasons, be continued, very serious and heavy losses are to be expected." His words came home to roost a few months later when, in the disastrous Convoy PQ17, fear of the *Tirpitz* led to one of the most tragic blunders of the war. In the mistaken belief that the battleship had put to sea, the convoy was ordered to scatter and its escorts headed off in the wrong direction to meet a non-existent enemy. To quote *Convoys to Russia, 1941–1945* by Bob Ruegg and Arnold Hague:

"What followed was a disaster, as the merchant ships were now sunk at leisure by aircraft and U-boats who were enabled to roam the outward route of the convoy with impunity, seeking out and sinking the near defenceless merchant ships at will."

Of the thirty-seven merchantmen which had set out with PQ17, twenty-four were sunk. As a result of this fiasco, the number of convoys sailing during the long hours of summer daylight was scaled down and the number of convoys trying to slip through undetected during the long hours of winter darkness was increased.

By the time 835 Squadron arrived in the Arctic the scenario had undergone a radical change. With the crippling of the *Tirpitz*, the threat from German surface warships had greatly decreased, but the threat from the U-boats remained. This in fact always had been and always would be the major danger, and there were now about twenty-five U-boats based permanently in Norway, and perhaps half as many from other bases operating in the Arctic. Many of them were of the latest Type XXI, equipped with "Schnorkels" (to enable them to recharge their batteries underwater) and armed with acoustic torpedoes. The threat from the air had, if anything, increased; for as the battleground in Europe contracted, German squadrons which had been serving in places like the Mediterranean now found themselves being pulled back to Norway. By the autumn of 1944 the *Kriegsmarine* had at its disposal between Bergen and North Cape upwards of forty reconnaissance planes, and the *Luftwaffe* upwards of 120 bombers and torpedo bombers.

As the nature of the threat from these German forces changed, so the defensive measures taken by the Navy also changed. To protect their convoys they came to rely more and more on aircraft-carriers.

American-built carriers, however, were not sufficiently robust to operate in the Arctic. This meant that the burden of protecting the convoys to Russia was about to fall almost entirely on the three British-built carriers, *Vindex*, *Campania* and *Nairana*.

It was, as we were about to discover, a demanding job, even when (as on our first convoy) there was little enemy activity and comparatively little flying.

★ ★ ★

*Nairana* arrived in Scapa Flow on 16 October, and it wasn't long before the rumours about our destination were confirmed. We were, we were told, about to provide air cover for Convoy JW61 to Murmansk.

A week later we stood north-west from the safe haven of the Fleet anchorage, and rendezvoused with the convoy in the not-so-safe waters of the Iceland gap.

JW61 turned out to be a medium-sized convoy: thirty merchant vessels, with their Commodore flying his flag in the *Fort Crèvecoeur*. And what an escort had been assembled to protect them! As we took up our position in a box, between lanes 3 and 7 and towards the rear of the convoy, we could see more warships than merchantmen. There were no fewer than three escort-carriers: *Vindex*, *Tracker* and *Nairana*. In the convoys of 1942 and 1943 there had seldom been even one. Even more remarkable was the fact that the officer commanding the escort, Vice Admiral Dalrymple-Hamilton, was flying his flag in *Vindex*. This was the first time a carrier had been chosen as flagship of a convoy, an indication of the importance now attached to this hitherto neglected branch of the Navy.

We were told that each carrier would do eight hours flying a day, eight hours standing-by and have eight hours resting. This was fine in theory. However, in practice the inability of *Tracker* to operate her Avengers in bad weather, and the disintegration of *Vindex*'s 811 Squadron, meant that in the end *Nairana* found herself doing all the flying and all the standing-by and having none of the rest.

From the moment we joined the convoy the weather was foul: low ten-tenths cloud, with poor visibility, high winds and heavy seas. And what seas they were! Great waves three-quarters of a mile from crest to crest and up to thirty feet in height thundering in endless succession over the horizon. They hit us beam on. Soon the top-heavy carriers were rolling to over 35°. Even worse off were the diminutive frigates on loan to the Russians as sub-chasers; they were tossed about like the proverbial corks, shipping it green and at times disappearing from sight. The fact that they managed to stay with the convoy is a tribute to the expertise of their builders and the skill and courage of their crews.

Val Jones, who invariably took on the most hazardous flights himself rather than risk the lives of his aircrew, flew the first patrol with one of the squadron's most experienced pilots, George Sadler. It was pitch dark when they took off at 0700, and very nearly as dark when, a couple of hours later, they returned to land-on. For at this latitude at this time of year there are barely three hours of daylight. At 1000 hours our night deck-landing lights were still switched on; by 1400 hours all ships were darkened. In spite of the appalling conditions George and Val got down safely, as did John Defrates and David Beal who flew the second patrol.

By the time it was the turn of one of the other carriers to take over, conditions had deteriorated still further. It was now impossible for *Tracker*'s Avengers to get off the deck, and *Vindex* reckoned conditions were so dangerous she declared her planes grounded. It didn't matter. The weather was too bad for the Germans too. For forty-eight hours the convoy ploughed on into the teeth of a north-easterly gale, battered but unmolested – "wind 45/50ks, gusting 67/70" Mike Arrowsmith wrote in his Met forecast. It grew colder. Among little nooks and crannies in the catwalks the spray began to solidify to ice. Then, unexpectedly, the clouds dispersed. The seas remained as high as ever and the wind as malevolent; but one moment the sky was filled with cloud, next moment it was wiped clean as a blackboard cleansed by a damp cloth. And late that evening we saw the Northern Lights.

> "Magnificent display of *Aurora Borealis*," Mick Murray wrote in his Diary. "Like a huge flame-thrower tossing bands of red, green and purple all over the sky. The bands wavered, shimmered, and gradually subsided into a layer of white semi-transparent light above the northern horizon. I wondered if it was the refracted image of the pack-ice?"

During the night of 25th/26th, as though to substantiate the idea that we were nearing pack-ice, the convoy altered course to almost due east. We were now coming up to the danger area.

Although the clouds had dispersed, gale-force winds and mountainous seas continued to buffet us. Conditions aboard were chaotic. To quote one of the observers:

> "Everyone had to work eat and try to sleep in a world that was constantly rolling through 80° – first a roll of 40° to port, then a roll of 40° to starboard. Although flying was not yet possible, we were told that U-boats had been reported ahead of the convoy. So a lot of our aircrew spent a lot of the time in flying gear in the darkened Ready Room [darkened to get their eyes accustomed to lack of light] ready to take off at a moment's notice. It was

impossible to get any sort of rest in these conditions, and already some pilots and observers were suffering from lack of sleep."

By the night of 27 October the convoy was approaching the last leg of its journey: the corridor between the Arctic pack-ice and the Norwegian shore. There were now reports of more than a dozen U-boats in the offing, and, although conditions for flying were appalling, it was agreed that the merchantmen *must* have air cover. At 0400 three of our Swordfish took off to patrol ahead of the convoy and from that moment *Nairana* and the other carriers provided continuous protection until JW61 reached the safety of Kola Bay. The number of patrols that we flew was small. But what patrols they were!

To say that conditions were difficult would be an understatement. For the wind was still a full gale; the seas were still enormous; and it was now pitch dark for nineteen hours out of twenty-four, and a sepulchral twilight for four hours. For we were now 400 miles to the north of the Arctic Circle.

First to take off at 0400 were Supple and Strong, Cowsill and Holley and Whittick and Worrell – the last two inexperienced aircrew being almost too literally "thrown in at the deep end". They carried out a series of searches ahead of the advancing ships. No U-boats, however, were detected, probably because the weather was too bad for them to surface. All three planes stayed airborne for a couple of hours and managed to find their way back to the carrier and land safely. The next three were not so lucky. McEwan and Eames, Sadler and the CO, and Urwin and Legood took off at 0530. The Fair Flying Log records the tasks they were given: "Alligator" . . . "Cobra 25" . . . "Adder 25 stbd"; these were codenames for different types of patrol – some circling the convoy, some patrolling up and down in parallel lines ahead or astern, some screening the port or starboard flank. All three aircraft remained airborne upwards of three hours, and by the time they got back to the carrier, the pilots and observers in their open cockpits were numb with cold and exhaustion. As McEwan came in to land, the stern of the carrier swung violently up to meet him, smashing his tail oleo and landing hook. A few minutes later Pat Urwin landed even more heavily and his undercarriage disintegrated, leaving the Swordfish squelched like an overripe plum on the flight-deck.

These, we reckoned, were good landings – because the aircrew walked away uninjured!

Later that morning, in the grey half-light that passed for dawn, John Cridland had an even closer shave.

"I was," he wrote, "coming in to land after a three-hour patrol. Although the carrier was pitching heavily, Bats seemed to think my approach was OK. I was within a few feet of the flight-deck, and within perhaps a second of being given the signal to cut, when the carrier dipped suddenly into an extra-deep trough and corkscrewed away from me. One moment I was poised over the round-down. Next I was heading straight for the bridge. I rammed the throttle full open, banked violently to starboard, and the bridge flashed by within inches of my wingtip. Indeed I was so close that my wing caught the radio and D/F aerials slung between the masts. No other aircraft could have survived and stayed airborne. But in spite of my damaged wing I was able to keep the faithful old Swordfish under control and go round again and make a normal landing. I think the only people NOT impressed were the Chief Petty Officer (Signals) and his ratings who had to re-rig the aerials in a howling 45-knot gale, lashed by sheets of spray."

It was about this time that *Tracker* took over flying-duties and, in spite of the heavy seas, managed at last to get her Avengers into the air. And one of them came near to achieving the success that had so far eluded us. It sighted a U-boat on the surface.

The U-boat crash-dived. The Avenger came swooping down and dropped its depth-charges in what it reckoned was the right spot. But the sea that morning was a mass of "white horses" and driven spume. It was hard to identify the tell-tale patches of slick which remain briefly on the surface of the sea after a U-boat has dived. No oil or wreckage came floating to the surface. And the attack was therefore classified as "inconclusive". (German records have subsequently confirmed that the U-boat did indeed receive no more than superficial damage.)

With the knowledge of hindsight, it seems likely that the U-boat picked up the approaching plane on its radar, but thought it must be the usual slow-moving Swordfish; this would have given it plenty of time to dive. Its crew must have had the shock of their lives when the much faster Avenger came swooping down on them out of the murk.

Soon it was pitch dark and our Swordfish were again circling the convoy. Conditions could hardly have been worse: heavy seas, strong winds, a sub-zero temperature and the horizon obscured by sea mist. To stay airborne the pilots had to rely on their instruments. And these, in spite of the efforts of our groundcrew, were beginning to prove fallible. Mick Murray and his observer John McEwan took off at 1530 hours, and almost at once suffered a complete radar and radio failure. It took John half-an-hour to rectify the fault, and the moment this was done they picked up a contact only fifteen miles from the convoy. They homed on it expectantly, but it turned out to be one of our destroyers hovering over the spot where *Tracker*'s Avenger had attacked the U-boat. This was not the end of their adventures. For, coming in to land, Mick hit the deck hard, ballooned over the first five arrester-wires, and was heading at forty knots straight for the barrier, when his landing-hook caught the Jesus Christ wire and, within a dozen feet, the plane was jerked to an exceedingly abrupt stop. Damage was limited to the Swordfish's longerons and Mick's head as it hit the windscreen.

A couple of hours later we picked up H/F D/F bearings on a U-boat which was transmitting from the surface, homing its colleagues on to the convoy. Three planes were flown off to silence it. The first two (George Sadler and Val Jones and Eric McEwan and John Eames) got off the deck safely; but as the carrier slewed sideways in a particularly vicious swell, the third hit the bridge on take-off. The tip of the Swordfish's wing was torn away. However, the pilot, Johnny Provis, not only managed to stay airborne but continued his search. Nothing was sighted, but the U-boat stopped transmitting and no more was heard of it. At the end of a two-hour search Johnny Provis managed to land his damaged Swordfish safely – a fine piece of flying.

At midnight *Vindex* took over as duty carrier, and it was her planes that protected the convoy as it entered the final leg of its journey: down the swept channel through the minefields at the approaches to Murmansk.

Not a great deal of actual flying had been done to protect JW61: only seventeen patrols involving some fifty hours in the air. These patrols, however, had been made in difficult conditions, and, in the last thirty-six hours of voyage, had been vital in keeping the U-boats at bay. And it is worth remembering that for every hour our pilots and observers spent in the air they spent at least half-a-dozen hours, in taxing conditions, either in the darkness of the Ready Room or strapped into the cockpits of their aircraft prepared to take off at a moment's notice. No wonder, as on the morning of 29 October we dropped anchor in Kola Inlet downriver from Murmansk, we were looking forward to some rest and some shore leave.

We got to know Murmansk and its environs quite well in the next six months. The town straddles the Kola River, about fifteen miles from its mouth. Its latitude is 69°N and its longitude 33°E, which means it is well north of the Arctic Circle and some way east of Suez. Before 1930 it was little more than a sprawling fishing village, with wooden quays and wooden houses. However, as part of an ambitious programme of modernization, it was decided to turn it into Russia's major ice-free port. Roads and railways were built, linking the town to Moscow and Leningrad (Saint Petersburg); concrete quays were laid down, and part of the town was rebuilt in brick and cement. The outbreak of war brought this work to an end, and in 1942 Murmansk was subjected to the most severe bombing ever inflicted on any European city. The fires burned for three months and totally destroyed 98 per cent of the wooden buildings. Cement, in Arctic conditions, tends to be brittle, and the brick and concrete structures collapsed under bombing like the proverbial packs of cards. Not one house in the entire city remained intact; most were reduced to rubble. Neither the docklands of London nor the heart of Dresden suffered such complete devastation.

By the time we arrived in the city in the autumn of 1944 some repairs had been effected and some rebuilding attempted. However, there were no shops and food rations had to be drawn daily from communal centres; there was virtually no social life; and most of the city's hundred-thousand-odd inhabitants seemed to be living in scooped-out holes in the ground surrounded by rubble. Snow fell almost continuously for eight months out of twelve. The average temperature was -5°F by day and -15° by night. It would be difficult to imagine a more depressing existence.

Our first contact with the Russians was when a river pilot came aboard to guide *Nairana* to her moorings. He was invited to dinner in the wardroom, and managed to consume with his meal no fewer than twelve bread rolls ("I don't believe," Bob Selley told me, "he had ever seen white bread in his life") and almost as many double whiskeys. Our only conversation was in German, with George Gordon as interpreter.

This set the pattern for our relationship with the Russians. They were not unfriendly, but communication was difficult and they were so preoccupied with the business of survival that they had neither the time nor the wherewithal to offer us hospitality. We heard, for example, that there was an "officers' club" on the way to Murmansk, but when Sam Hollings and some of his friends paid it a visit, they were nearly shot by a trigger-happy sentry, and all they found in the "club" were a few broken chairs and a billiard table with no pockets.

There were, however, two ways in which the Russians did us proud. They provided us with skis and their Red Fleet Choir turned on a truly magnificent concert. Murmansk is hardly the ideal ski resort; it is too flat, too rocky, and the snow is in good condition only between January and mid-April. On this our first visit the snowfields were sparse and soggy. However, we were loaned cross-country skis and the more energetic members of the squadron can now boast to their grandchildren that they learned their skiing north of the Bering Sea and east of Suez.

On our last evening in Kola Inlet the North Russian Red Fleet (all male) Choir came aboard and gave a performance in *Nairana*'s hangar which would have won acclaim in the Albert Hall. The singing, dancing and burlesque were of a very high standard indeed, and – with due respect to ENSA – something altogether different from the usual fare offered to British troops. Inevitably there were moments of confusion. An offstage interpreter provided a running translation, and his announcement of one song as "Oh Happy Sailor, far out to sea" produced a burst of sceptical laughter, coupled with one or two observations (fortunately untranslated) about the absence of the Red Fleet sailors far out to sea. The interpreter, nonplussed, doubtless thought us a strange people. After the performance the officers and their political commissars were entertained in the wardroom where they valiantly resisted the efforts of their hosts to drink them under the table!

Next day, 2 November, we weighed anchor in readiness to join the homeward bound RA61.

This was another medium-sized convoy, thirty-three merchantmen, with the Commodore flying his flag in the *Edward A. Savoy*. The escort consisted basically of the same warships that had protected the outwardbound JW61: three escort-carriers, one cruiser, seven destroyers, and some dozen sloops, frigates and corvettes. Dalrymple-Hamilton again flew his flag in HMS *Vindex* – though this was probably a decision he was soon to regret!

The official report on the convoy reads:

> "18 U-boats were assembled off the mouth of Kola Inlet, in an attempt to mount an attack on the convoy as it left the safety of Russian minefields. The frigates and carriers therefore sailed early to 'put down' these attackers. However, Asdic conditions were poor, and despite the strength of our forces no U-boats were sunk. We lost HMS *Mounsey*, torpedoed by *U-295*. Thanks to the efforts of carrier-borne planes no attack was mounted against the convoy. . . . During an uneventful passage home bad weather was experienced. . . . The convoy arrived without loss in Loch Ewe on 9 November."

For the aircrew of *Nairana* and (in particular) of *Vindex*, there was more to it than that. Both carriers on the evening of 2 November flew a continuous succession of patrols as the convoy stood out of Kola Inlet. Ours were successful. *Vindex*'s were disastrous.

It was pitch dark as, at a little after 1600 hours, our first three Swordfish took-off to circle the convoy. Conditions, as usual, were difficult: heavy seas, mist and the aircraft compasses susceptible to excessive magnetic variation. And to add to our troubles, two out of the first ten planes to get airborne had to return with their engines running roughly. Ted Pitts had barely sufficient power to get back to the carrier. Nevertheless all patrols were successfully completed, and all aircraft landed safely.

It was a different story for the unfortunate *Vindex*. She too had a composite squadron aboard: the twelve Swordfish and four Wildcats of 811 Squadron. 811 Squadron had a fine record – far more prestigious to date than ours! Earlier in the year they had been part of a "hunter killer" group which had accounted for several U-boats in the North Atlantic. Their standard of flying was second to none. However, many of their more experienced aircrew had recently been given shore appointments, and when, in October, 1944, they set out for Russia, about half the Squadron consisted of pilots and observers who had little operational experience. On the voyage home, within the span of forty-eight hours, the Squadron suffered such terrible losses that as a fighting unit it ceased to exist.

Their first two Swordfish that flew off to protect RA61 got lost. When, at the end of their patrols, they returned to what they thought was the convoy, they found they had been circling a rain cloud. They began a square search, but after four hours there was still no sign of the convoy. Desperately short of fuel, they asked by radio for a homing bearing and this they were given. By the time they sighted the pale blue landing lights of the *Vindex*, they had been flying for 4¾ hours and were numb with cold and exhaustion. Somehow they got down safely. "Somehow" because both pilots and observers were found to be literally frozen solid; they had to be cut free and lifted out of their cockpits.

Next morning in the brief couple of hours of daylight, one of the squadron's most experienced fighter pilots took-off in an attempt to intercept a shadowing aircraft. The light was poor and layers of low cloud and sea mist made it impossible to tell where the horizon was. The Wildcat flew straight into the sea. A destroyer was sent to try and rescue the pilot who had been seen in the water, but in the four minutes it took the warship to reach him, he had died of exposure. A couple of hours later a Swordfish trying to take-off toppled over the bow and into the sea. Its RATOG had failed to operate. Both pilot and observer were killed. Soon afterwards a Swordfish coming in to land went over the side. For perhaps thirty seconds it hung suspended by its landing hook which had caught on one of the arrester-wires. Then the strain was too much; the hook was torn from the fuselage and the aircraft plummeted into the sea. The pilot was saved, but the observer drowned; it was their second operational patrol. In the next twelve hours another Swordfish ended up in the barrier, and yet another shattered its undercarriage.

Then, from the point of view of keeping the Squadron operational came the ultimate disaster. It was midday and two out of the squadron's three remaining Wildcats had been brought up to the flight-deck in case they needed to be scrambled quickly in an emergency. They were being manhandled into position and lashed down when the carrier started to roll even more violently than usual in a series of enormous waves. The Wildcats, with folded wings and narrow undercarriages, were unstable. And they were heavy. One of them started to glissade, out of control, across the ice-coated deck. The flight-deck handling party flung themselves on to it, fighting to hold it and lash it down, but, as the carrier rolled through 80°, the plane broke free, tossing off the handling party as a rolling log tosses off sparks. Then the other Wildcat too broke loose. And both aircraft, gathering momentum, went crashing into the catwalk and over the side, fortunately minus their pilots who had leapt clear at the last second.

On the morning of 2 November 811 Squadron had been an efficient if somewhat inexperienced flying unit. By the evening of 3 November it had written off or seriously damaged seven out of its twelve Swordfish and lost three out of its four Wildcats.

The final nail in its coffin was the breakdown of *Vindex*'s lift. This meant that there was no way of moving even the few aircraft which were undamaged between the hangar and the flight-deck. Both carrier and Squadron were hamstrung.

*Tracker* too was incapacitated. Due to her open design and lightweight construction, she was pitching and rolling even more violently than her British-built counterparts. There was no way that her Avengers could get off the flight-deck, let alone land on it. Dalrymple-Hamilton therefore signalled the carriers to stop flying.

Captain Surtees, however, saw fit to query this order: "My boys," he told the Admiral, "can still fly." As a result of his keenness, optimism, rashness, ignorance, devotion to duty or call it what you will, *Nairana* now found herself saddled with the job of providing air cover for RA61 singlehanded.

It was a challenge, and the Squadron rose to it. The weather was too bad for our Wildcats even to think of flying; but whenever conditions permitted, over the next few days, it was *Nairana*'s Swordfish and *Nairana*'s Swordfish alone which circled and protected the convoy.

Val Jones, with George Sadler as his pilot, was first to take-off – "to see if flying was possible" – a two-hour Cobra in the small hours of 4 November. And where he led, his Squadron followed.

It would be no exaggeration to say that every one of the patrols flown during the next couple of days called for airmanship of the highest standard. If there had been the slightest error in an observer's navigation or in his use of his ASVX, that would have been the end of *that* crew. If there had been the slightest misjudgement or slowness of reaction on the part of a pilot as he took-off or landed, that too would have been fatal. As it was, the Swordfish flew fourteen patrols in forty-eight hours, providing more or less continuous air cover for the convoy during a vital part of its route where no land-based aircraft could guard it. The wonder is not that there were *some* accidents but that there were not more. Inevitably it was the less experienced aircrew who came to grief.

Sid Cowsill didn't so much hit the barrier as land on top of it. "Barrier landing," records the Fair Flying Log, "aircraft a total write off."

Dave Whittick arrived in an even more spectacular manner. Coming in to land at the end of a three-hour patrol, he made a good approach and was given the signal to cut; but at the last second the deck swung up to meet him. He hit it hard, missed the arrester-wires, ballooned high into the air, and suddenly found himself half-stalled some thirty feet above the flight-deck and heading straight for the *top* of the barrier. Seeing that if he didn't do *something*, he and his observer would almost certainly be killed, he rammed open his throttle, leapfrogged *over* the barrier, and just managed to pick up sufficient flying speed to stay airborne. Coming in a second time, he made a perfect landing. "Jumped barrier and went round again!!!" records the Fair Flying Log, the number of exclamation marks in this most prosaic of journals reflecting a mixture of disapproval, disbelief and reluctant admiration. It will be remembered that our former CO, the unfortunate T.T. Miller, tried to do much the same thing. *His* hook caught the top of the barrier and he wrote off his Swordfish and a Sea Hurricane and ended up under cabin arrest. Dave was lucky, because those who watched his landing are all agreed that his hook missed the barrier by inches rather than feet.

One other *Kamikaze*-type patrol is worth recording. On the evening of 3 November a German reconnaissance aircraft found and started to shadow the convoy. It shadowed us hour after hour, round and round. Every now and then, reminding us of what was going on, we could hear above the roar of the wind and the pound of the sea the not-quite-synchronized beat of its engines. It was far too dark and too stormy even to think of flying off our Wildcats, but Bob Selley and Dave Newbery volunteered to masquerade as a night-fighter in their Swordfish and try to drive it away. Their only armament was an ancient sub-machine-gun, which Dave Newbery managed (with some difficulty) to cram into his already overcrowded cockpit. Then they took-off and were vectored by Alan Kerry towards the shadower. And the German aircraft fled! Maybe it picked up Alan Kerry's transmissions and thought that a *bona fide* fighter was about to attack it; maybe it spotted the vague shape of the approaching Swordfish and mistook it for a Wildcat. At any rate and for whatever reason, the blip disappeared from our screen and didn't trouble us again. With considerable relief, Bob and Dave flew back to the carrier and landed safely after what was surely one of the more bizarre "fighter patrols" of the war. As Dave Newbery remarked as he returned his sub-machine-gun to Stores, "It's lucky for us all cats are grey in the dark!"

The bad weather meanwhile showed no sign of abating. Indeed if anything it got worse, and the speed of the convoy had to be reduced. Even so, many of the merchantmen, in ballast, were flinging their screws clean out of water as they nosedived into the swell.

Aboard the unwieldy carriers conditions were chaotic. One of *Nairana*'s rolls was measured at 54°; in other words she tipped from port to starboard through an arc of over 100°. This, according to the book, should have made her turn turtle. Conditions in the hangar were beyond belief, with the maintenance crew having to secure every aircraft and every item of equipment with treble lashings. In the wardroom too we had our problems. Our gallant gunnery officer was unable to enjoy his daily tipple until he had lashed himself to a stanchion!

For three consecutive days we were duty carrier. Then, on 6 November, *Vindex* at last got her lift working and was able to help us. Next day aircraft of Coastal Command, operating from the Shetlands, were circling the convoy. And the day after that we sighted the northernmost islands of the Orkneys.

As we entered Scapa Flow it was still blowing a full gale and snowing as though it would never stop. The elements, it seemed, were reluctant to admit we had escaped them.

While protecting this homewardbound convoy we had flown thirty-three anti-submarine patrols and searches: not, you might rightly say, a lot of flying. Yet most of the patrols had been at night, all had been in difficult conditions, and we had lost only one aircraft and none of our aircrew.

The three carriers didn't tarry in Scapa but stood south at full speed for the Clyde: full speed because we reckoned that leave was in the offing. We must have been an impressive sight as, screened by our destroyer escort, we swept in perfect formation past the Mull of Kintyre. *Nairana*, however, had difficulty maintaining the requisite fifteen knots. Our Chief Engineer had to order "continuous maximum revolutions", and this produced a curious rhythmic surge in the engines and a curious up-and-down movement – known as "the honeymoon motion" – in the ship.

As we approached our berths at Greenock, *Vindex* must have been thankful that RA61 was over. However, she was to suffer one final indignity. In front of the watchful eyes of the welcoming Vice Admiral, she fouled

34. A Swordfish armed with 'Oscar' crashes. Note that the outline of the secret acoustic torpedo has been scratched out by the censor.

35. Joe Supple nearly goes over the side.

36. Bill Armitage nearly goes over the side in his Sea Hurricane.

37. Pete Blanco and his Wildcat end up in the barrier.

38. Swordfish taking off on a dawn patrol...

39. ... and landing.

40. A Swordfish, its wings folded, is 'struck down' aboard HMS *Battler* into the hangar below the flight deck.

41. A Swordfish revs up in preparation for take-off.

42. Officers of HMS *Vindex* clear the flight deck of snow.

43. Clearing the snow from HMS *Campania*'s flight deck.

44. HMS *Nairana* in heavy seas on the way to Russia.

45. Mist rising from the sea around merchant ships on a Russian convoy.

46. *Nairana*'s ship's bell, now hanging in the Fleet Air Arm Museum, Yeovilton.

47. Seamen clear the flight deck on an escort carrier at Kola Bay, illustrating the conditions which hampered flying in Arctic operations.

48. In 1949 HMS *Nairana* was converted to the MV *Port Victor*.

49. Forty years on! Lansdown Grove Hotel, Bath, 9 May, 1989.
L. to R.: John Lloyd, Norman Sargent, John Roberts, Barry Barringer,
Sam Mearns, Jack Teesdale, Al Burgham, Willie Armstrong, Bob
Selley, Ken Atkinson, Jock Bevan, John Cridland, Eric McEwan,
George Arber, John Eames, Teddy Elliott, David Newbery, Val Jones,
Charles Gough, Donald Payne. Hank Housser also attended but missed
the photograph.

the boom. We reckoned it was the Almighty's passing shot at Dalrymple-Hamilton for not having flown his flag in *Nairana*!

That night we had a distinguished visitor. Almost as soon as we had dropped anchor, Lumley Lyster came aboard to congratulate us. We were, he told us, "the first convoy to get to Russia and back without losing a single merchantman". (Lyster, in fact, was not strictly right about this. A couple of small and very early convoys were never attacked at all. A stickler for accuracy would therefore say that Lyster ought to have told us we were the first convoy that was *attacked* and got through without loss.) Anyhow, his praise meant a lot to us. As did nine days' leave.

On returning to *Nairana*, we were told to fly to Machrihanish for the inevitable working up.

Our Wildcat pilots were glad to get into the air – during JW and RA61 they hadn't once got off the deck (although they had spent a total of nearly fifty hours strapped into their cockpits or in the Ready Room) – and they now gave priority to practising dawn and dusk landings. For rumour had it that we might soon be providing air cover for another convoy to Russia, and it was obvious that in midwinter in the Arctic there would be little daylight-flying for the Wildcats. For the Swordfish there were dummy-night-deck-landings for the pilots, and swinging compasses for the observers; and we now carried out these routine assignments with more than usual care; for it was obvious that deck-landings and compasses were matters of life or death.

Soon we were en route a second time to Scapa Flow. While waiting here for our convoy to assemble there were changes in personnel among both the squadron's and the ship's officers. We lost two stalwarts, George Sadler and Dave Newbery; both were given shore appointments. And we lost Commander Healey, an able and understanding man, who had managed to be both efficient and popular. His successor, Commander F.J. Cartwright (known as "Fat Jack") may have been efficient but he was certainly not popular, for he tried to impose a formal Dartmouth-type régime in the wardroom. To give just one example: he decreed that meals – as in a peacetime battleship – should be served punctiliously at set (and very restricted) times. When he was told that aircrew might be flying at these set times, he replied that was too bad; if they couldn't be in the wardroom on time they could go without. And when he was told that aircrew not only had to fly but often had to spend long hours in the Ready Room (which they were not permitted to leave) waiting to take-off at a moment's notice, he replied that also was too bad and they would still have to go without. (How very different from the way the RAF treated *their* aircrew.) We could tolerate this in harbour or when we were working up, but *not* on operations, when our pilots and observers needed all the sleep and all the decent food they could get. A confrontation was certain as thunder after lightning. It was the quiet, equable and well-balanced Al Burgham who at last said what all of us had been longing to say.

"You'd better remember," he told "Fat Jack", "the ship is here for pilots to fly off, not for you to try out your Dartmouth rules and regulations."

In view of the criticism that was later levelled at our captain, it ought to be said that it was Cartwright not Surtees who favoured these restrictions. At the end of the convoy, in his "report of proceedings" to Vice Admiral Aircraft Carriers, Surtees wrote:

"I am not satisfied with the present arrangements for meals for aircrews, due in part to internal organization, lack of suitable accommodation and approved complement of cooks and stewards. This is being gone into, and a separate report will be rendered."

In the small hours of 30 November we left the Fleet anchorage at Scapa Flow and rendezvoused with Convoy JW62. This was another fair-sized convoy: thirty-one merchantmen, with the Commodore flying his flag in *Fort Boise*. Again the escort was powerful: one cruiser, three sloops, four corvettes, eleven frigates, fourteen destroyers, and the aircraft carriers *Nairana* and *Campania*, the latter flying the flag of Rear Admiral McGrigor. *Tracker* had been left behind, since both she and her Avengers had proved ill-suited to winter flying in the Arctic, while *Vindex* and her shell-shocked squadron were being very sensibly rested. The fact that once again there were more warships than merchantmen is evidence of the importance attached to these Russian convoys and of the difficulty that was anticipated in getting them through.

A report on JW62 reads:

"Although *Tirpitz* had been eliminated, removing the necessity of maintaining the Home Fleet at strength and using it to support the Russian convoy route, the enemy had replaced one threat with another by moving to North Norway a substantial force of Ju 88 torpedo-bombers. The U-boat threat, as always, remained great in this theatre. In spite of his formidable strength, however, the enemy was not able to make any impression on JW62 which arrived unscathed in Kola Inlet."

835 Squadron, however, were by no means unscathed. And it was on this convoy that the friction between Val Jones and Surtees came to a head.

Our first convoy to Russia had followed a direct route which had taken us close to the Norwegian shore. This time we followed a far more westerly and northerly route, skirting Bjornaya or Bear Island (so called because the Dutch who discovered it in 1596 found there "a great white bear, which we came at with muskets, halberds and hatchets and killed after a two-hour fight"). This detour added three hundred miles and a couple of days to our voyage, but we hoped it would make things difficult for the Ju 88s, whose arrival at Bardufoss and Banak had not escaped the notice of Norwegian resistance agents.

During the first couple of days we didn't do a great deal of flying, no more than four patrols; for it was now official policy, we were told, to conserve aircrew in the early stages of the convoy so that they would be in good shape to cope with the more difficult later stages when we were likely to be beset by U-boats, Junkers, pack-ice and sea mist, the warships' Asdic would be ineffective, and our aircraft would be the merchantmen's most effective, and indeed their only, defence. However, on our second day out from Scapa, in the early hours of the morning, two enemy aircraft appeared on our Radar screen. There was not much cloud and a certain amount of moonlight; our Wildcats had been practising dawn and dusk take-off and landing and, although it wouldn't be dawn for several hours, it was decided to scramble the two pilots who were standing-by – Bill Armitage and Norman Sargent – to see if they could make an interception. There was a strong wind and *Nairana* was pitching heavily; nonetheless Bill and Norman managed to get airborne and were vectored towards the German aircraft. Now it could have been that the Germans were short of fuel and that is why they turned for home; it could be that they saw the Wildcats coming; or it could be that they picked up *Nairana*'s homing signals. Whatever the reason, they suddenly headed back for Norway. Bill and Norman never managed to get within a mile of them. They did, however, manage to stay airborne for another couple of hours, until dawn brought a hint of light, and that made landing a bit (but not much) easier. They got down safely.

However, it was clear that the convoy had been discovered, that its course and its strength were known and that there was likely to be trouble ahead.

*Nairana* and *Campania* between them kept up a succession of patrols over the next few days. Then the weather worsened. And to make things even more difficult our Swordfish (hitherto so reliable) began to suffer a spate of engine, radio and ASV failures. This was not because of any shortcomings among our maintenance personnel; it was because of the testing conditions in which the aircraft had to be maintained, ranged on the flight-deck and flown. A glance at the Fair Flying Log reveals that, within the span of twenty-four hours, we could, all too easily, have lost a quarter of our aircrew.

| Date | Aircraft | Pilot | Observer | Time off | Duration | Duty |
|------|----------|-------|----------|----------|----------|------|
| Dec 6 | NR939 | Selley | C.O. | 0005 | .35 | A/S Patrol. Returned engine failure. Hit barrier. |
| " | NR897 | Brown | Eames | 0245 | 3.25 | Cobra 25 |
| " | NR859 | Wilson | Strong | 0645 | 2.55 | Cobra 25 Returned, engine trouble |
| " | NR897 | Urwin | Legood | 0800 | 2.40 | Crocodile 25 |
| " | NR916 | Cowsill | Holley | 0920 | 2.00 | A/S Search Returned, engine trouble |
| " | NR874 | Cridland | Hall | 0930 | 1.15 | A/S Search |
| " | NR864 | Whittick | Worrell | 0930 | 3.20 | A/S Search |
| " | NR999 | Provis | Rose | 1030 | 2.20 | Crocodile 25 |
| " | NR186 | McEwan | Hankin | 1030 | 1.40 | A/S Search Total R/T failure |
| " | NR897 | Selley | C.O. | 1120 | 1.40 | A/S Search (recalled) |

Of the ten Swordfish to fly that day one suffered a complete and unnerving R/T failure which severed contact between plane and carrier, one was recalled because of worsening weather, and three suffered the sort of engine-trouble which might all too easily have resulted in the plane having to ditch some way from the convoy, in which case the aircrew would have been unlikely to survive.

The strain of having to face this sort of danger day after day was cumulative and our senior medical officer, Lt-Cdr Waterman, was not unaware of the fact that the health of the squadron aircrew, both physically and mentally, was now beginning to deteriorate. It seems likely that three factors exacerbated this deterioration: the weather, our failure to sink a U-boat, and the unreasonable demands of Captain Surtees.

We escorted three convoys to Russia that winter in relatively quick succession and the weather on each of them seemed to get progressively worse. Week after week we had to live with huge seas, gale-force winds, numbing cold, and some nineteen hours each day of absolute darkness; even when it was light there was never a glimmer of sun. After a while it became depressing, and we depressed.

If we had sunk a U-boat that would have gone a long way towards making it all worthwhile. Just about every other squadron in the Fleet Air Arm seemed to have sunk one, and goodness knows how many times we had picked a contact up on our ASVX, homed on it and sometimes sighted it and attacked it. Yet we could claim no definite kill. We began to think of ourselves as Jonahs.

An understanding captain would have got us to snap out of it. But whatever virtues Surtees may have possessed, understanding the needs of his aircrew was not among them. With his obsession to keep the squadron flying at all times and in all circumstances, he made life even harder for us than it need have been. What happened on the night of 9 December was typical. Conditions were appalling: wind 60 knots gusting 100, heavy squalls of snow, and a layer of stratus (and icing) at 500 feet. No U-boat could have been anywhere near the surface and survived, and *Campania* had very sensibly cancelled flying. But not Surtees. He ordered a Swordfish to patrol ten miles ahead of the convoy. It was of course Val Jones and his long-suffering pilot, Bob Selley, who "volunteered" for what at best was a highly hazardous assignment. Taking-off from a wildly-pitching carrier in total dark and a 60 knot snowstorm isn't easy, but Bob managed it. He then did his best to reach his designated patrol-area ahead of the convoy. The trouble was that the convoy was heading almost directly into wind, and after about ten minutes Bob got a plaintive request from his observer:

"Can you put your foot down? On the accelerator?"

Bob checked his throttle-setting which was almost at maximum revs, and his airspeed which was also very nearly at maximum. "I'm doing my best. Why?"

"We're barely," Val told him, "keeping pace with the convoy!"

Bob pushed his throttle-lever right through the gate, the Swordfish's airspeed increased to 95 knots, and the plane began very slowly to draw ahead of the advancing merchantmen. Suddenly the engine cut stone dead. One second the noise of the storm was muffled by the throb of the Pegasus XXX, next second there was only the storm.

Val transmitted a Mayday distress call. Bob jettisoned his depth-charges and flares. (This was standard procedure for an aircraft about to ditch; otherwise when the plane hit the water it was liable to be blown up by its own depth-charges and set on fire by its own flares.) Depth-charges could be jettisoned "safe"; flares could only be jettisoned live. And now, to Val and Bob's horror as the bright white flares suspended by their parachutes were swirled away downward, they lit up the advancing convoy. For, although the Swordfish had been airborne for more than a quarter of an hour, it had made little headway against the wind. However, for the moment the convoy was the least of Bob's worries. He made all the checks that were in the book – and several that weren't – flicking his ignition switches, shifting his fuel cock, operating his primer. But to no avail. The Swordfish lost height. However, due perhaps to the force of the gale, the propeller was still windmilling, and suddenly and for no apparent reason, when they were down to 300 feet, the engine burst into life. They were now almost directly over the centre of the convoy and Bob made a beeline for *Nairana*, his one thought to land-on before his engine failed a second time. In spite of the darkness, the 60 knot wind, the snow, the fact that *Nairana* wasn't exactly into wind, and a coughing engine, he managed, by a combination of luck and skill, against all the odds, to get down safely.

He and Val were at once summoned to the bridge. Here, instead of being congratulated by Surtees on a fine piece of flying, they were berated for having lit up the convoy. This was just one example of Surtees' inability to understand what could reasonably be expected of his aircraft and his aircrew.

Other examples were to follow. Next day JW62 reached its destination safely and without loss. No sooner had we dropped anchor than we were told we would be staying in Vaenga (the port for Murmansk) for three or four days and then escorting another convoy back to the UK. On our first night in harbour our maintenance crews were looking forward to being able to service their Swordfish in peace and quiet. Captain Surtees, however, had other ideas. He ordered the hangar to be cleared of aircraft so that the ship's company could enjoy the showing of a film. In spite of Val Jones' protests our already deteriorating Swordfish were taken up to the flight-deck and parked there for more than five hours, exposed to the driving snow and sub-zero temperature of the Arctic night. This did them no good at all. To quote Val Jones:

> "It was a crass decision. Anyone in his right mind would have realized that by hazarding his aircraft he was hazarding not only the lives of his aircrew but the safety of his ship; for the whole *raison d'être* of a carrier is to operate aircraft, and without its aircraft a carrier is like a tiger devoid of claws and teeth."

So *was* Surtees in his right mind? Val Jones was not the only person to ask himself this. For improbable and theatrical as it sounds, during our brief stay in Vaenga Commander Cartwright and "Doc" Waterman got together and seriously discussed the possibility of declaring *Nairana's* captain insane. If they had done this – as readers of *The Caine Mutiny* will recall – they would have been empowered to relieve him of his command.

What particularly concerned the doctor was the deterioration in the health of the aircrew, and this he attributed very largely to Surtees' insistence on keeping them flying no matter what the circumstances. However,

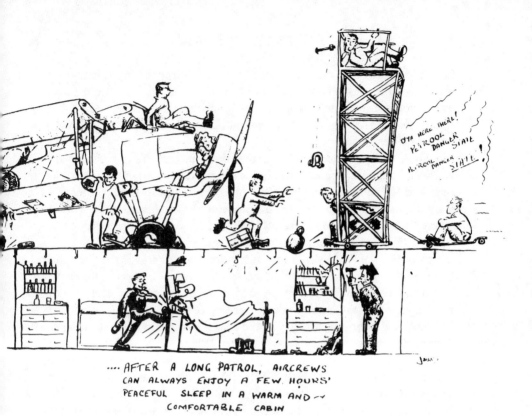

.... AFTER A LONG PATROL, AIRCREWS
CAN ALWAYS ENJOY A FEW HOURS'
PEACEFUL SLEEP IN A WARM AND ~
COMFORTABLE CABIN

after considerable personal agonizing, "Doc" Waterman decided, I believe rightly, to let things be.

No sooner had he made his decision than *Nairana* weighed anchor, and, screened by the 6th Destroyer Flotilla, stood out to sea. It transpired that Surtees had volunteered to leave harbour forty-eight hours ahead of the convoy and disperse the U-boats which were known to be congregating at the mouth of Kola Inlet. *Campania* was not involved in this venture. So before the convoy even put to sea, our squadron had to face the prospect of two days of intensive flying single-handed. And what days they were!

During the next forty-eight hours our Swordfish flew twenty-five patrols and searches. Sometimes as many as four planes were in the air at the same time; hardly ever was there less than one. Sometimes as many as four aircrew were standing by in the Ready Room; never were there less than two. What made this programme particularly demanding was (a) the weather – high seas, intermittent snow, low cloud and sea mist; (b) the darkness – because it was midwinter and we were so far north of the Arctic Circle the sun never rose above the horizon; (c) the unreliability of our aircraft: of the twenty-five Swordfish to take-off two suffered electrical or radio failure and three suffered partial engine failure; (d) the fact that our senior naval officer knew so little about flying. To quote one of our pilots: "At the back of our minds was the fear that because Surtees had so little experience of operating aircraft he would land us in a situation where our lives would be put needlessly at risk."

Of all our aircrew none had better reason to endorse this judgement than Brown and Eames. Their first patrol was aborted and they were recalled because of worsening weather. Next morning, at 0300 hours, they were off again, with orders to patrol some seventy miles ahead of the carrier; navigation and fuel, they were told, should be no problem because the carrier would be maintaining a steady westerly course towards them. At the end of their allotted two-and-a-half hours Brown and Eames returned to the place where the carrier ought to have been. It wasn't there. On one side (invisible of course in the dark) lay the Norwegian shore at the approaches to North Cape; on the other side (equally invisible) lay a mass of pack-ice extending all the way to the Pole – not ideal terrain for a forced landing. Brown and Eames switched their IFF to "distress" and tried to gain height with the idea of picking up *Nairana* on their ASV. Gaining height, however, led to problems. Immediately above them was a layer of cumulus in which icing was heavy; after only a few minutes their Swordfish was so sheathed in ice that she became difficult to control. However, they picked up the image of the carrier and homed on it. They had been flying for nearly three-and-a-half hours and were getting low on fuel when at last they spotted the *Nairana* – heading not west but east. They requested permission to land – and were refused.

What happened next beggars belief. Brown and Eames circled the *Nairana*, their IFF at "distress" and their navigation lights flashing. Again and again they asked permission to land. When they were down to their last few gallons of fuel they started transmitting "Maydays". Nobody took any notice of them. Eventually they ran out of fuel and crashed into the sea.

What had been happening meanwhile aboard the *Nairana* was this. When our Operations Officer, Dick Mallett, was planning how best to fly the patrols that Surtees wanted, he was told that for the next few hours the carrier would be heading due west: i.e. it would be steaming towards the aircraft which was patrolling ahead of it. However, after this aircraft (Brown and Eames's) had been airborne for about an hour and a half, *Nairana*'s navigating officer thought that there might be shoal water ahead. He therefore ordered the carrier to reverse course. Nobody, however, bothered to tell Brown and Eames that instead of steaming directly *towards* them, their landing-strip was now steaming directly *away* from them. When, by a combination of luck and navigational expertise, they managed to locate

*Nairana* and catch up with her, they ought to have been landed-on at once because they were short of fuel. Surtees, however, wanted to have aircraft continuously in the air. He therefore ordered the next two Swordfish that were due on patrol to take-off before Brown and Eames landed. This would have been OK (a) if Brown and Eames had had plenty of fuel and would have been happy circling the carrier, and (b) if the two Swordfish could have been flown off quickly. However, Brown and Eames did *not* have plenty of fuel and one of the Swordfish due to be flown-off refused to start. The recalcitrant aircraft ought to have been moved out of the way – either by pushing it for'ard of the barrier or striking it below into the hangar. However, it remained in the middle of the flight-deck, blocking the landing area and surrounded by mechanics trying to start it. They were still trying to start it as Brown and Eames crashed into the sea.

Ron Brown did everything right. He managed to ditch so skilfully that he and his observer were able to get into the aircraft dinghy before the plane went down. And he ditched in exactly the right place: on the *Nairana*'s port quarter, where the rescue ship should have been waiting to pick them up. There was no rescue ship.

It was standard procedure (and Admiralty Instructions) that, whenever landing-on or taking-off was in progress from a carrier, a rescue ship should *always* be in position to rescue the aircrew in emergency. Surtees, however, was so obsessed with his quest for U-boats that he failed to take this obligatory safety measure. Even after the Swordfish had ditched, little apparent attempt was made to rescue the aircrew. About the only person aboard the *Nairana* to act positively was Bob Mathé who, with commendable presence of mind, flung his illuminated bats into the sea in an attempt to mark the spot where the plane had gone down.

It was as well for Brown and Eames that they were wearing their recently-issued rubber-immersion suits, otherwise they wouldn't have survived for more than a few minutes. As it was, they crouched in their dinghy, firing off distress signals and watching *Nairana* grow smaller and smaller until she disappeared into the night.

John Eames relates what happened next: a saga not of hours but days.

"Our depth-charges hadn't gone off, but our flares burned brightly. Into this somewhat apocalyptic scene came HMS *Cassandra* (Lt Leslie, OBE, RN) with roving searchlight. He very sportingly made his ship alarmingly visible as he stopped to pick us up. Our hands were so numb we couldn't grasp the lifelines thrown to us, but *Cassandra*'s seamen jumped into the icy water to secure us and haul us to safety. We were a bit chilled but undamaged.

"It was too rough for us to be transferred back to *Nairana*, so next night we borrowed pyjamas and settled down for a comfortable kip.

"I woke not in my bunk, but in the corner of the cabin where I had been flung by the force of the explosion. *U-365* had torpedoed *Cassandra*, cutting the destroyer in two. The bow section sank immediately, with heavy loss of life – all those in the for'ard messdeck. The after section remained afloat, and we began to try and limp back, sternfirst, towards Kola Inlet about 200 miles away. The frigate *Bahamas* took us in tow, but in the heavy seas the two ships were more often on parallel courses than in line ahead. After twenty-four hours we had been blown thirty miles farther from Kola than when the tow started.

"We had a lot of injured. Two died, and we buried them on the second day. The usual quiet ceremony, made more dramatic and somehow more poignant by the huge seas, stormy sky and twilight at noon.

"Eventually a Russian tug came to our rescue, and we got back to Kola I forget how many days later.

"After kicking our heels here for almost a week, we were given passage home in *Bahamas*, and arrived in Londonderry after a solo voyage uneventful except for one brief encounter with a mine."

It is an indication of the spirit and camaraderie in the Squadron that both pilot and observer declined to take the survivors' leave to which they were entitled, but reported back as soon as they could to *Nairana*.

Meanwhile aboard the carrier, Captain Surtees' sortie was grinding to a halt; for at the end of forty-eight hours' continuous flying virtually all the squadron's Swordfish were unserviceable. *Nairana* therefore returned to the entrance to Kola Inlet to await the convoy now due any moment to emerge from behind the protective barrier of the Russian minefields.

It is perhaps only fair to point out that although no one in the squadron thought much of Surtees' venture, and although he himself admitted in his official report that it "proved a great strain on all concerned," it is possible that it *did* disrupt the U-boats. For, although once again we made no "kills", our constantly patrolling planes kept the submarines submerged and on the defensive.

The homewardbound convoy (RA62) which on the morning of 11 December stood west out of Kola Inlet was a medium-sized one – twenty-nine merchantmen with their Commodore in *Fort Crèvecoeur* – and it was to prove our most eventful to date.

Within an hour of clearing the minefields the corvette *Banborough Castle* attacked and sank *U387* (Kapitän Buchler); there were no survivors.

Over the next couple of days *Nairana* and *Campania* did their best to provide air cover, turn and turn about. However, flying conditions were "at the very limit of possibility," and the serviceability of our Swordfish was a constant headache. Nonetheless on the morning of 11 December we came our closest yet to success.

Joe Supple and Johnny Lloyd took-off at 1000 hours, in what passed for dawn. There was a lot of mist about and, with poor visibility and an indeterminate horizon, Joe had to fly most of the time on his instruments. They had been airborne about an hour when they picked up a contact at a range of nine miles. They homed in on it. Most contacts as a plane approached usually disappeared. This one remained on their screen and it occurred to John Lloyd that, if it *was* a U-boat, its kapitän probably reckoned the weather was too bad for aircraft to be flying. With the range down to less than a mile, the contact was still on their screen.

Suddenly they saw it – a surfaced U-boat at a range of no more than 500 yards – looming surprisingly large out of the mist. The U-boat must have seen them at the same moment as they saw it, for, as Joe dived in to the attack, it began to submerge. As ill luck would have it, their Swordfish was armed with rocket projectiles (which were best against a surfaced target) rather than depth-charges (best against a submerged one), and, although Joe obtained at least a couple of underwater hits, the submarine was damaged rather than sunk.

John Lloyd had just transmitted the news of their attack to *Nairana* when the Swordfish suffered a total radar, radio and electrical failure. He switched his IFF to "distress", circled the spot where the U-boat had been attacked, and hoped that the carrier would guess what had happened.

Aboard *Nairana* a strike force of two Wildcats and two Swordfish was quickly flown off in the hope of detecting and finishing off the U-boat, but no trace of it could be found. The strike force did, however, find Supple and Lloyd, and the stranded Swordfish formed up on them and was guided back to the carrier. Landing-on was not easy because the plane had no wing lights, but between them Joe Supple and Bob Mathé got it safely on to the flight-deck. This U-boat was officially classed as "damaged".

Next day the threat of German submarines receded, but the threat of German torpedo-bombers increased. For the convoy was now passing North Cape with its airfield at Banak, and would soon be turning south-west which would bring it close to the airfield at Bardufoss. And sure enough, late that night, we were picked up by a pair of German reconnaissance planes. They circled us hour after hour, well out of range of our ack-ack, reporting, we didn't doubt, our composition, course and speed.

It looked as though, next morning, we would be in for a dawn attack. Action stations were piped at 0600 and, although it was pitch dark, four Wildcats were ranged hopefully on the flight-deck.

It was not, however, the expected torpedo-bombers which were first to materialize on the morning of 12 December, it was another shadower, a Blohm and Voss 138 reconnaissance plane. It appeared on our radar screen a little after 0800 and started to circle the convoy. At 0830, although it was still almost pitch dark, Bill Armitage and Norman Sargent were scrambled to try and make contact with it. They had a hard time taking-off, a hard time staying airborne, and an even harder time trying to catch the Blohm and Voss. Wildcats were *not* night fighters – "on no account," reads an Admiralty Fleet Order "are Wildcats to be flown at night under operational conditions" – they had none of the sophisticated instruments which enabled Swordfish to "see in the dark"; they needed to be flown visually. In poor light they were difficult to control; in particular when flying at low level in and out of cloud with an ill-defined horizon, it was all too easy to end up in the sea. Another problem – assuming they did spot an enemy aircraft – was the difficulty of lining up their reflector gunsights, a problem aggravated by the fact that, in poor light, the flames from their uncovered engine exhaust ports affected the pilot's vision. A final disadvantage for them in poor light was that it was almost impossible to operate in pairs. So no wonder, that morning, to quote Bill Armitage, "we chased the bugger all over the sky but couldn't catch him!"

An hour later, at 0940, another pair of Wildcats was scrambled. George Gordon and Pete Blanco were the pilots, and they too were vectored towards the circling aircraft. By now the light was better, and they spotted it, spotted it in a patch of open sky and swooped down on it before it could escape into cloud. It was all over in seconds. George closed right in and, with an inspired burst of shooting, set fire to one of the Blohm and Voss's engines. The great plane crashed in flames near the periphery of the convoy. There were no survivors. It was George Gordon's 21st birthday.

That afternoon, as though in retribution, "blips" came swarming on to our radar screen. In one group, coming in from the north-east, it looked as though there were nine or ten aircraft; in another, coming in from the south-east, it looked as though there were about the same number. It seemed we were about to face a well-organized, co-ordinated attack. *Nairana* quickly landed-on her patrolling Swordfish and ranged her Wildcats.

Then came a problem. Should the Wildcats be flown-off? It was after 1330 hours, already dark, and getting quite rapidly darker. It was also one of those afternoons, with low cloud, sea-mist and poor visibility, when conditions were particularly hazardous for the Wildcats. Al Burgham and

Dusty Miller were strapped into their cockpits, ranged and ready for take-off. But were conditions too bad for them to have any realistic chance of making an interception? Surtees, needless to say, wanted the aircraft flown-off. Val Jones thought it too risky. Nigel Ball came running across the flight-deck to ask the pilots what *they* thought. The cautious and experienced Al Burgham thought "no"; the eager and less-experienced Dusty Miller thought "yes". Before their views could be relayed to the bridge, Surtees ordered "fly off".

Both Wildcats got away safely and within five seconds of clearing the flight-deck, they had disappeared into the murk. Al Burgham knew what to expect. As sun, sky, clouds and horizon merged into a kaleidoscope of grey, he concentrated on his instruments. Over his R/T came instructions to climb to 3,000 feet and head west, and almost at once, through a gap in the clouds, he spotted high above him a solitary JU88. He climbed to 9,000 feet, trying to keep in visual contact, but, with eight-tenths cloud and ten-tenths murk, it was impossible. After three or four minutes flying blind in cloud, he decided to drop down to sea level near the fringe of the convoy in the hope of intercepting the Junkers as they came in to launch their torpedoes. Several times he called up Dusty Miller, but there was no reply.

When the Junkers *did* come in, visibility was so bad that Al could hardly see them, let alone intercept them, before the attack was over. Though he flew this way and that in the gap between cloud-base and sea, he never managed to get a plane in his sights.

However, the convoy's ack-ack turned out to be an effective deterrent. As the first wave of about a dozen planes came skimming in at sea level the merchantmen and their escorts threw up a curtain of enthusiastic if not very accurate fire. Not very accurate because by now it was so dark that it was difficult to spot the attacking aircraft until they were almost overhead. The attack was pressed home with considerable skill and determination, most of the planes managing to launch their torpedoes effectively. Four were aimed at *Nairana*. It was lucky for us they weren't acoustic, and by zigzagging frantically we managed to avoid them; we also avoided a radio-controlled glider-bomb which exploded harmlessly in our wake. One moment the sky was filled with the roar of planes and the stench of cordite, next moment it was empty. We expected a second attack from the other group of Junkers but in the bad light they failed to find us. Although there had been several near-misses, no ships had been hit, and at least three enemy aircraft had been shot down.

As soon as it seemed certain the air attack had ended, Al Burgham was given permission to land. He managed to get down safely, but as he climbed out of his cockpit he was met by Sam Mearns and a group of squadron pilots and observers almost beside themselves with grief and fury. It seems that only a few minutes earlier, as the last of the Junkers disappeared, they had seen a Wildcat, its navigation lights glowing brightly, waggling its wings and approaching the convoy in a three-point attitude – presumably trying to ditch among the warships and merchantmen. As the plane came level with HMS *Bellona* the cruiser opened up with every gun it could bring to bear and shot the plane into the sea. All those who saw the incident were unequivocal about what happened. And the Wildcat could only have been Dusty Miller's.

In his official report Surtees wrote that "Miller died gallantly attacking enemy aircraft". Rear Admiral McGrigor, however, wrote in *his* report "next time single-engined aircraft must not, repeat not, be fired on" – an indication that some people at least knew what had happened.

This tragic story has a rather inconclusive postscript. Checking *Luftwaffe* records after the war, it seems that one of their three missing aircraft *may* have been shot down by a Wildcat. Since Al Burgham says that he never got near one, it could be that Dusty Miller did indeed destroy a Junkers before he himself was shot down by the very people he was trying to protect. More evidence, if more was needed, that war is seldom fair and "never chooses an evil man, but the good".

For several hours Surtees kept a searchlight beamed vertically on to the cloud base in the hope that the missing Wildcat might still be looking for us, but it was a forlorn hope. When the searchlight was switched off, we knew that Dusty Miller was dead.

Almost as soon as the Junkers vanished, the U-boats returned. And that evening, while *Campania* was duty carrier, her Swordfish reported as many as four contacts. However, in the difficult flying conditions no U-boats were sighted and no attacks made. Next morning, soon after *Nairana* had taken over flying, we picked up high-frequency, direction-finding bearings on a surfaced U-boat which was transmitting to its base. Doc Wilson and George Strong were scrambled, with orders to fly down the reported bearing.

They picked up a radar contact at a range of seven miles. Doc Wilson pushed his throttle-lever through the gate, and with maximum over-ride closed in at his top speed – all of ninety-five knots! It was midday. Visibility was good and they sighted the wake of their target at a range of three miles. To their surprise, the U-boat made no attempt to submerge. She stayed on the surface, evidently determined to fight it out. As the Swordfish started its attack, tracer and ack-ack, uncomfortably accurate, came streaming up at them. Doc had to take violent evasive action, weaving this way and that as the multicoloured ribbons of light flashed past his wingtips. He fired his first four rocket-projectiles from 400 feet at a range of 800 yards.

One hit the U-boat squarely aft of the conning tower. There was a bright white flash. The ack-ack stopped. Then the U-boat, obviously reckoning it wasn't getting the better of things, crash-dived. It crash-dived so fast that it disappeared beneath the waves before Doc had time to launch his second lot of rockets. Nevertheless he fired them and saw them enter the water at the spot where, only a few seconds earlier, there had been a conning tower. The Swordfish circled hopefully, pilot and observer scanning the sea for signs of oil or debris, but the sea remained empty. After about ten minutes their engine started vibrating and running roughly, almost certainly as a result of being flown at maximum revs; so they marked the position of their attack and headed for *Nairana*. They had, of course, been keeping in touch with the carrier by radio and on their way back they passed a strike force of two Swordfish and two Wildcats which had been scrambled in the hope of finishing the U-boat off. The strike force searched for more than an hour but found nothing and eventually all five planes had to admit defeat. The submarine was classified as "damaged". It has since come to light that in fact it was damaged quite badly and had to return to base without taking further part in attacks on the convoy.

In the small hours of the morning, as the weather again worsened, the usual shadower appeared on our radar screen. It closed to within a couple of miles of us. At first light a pair of Wildcats was brought up and ranged on the flight-deck. It seemed that Surtees had hopes of making an interception. Conditions by now were if anything worse than when Dusty Miller had been killed. And after consulting with the senior fighter pilot, Val Jones went to the bridge and told Surtees that he was against flying off the Wildcats. Surtees waved him away. Val, however, stuck to his guns. He insisted that if the Wildcats *were* flown-off, it should be officially recorded in the ship's log that the flight was being made contrary to his advice and wishes. Surtees could have overruled him, but he reluctantly gave way. (This, it seems, may have been one of the reasons why the Captain subsequently wrote a scathing official report on Val's capabilities as a Squadron CO.) Anyhow, and much to our fighter pilots' relief, the Wildcats were struck down.

The Swordfish, however, continued flying, and that afternoon *Campania*'s 813 Squadron achieved the success which had so far eluded us. One of her Swordfish sighted a U-boat and attacked it with depth-charges. This attack was inconclusive, but almost at once, as the Swordfish resumed its patrol, it sighted another U-boat, fully surfaced and closing in on the convoy. Having dropped its depth-charges, the Swordfish could only shadow its quarry and call for reinforcements. By now it was too dark for Wildcats to be airborne, but a strike force of two Swordfish was flown-off from the *Campania*. They homed in on the U-boat and in a skilful and co-ordinated attack – with one aircraft illuminating the submarine with flares and the other straddling it with depth-charges – *U365* (Kapitän Todenhagen's U-boat which had so nearly sunk the *Cassandra*) was sent to the bottom. There was a great deal of oil and debris, but no survivors.

Of the ten Swordfish from *Nairana* which took off in the next twenty-four hours two returned with radio or ASV failure and three returned with engine trouble. It was little short of a miracle that neither aircraft nor aircrew were lost.

Wilson and Strong took-off at 0100, less than twenty-four hours after their attack on the U-boat. Almost at once their engine started coughing and misfiring. They returned and made a successful emergency landing.

A couple of hours later John Defrates and David Beal were returning from patrol when they picked up a radar contact 20 miles astern of the convoy. They went down to sea level and homed on it. It was pitch dark, there was no moon, and they were almost on top of the U-boat before they spotted it, fully surfaced and on much the same course as they were. John dived on it from dead astern and released his depth-charges and marker flares. It should have been the perfect attack, but, as ill luck would have it, his bomb distributor malfunctioned, with the result that the bombs and flares were dropped simultaneously. There was a huge explosion, a blinding coruscation of light and the U-boat vanished. John and David circled the area in the hope of sighting oil or wreckage, but the sea remained empty. After a while the Swordfish engine began to vibrate and lose power, and, to add to John's problems, his bomb distributor detached itself from the instrument-panel and started bouncing about in his lap. He had just enough power to get back to the carrier and make another emergency landing. (After the war it was confirmed that this U-boat – attacked in 69°22'N, 5°35'E – suffered "some damage", with the result that it took no further part in operations against the convoy.)

The next crew to take-off were Eric McEwan and the CO. They had just begun to circle the convoy when Eric noticed that two of the upper cylinders of his Pegasus XXX were glowing a dull red. With the possibility of their engine bursting into flames, Eric and Val returned *post haste* to the carrier and made the third emergency landing in as many hours.

Their replacements, Cowsill and Holley, took-off at 0430, and had to return an hour later with their ASV inoperative.

*Their* replacements, Cridland and Hall, stayed airborne even more briefly; at the end of half an hour they landed back with their ASV *and* their radio both out of action.

However, the shortest and most eventful patrol of all was by John Defrates and David Beal, who took-off at dawn in their Swordfish NR 897. This was the plane in which, only twelve hours earlier, they had attacked the U-boat. Its engine was *supposed* to have been repaired, but the moment they lifted clear of the flight-deck, it began to vibrate and tremble. They lost power and height, and John had to use his override boost to stay airborne. He was cleared for yet another emergency landing, quickly jettisoned the flares and depth-charges in the middle of the convoy, and was back on the flight deck within five minutes of leaving it.

Any one of these patrols could have resulted in the loss of a Swordfish and its crew, and such losses were averted only by a combination of good fortune and skilful flying.

By our seventh day out from Kola Inlet both aircraft and aircrew were at the end of their tether and it was just as well that conditions now became so bad that even Surtees could no longer contemplate flying.

That evening the wind increased to a full gale; the sea became higher, and by midnight *Nairana* was pitching into a succession of huge thirty-foot rollers and shipping it green over her flight-deck. In the small hours two enormous waves broke flush on our port wingbridge. Water, cascading below-decks, caused serious flooding and a short-circuit and fire in the generator room. The ship was plunged into darkness and wreathed in smoke. We had reason now to be thankful for Surtees' emergency fire drills, and the flames were quickly brought under control.

Soon the convoy was forced to reduce speed to no more than three knots – just enough to keep the ships head-on to the swell. And now it was the turn of *Nairana*'s watchkeeping officers to have a hard time. Carriers in heavy seas and strong winds are difficult to control. Being top-heavy, they roll far more than other warships, while their tall slab-sides make them reel under gusts of wind that more streamlined vessels hardly notice. Maximum rudder and huge fluctuations in speed were often needed to keep *Nairana* in station, and altering course and position within the convoy to fly aircraft on and off became a hazardous operation. A four-hour watch, lashed by sheets of spray, in gale force winds and sub-zero temperatures was not much fun, but at last the storm blew itself out.

By this time we were south of the 65th parallel and beyond easy reach of the Junkers, while the U-boats had evidently decided we were too tough a nut for them to crack. The last forty-eight hours of our passage home were uneventful. On 17 December aircraft from Coastal Command took over convoy-protection duties, and next morning in calm clear weather – the first time we had seen the sun in three weeks – we dropped anchor in Scapa Flow.

That evening we had a glimpse of the more human side of Surtees. He cleared the lower deck and spoke to the ship's company, congratulating us on our "splendid achievement"; he then joined a party in the wardroom, taking off his jacket to indicate that rank had been abandoned, and singing with enthusiasm the bawdiest of our songs. It was some time before we had the nerve to strike up our favourite, sung to the tune of "Stand up, stand up for Jesus".

> "Fly off, fly off for Christ's sake;
> The Captain wants a gong.
> Fly off, fly off for Christ's sake;
> The Captain can't be wrong."

The irony can hardly have escaped him, yet he sang with gusto, and later chatted amicably with several of our pilots and observers. There was one revealing moment when he was talking to Eric McEwan. They were discussing "after the war" – a favourite topic in the winter of '44/'45 – and Surtees told Eric he was lucky because the whole world was open to him, whereas he himself knew no other life than the Navy and would have to stay on in the Service. The remark, it seems to me, of a lonely man. Looking back, I don't think it occurred to many of us in those days that the loneliest place in a warship can be the captain's cabin.

Another to congratulate us was Rear Admiral McGrigor, who wrote in his report:

> "This convoy was run at the darkest period of the year. Aircraft patrols and attacks on U-boats were almost all made in total darkness, and I wish to record my admiration for the efficient and enthusiastic manner in which they were carried out by *Nairana* and *Campania*, often in conditions when flying was barely practicable owing to the state of wind and sea. . . . There had been some doubt before this convoy as to whether the inclusion of escort-carriers was worthwhile in midwinter; but without question they were of the greatest value, both for safeguarding the convoy and for killing and damaging U-boats. However, it should be borne in mind that only squadrons as expert and experienced in night flying as those in *Campania* and *Nairana* could have coped with the exacting conditions which prevailed."

Soon after our arrival in Scapa the squadron was given seven days' leave and this triggered off another row between Val Jones and Surtees. Val argued that the aircrew deserved, and indeed needed, as much leave as they could get, and he pointed out that *Campania*'s 813 Squadron, who had done less flying than we had, had just been given twenty-one days. Surtees, however, insisted that each watch aboard the *Nairana* was getting only seven days and that Squadron officers should be treated the same as the rest of the ship's company.

Returning from leave we found several new faces among the aircrew: Sub-Lts(A) Charles Gough, Donald Payne and Norman Wylie had come to us from *Vindex*'s 811 Squadron, which had just been disbanded, while early in the New Year we were joined by Leslie Paine, John Roberts and John Rogers. We also found that, whereas our aircraft had been left at Ayr on the Firth of Clyde, our carrier was en route for Scapa Flow in the Orkneys, in preparation (rumour had it) for another venture into the Arctic. We flew north to join her.

Our route, via Fearn (just south of the Moray Firth) and Hatston (just north of the Pentland Firth) lay over the Highlands. It was midwinter, the sun was shining and Scotland lay deep in snow. It was one of those days when if you were flying low in an open-cockpit plane, vista after magnificent vista opened up in front of you, a cornucopia of peaks like pyramids of diamonds, rivers blue with ice and cliff-faces dark as seams of coal. After our recent experiences in the Arctic, it made us doubly glad to be alive. Arriving at Fearn, our Wildcats "beat up" the airfield with a spectacular display of low flying and aerobatics, while the arrival of our Swordfish was equally impressive: ten planes peeling off from tight formation and stream-landing so close together that the last plane had touched down before the first had reached the end of the runway.

"In all my years with the Air Arm," Fearn's Commander Flying told Val Jones, "I've never seen such a well-drilled squadron!"

We were given VIP treatment, transport to the wardroom and a first class lunch, so good a lunch in fact that it was late by the time we took off and dark by the time we landed at Hatston.

During the next few days we flew sometimes from the airfield and sometimes from the *Nairana*, which by now had reached the nearby anchorage of Scapa Flow. We practised, among other things, formation flying. And in their spare time both our fighter pilots and our Captain tried their hand at small boat sailing.

When it came to sailing a dinghy, our Wildcat pilots displayed more exuberance than expertise. Downwind they made rapid progress, but when it was time to go about and tack in and out between the warships at anchor in the Flow, they soon found themselves in difficulty. First they almost capsized, then they rammed the pukkah HMS *Diadem* amidships. In some disarray they grabbed hold of the cruiser's quarterdeck gangway, but were at once dislodged from this safe haven by a scandalized Officer of the Watch, who ordered them to "cast off", because the Admiral's barge was expected alongside. It was lucky that *Nairana*'s Officer of the Watch spotted their predicament and sent a motorboat to the rescue.

Next day it was the turn of our Captain to go out in one of *Nairana*'s dinghies. Surtees' credentials for small-boat sailing were of course impeccable. However, he turned up dressed in an old jersey and disreputable baggy trousers, and armed with a bottle of sloe gin. Three or four hours later, on his way back, his dinghy happened to pass our sister carrier *Campania*. It had obviously not escaped Surtees that there was a good deal of friendly rivalry between the two carriers. (Our view was that we did all the flying, they got all the leave.) And, as his dinghy passed astern of *Campania*, Surtees rose to his feet, brandishing his now empty gin bottle.

"Up the *Campania*!" he shouted.

This salutation was not appreciated by *Campania*'s Officer of the Watch and when our gallant Captain returned to his ship, he found waiting for him a signal complaining of the "reprehensible behaviour" of the occupant of one of *Nairana*'s boats. Surtees signalled in reply, "Suitable action has been taken."

Next day, in company with the aircraft carrier *Trumpeter*, the cruiser *Berwick* and a strong escort of destroyers, we left Scapa and headed north, our objective this time not to protect another convoy to Murmansk but to strike at enemy shipping among the Norwegian fjords.

It is difficult to know what to make of this shipping strike, which went under the codename of Operation Sampler. At the time several of the Squadron felt there was an air of unreality about it. It seemed a somewhat pointless exercise, and the fact that we were given escape kits, revolvers, hidden compasses and Norwegian currency, and briefed on how to build a snow igloo in the event of our being shot down, made us feel we were about to embark on some Hollywood epic. In retrospect the whole operation seems even more improbable. Our target, the fjords between Bergen and Trondheim, was within easy range of hundreds of modern RAF bombers, so why send in a squadron of antediluvian Swordfish? We intended to fly off within sixty miles of the Norwegian coast; why risk valuable warships in waters full of U-boats and within range not only of enemy bombers but enemy fighters? At the time we were told that troops and vital war supplies (in particular iron ore) were being moved from north Norway to Germany for a last-ditch defence of the Fatherland, and that the RAF could disrupt this traffic by day but not by night, because they lacked the navigational skill and the manoeuvrability to locate and attack shipping in the dark among the steep-sided fjords. This may have been true, but we were still left with the feeling that it was all "much ado about nothing". One member of the squadron has since come up with the theory that our objective was in fact to disrupt the shipment of "heavy water" from its processing plant near Narvik to the V2 launching pads on the Channel coast. If this is so, it would certainly go some way towards justifying the risks we were about to take.

If Operation Sampler had been a success it would have provided a much-needed boost to the Squadron's morale. But it was not a success. It was aborted. And the manner of its abortion brought matters between Val Jones and Surtees to a head.

Dick Mallett had drawn up a comprehensive blue-print for the operation, based on the assumption that a full moon would enable our strike force first to make a landfall on the Norwegian coast and then to locate its quarry among the fjords. In other words good weather was a prerequisite of success. However, as we stood out of Scapa Flow on the first day of 1945 the weather was not good and Mike Arrowsmith predicted it would get worse rather than better, for a succession of low fronts was moving in from the Atlantic, and his forecast was for heavy seas, strong winds, nine-tenths cloud and frequent falls of snow. And of course no moon. It should have been obvious that in these conditions Operation Sampler was a non-starter. Surtees, however, was unwilling to accept the obvious and our task force continued to head north-east for the coast of Norway. On 2 January, in a brief lull between the fronts, *Trumpeter* managed to fly off her Wildcats on a fighter-sweep, but that evening the weather again closed in. The wind strengthened, the cloud-base dropped to 400 feet and it began to snow. Surtees ordered the squadron to prepare for take-off.

Our Swordfish were armed with either four 250 lb bombs or eight 60 lb rockets. Four were ranged on the flight-deck. The rest were ranged in the hangar. All aircrew were at the ready, strapped into their cockpits. At 0400 on the morning of 3 January, against the advice of our met officer and our Commander Flying, the first four Swordfish were ordered to take-off. First to get airborne were Bob Selley and the CO; they were followed by Doc Wilson and George Strong, John Defrates and David Beal, and Joe Supple and Johnny Lloyd. Bob reckons it was a near miracle they all got off safely. However, once airborne, their troubles were far from over. They formed up and circled the carrier which almost at once disappeared in a blinding snowstorm. The four aircraft clung desperately together, snow dimming their navigation lights and, only partly dissipated by the slipstream, filtering into their open cockpits. Soon the Swordfish began to ice up; their controls became sluggish and Bob found it impossible to get his airspeed above sixty-five knots – barely enough to stay airborne. It was almost exactly an hour before it was decided to postpone Operation Sampler and try to bring the planes back. To quote one of the Squadron officers:

"It was a very fine effort by four frozen and badly shaken pilots to land their planes safely on the flight-deck, a feat which would have been impossible without the skill and devotion to duty of our Deck Landing Control Officer, Bob Mathé. The rear cockpit of a Swordfish is more open to the elements than the front cockpit, and all four observers were almost literally frozen solid on to their aircraft and had to be lifted out."

Although our met officer insisted that the bad weather would continue, with snow squalls becoming more frequent, Surtees refused to cancel the operation. He postponed it twenty-four hours. So the next night found us once again strapped into our cockpits at the ready. However, conditions during the night of 3/4 January were even worse than on the previous night. Yet Surtees was still reluctant to call it a day. He postponed the operation yet another twenty-four hours. Not until 5 January did a waning moon and some blunt talk from Val Jones convince him that the task force had no option but to return to Scapa.

There were two ways of looking at this aborted operation. Surtees felt that Val Jones had not been sufficiently eager to engage the enemy. Val Jones felt that Surtees had needlessly jeopardized the lives of his aircrew, and that anyone who knew the first thing about flying would have realized that in the prevailing weather the operation was impossible. This friction between our Captain and our Commanding Officer was not conducive to good morale.

No sooner had we dropped anchor in Scapa Flow than two bearded and disreputable-looking characters requested permission to come aboard. For a moment the Officer of the Watch was nonplussed. Then, behind the stubble and the scruffy clothes, he recognized the dapper Ron Brown and the scholarly John Eames, who were reporting back for duty after their adventures aboard the *Cassandra* and *Bahamas*.

"Good God!" he exclaimed not very tactfully. "We'd forgotten about you two!"

Forty-eight hours later *Nairana* was in the Clyde, and the Squadron had been flown ashore to Machrihanish.

Val Jones and Surtees now brought matters to a head. Val was seriously concerned, and it was soon to be proved rightly concerned, about the health of the Swordfish aircrew. He discussed the matter with the Commanding Officer of Machrihanish, Captain Howe, who at once arranged for Val to be flown to Lee-on-Solent for an interview with the Central Air Medical Board. As a result of what he told them, a team of naval doctors was sent *post haste* to Machrihanish to talk to the Squadron aircrew and give them medical tests. These tests were carried out within forty-eight hours, and when they had been completed, seventy-five per cent of our aircrew were declared unfit for flying! fifty per cent, it was decreed, were to be relieved of all operational flying at once and a further twenty-five to be relieved within a month. It was the end of the road for a lot of the squadron stalwarts – to mention only a few Bob Selley, Paddy Hall, Val Jones himself, Legood, McEwan, Murray, Pitts, Urwin and Wilson. They were sent on indefinite leave.

Surtees, meanwhile, had gone to the Admiralty and demanded that Val Jones be relieved of command of his Squadron. In furtherance of this demand, he put in a very adverse report on him, both as an officer and a commanding officer. The result was that Val was recalled from leave and ordered to appear before a Board of Enquiry.

With considerable courage, he refused to give evidence to the Board, but requested a full court-martial. For this, he reckoned, was the only way in which Surtees' shortcomings as the captain of an aircraft-carrier could be brought to light.

The Board were now in a dilemma. They wanted to be fair, but they wanted also to avoid scandal and uphold the traditional sanctity of seniority. In the end they asked one of their number, a retired and kindly Captain RN, to take Val aside and, in a relaxed and informal atmosphere, talk things over with him. The Captain admitted, unofficially, that the Board knew Val was in the right, but no good would come, he said, of a court-martial and, if Val withdrew his demand for one, the Board would endorse the stand he had taken against Surtees and appoint him CO of 737 Observer Training Squadron at Arbroath, an important post which many would see as promotion.

It was now Val Jones who was in a dilemma. He didn't like what he was being asked to do, but in the end, with considerable reluctance, he went along with the Board's proposal. There was one last and moving moment. He returned to the carrier to collect his personal belongings and, when the time came for him to leave in *Nairana*'s jollyboat, the whole ship's company mustered on the flight-deck to wish him God speed, for Val had been as popular below decks as among the aircrew. Three times his jollyboat circled the carrier, and three times as he passed the island the ship's company gave him an enthusiastic cheer. Surtees was conspicuous by his absence.

During the next couple of weeks there were many changes among the Squadron personnel, as one by one the "old hands" departed and new aircrew (several of them straight from training-school) arrived. One of the last to join us, in mid-January, was our new CO.

Lt-Cdr(A) John Godley was a Swordfish pilot with over three years operational experience; latterly he had been in command of a sub-flight of three Swordfish from 836 Squadron, operating from MAC ships in the Atlantic. He took over the Squadron at a difficult time, with morale not particularly high, and the more experienced aircrew mistrustful of the Captain. He tackled the job, in his own words, "with a mixture of apprehension and exultation", and it is greatly to his credit that he managed firstly to establish a *modus operandi* with Surtees and secondly to restore morale to something like its original high level.

After the usual spell of working up at Machrihanish, which this time included a number of operational A/S patrols round the mouth of the Clyde, the squadron rejoined *Nairana* on 22 January. The carrier at once stood north and that night Surtees called Godley to his cabin.

"It'll be full moon again in a couple of days," he told him, "and we'll be going back to Norway for another crack at enemy shipping in the fjords."

This time the weather was perfect. Our task force consisted of the carriers *Nairana* and *Campania*, accompanied by the cruiser *Berwick* and a strong escort of destroyers. The night before we left Scapa we were given a thorough briefing by Dick Mallet who explained that 835 Squadron from *Nairana* was to concentrate on shipping in Rovde Fjord, while 813 Squadron from *Campania* was to concentrate on shipping in Romsdals Fjord some fifty miles to the north. We were told what landfall to make, what height, course and speed to fly at and where the known ack-ack positions were. Finally Dick stressed that he wanted no heroics, no venturing into dark labyrinthine fjords and ending up splattered against the sheer-sided cliffs. Surtees attended the briefing, listened attentively and made no comment.

Late on 28 January we were in position to fly off, less than 100 miles from the Norwegian coast. It was a bright moonlit night, no cloud and no more than a gentle swell, as the carriers turned into wind. John Godley takes up the story.

> "At 2000 hrs I got my green light from the bridge. Chocks away, and I open up full throttle. After 80 yards I fire my RATOG and am propelled skywards into the brilliance of the night. I keep my airspeed below 70 and make a long sweeping turn to port, so that the others can quickly form up on me. (The CO of 813, to avoid any risk of collision, is doing the same to starboard.) In less than five minutes we are in extended echelon formation, and I settle onto a course of 042° at a comfortable 80 knots. . . . The moon is so bright it is almost like daytime, and soon we can see ahead of us the great snow-covered mountains of the Norwegian coast. . . .
> Our landfall, Riste Island, is now clearly visible. It is inhabited, Dick Mallett assured us, by nothing more hostile than farmers

and cows. But suddenly two batteries of Bofors ack-ack open up on us. Streams of multi-coloured tracer come streaking towards us: at first slowly, then with lethal acceleration. We should have been dead ducks. But our slow speed saved us. Accustomed to Mosquitoes flying almost four times as fast, the German gunners couldn't believe we were stooging in at 80 knots, and the tracer passed well ahead of us. I put my aircraft into a steep dive to port, and the rest of the Squadron follow without delay to the safety of the wavetops. . . . Now we are flying at zero feet up the narrow waters of Rovde Fjord. Lights come on ahead of us in homesteads on both shores as we are heard approaching, and men come to their doors as though to show us the way. The whole country is deep in snow, with the white mountains bathed in moonlight rising high above us on either side. At last we sight a target: a small merchantman sailing towards us on her own. I lead the sub-flight over her, hesitate, and decide to fly up-fjord in search of larger vessels. But the rest of the fjord is empty. We turn back and climb to 1500 feet, the perfect height for rockets. . . . It amazes me now that at the time I never thought of the men in that ship. It was wholly impersonal as I fired my rockets in a ripple of four pairs and watched them strike the merchantman along the waterline. My next two pilots, Roffey and Payne, also scored several hits. Now I know she had no hope of surviving. She is stopped and on fire. I call up the others and tell them to break off the attack and seek targets ashore. Gough and Supple chose the ack-ack positions, and silenced them so effectively they never fired again." (The first sub-flight now returned independently to the *Nairana*. Godley, however, remained in the fjord to guide in the second sub-flight.) "All around me the silent mountains, I can see each cottage on the rock-strewn shore. . . . Suddenly I spot two more merchantmen on the point of entering Rovde from a smaller fjord to the south. I call up my second sub-flight: three to attack each ship. . . . Summers, Paine and Cridland dive to attack one, scoring direct hits with at least six rockets. Provis with his bombs scores a direct hit and two near-misses on the other. The first ship is set on fire and beached. The second is settling rapidly. But I can't stay to observe them, I've been airborne for over three hours, and we still have to get back to *Nairana* and land-on."

Two aircraft, on their way back, had lucky escapes. No sooner had Leslie Paine and Derek Ravenhill made their attack than they suffered a complete electrical failure – radio, radar, homing beacon, the lot. They went down to sea level and circled an offshore island while they worked out what to do. There seemed to be only two alternatives: they could land in enemy-occupied Norway or they could try and find their way back to *Nairana* by dead-reckoning navigation. They agreed to attempt the latter. They were about to set course when, very luckily for them, they were spotted by Johnny Cridland. He realized they must be in trouble, went down to sea level and switched on his navigation lights. They formed up on him gratefully and the two Swordfish flew back together to the carrier. Leslie and Derek almost certainly owe their lives to Johnny Cridland. For *Nairana* had had to take evasive action to avoid a pack of U-boats; she was not in her expected position and it is extremely unlikely that Leslie and Derek would have found her by dead reckoning.

The other aircrew who were lucky, although they didn't realize it at the time, were Godley and Strong. When they got back to *Nairana* they had been airborne for over three-and-a-half hours; yet Godley's fuel gauge told him he still had about forty gallons of fuel left. He therefore decided to stay airborne and let his returning aircraft land ahead of him, one by one, as they arrived back from the fjords. So he was first to fly off (at 2000 hours on 28 January) and last to land on (at 0020 hours on 29 January). Later that morning, when he was in the hangar checking the serviceability of the Swordfish – not one had received so much as a scratch – his air fitter said to him casually:

"Did you know, sir, how much fuel you had left when you landed?"

"About thirty gallons."

The air fitter shook his head: "I took a reading with a dipstick, sir. You had so little left it didn't register. Your fuel gauge was U/S" (unserviceable). Another five minutes and their Pegasus would have cut stone dead. And there would have been no restarting it.

Our return to Scapa was uneventful, or, to be strictly accurate, it ought to have been uneventful. We were half-expecting an attack by torpedo-carrying Ju 88s, but it didn't materialize, and by late afternoon on the 29th we had passed the Shetland Islands and air cover was being provided by RAF Spitfires from Grimsetter. Our Wildcats, which had been ranged all day at readiness, were being struck down. The last pair were about to be wheeled onto the lift when there was a sudden order to "Scramble". Al Burgham and Bill Armitage happened to be in the Ready Room. They thought there must be an emergency, grabbed their helmets, sprinted down the flight-deck, tumbled into their cockpits and took-off while the carrier was still turning into wind. Once airborne, they waited for instructions to intercept enemy aircraft. But no instructions were forthcoming and the only aircraft they saw was the slow, peaceful and decidedly friendly Orkney-to-Shetland "airbus" en route to Lerwick. Al was not amused to learn subsequently that the moment Surtees learned that a "blip" had appeared on *Nairana*'s radar he had ordered the Wildcats to be scrambled without waiting for the "blip" to be identified. It was, as John Defrates succinctly put it, "typical of the Captain's determination always to be first to engage the enemy whether he was there or not".

It was quite dark by the time we dropped anchor in the safety of Scapa Flow. "Everyone," according to Godley, "was in high spirits. We'd had success just when we needed it."

At the time most of the squadron reckoned our success had been modest. However, German records indicate that three ships (having a total displacement of over 5,000 tons) were sent to the bottom. This made the operation *per se* worthwhile. And it could be that its intangible results were of even greater significance than its tangible. For our Norwegian strike did undoubtedly help to bring about a *rapport* between Surtees and Godley, a rapport which had been conspicuously absent between Surtees and Val Jones.

And it was as well that our Captain and our Commanding Officer *were* on the same wave length, for we were about to embark on the last and most eventful of all our convoys: escorting the outwardbound JW64 to Murmansk and the homewardbound RA64 back to the UK.

We spent a week at Hatston – the usual dummy deck-landings and low-level bombing for the pilots, and swinging compasses for the observers. Then on 5 February, together with the *Campania*, the cruiser *Bellona* and a strong destroyer escort, we left the Flow to rendezvous with JW64.

This was another fair-sized convoy – twenty-nine merchantmen, with the Commodore flying his flag in the *Fort Crèvecoeur* – and even before we joined them they had an escort of almost twenty destroyers, sloops and corvettes. So once again warships outnumbered merchant ships. It was, for Godley, a marked contrast to the Atlantic convoys that he had flown on less than a year ago, when four corvettes and a couple of MAC ships had shepherded more than 100 merchantmen.

On our way to the rendezvous we were joined by a last minute replacement for Dusty Miller. Sub-Lt Moss had arrived at Hatston that morning only to find *Nairana* and the squadron that he was supposed to be joining had already sailed. Joe Supple was sent to pick him up in his Swordfish. Returning with his passenger to the carrier, Joe had trouble with his arrester hook, which refused to drop. However, he made a perfect landing without one, managing to pull up well short of the barrier and greatly impressing our "new boy" with the Squadron's expertise in deck-landing.

We joined the convoy a little after midday, took up position in our usual central "box" among the merchantmen and flew-off a pair of Wildcats to give their customary and morale-boosting display of low flying and aerobatics.

It had been agreed that our two carriers would operate turn and turn about, twelve hours flying and twelve hours standing by, with both of us putting planes in the air in the event of an emergency. There was an emergency almost at once.

*Campania* had taken over as duty carrier and several of our aircrew had jut started a game of deck-hockey when a "bogey" was picked up on our radar, a single plane coming in high from the east. The Wildcat pilots dropped hockey sticks and dashed for their planes; the carrier swung into wind and Mearns and Moss took-off and were vectored towards the approaching plane. But *Campania*'s fighters, who were already airborne, got to it first. Guns clattered. Smoke spirals patterned the sky and two planes, one Ju88 and one of *Campania*'s Wildcats, fell torchlike into the sea.

The question was, had the Junkers managed to transmit a sighting report before it was shot down? Admiral McGrigor (who once again was in command of the convoy escort) assumed that it had and next morning he called all ships to action stations to meet the expected dawn attack.

The first attack came at first light: about a dozen torpedo-carrying Junkers coming in so low they were within a dozen miles of us before they were picked up. Mearns and Moss, once again, were the duty pilots and they had barely time to get airborne before the Junkers were bearing down on the convoy. The escorts put up a fearsome barrage. At least one Junkers was shot down and the others, harried by our Wildcats and disconcerted by our ack-ack, dropped their torpedoes inaccurately at long range and sought the safety of cloud. No ships were damaged.

About an hour later there was another attack, again by roughly a dozen Junkers. By now Mearns and Moss had landed. Armitage and Sargent were on patrol and the moment the German planes spotted them they, like their predecessors, dropped their torpedoes at long range and made for the safety of the clouds. One wasn't quick enough. Hit repeatedly by the Wildcats' cannon fire, it disappeared into a cloudbank, smoke pouring from both engines. This, at the time, was claimed only as a "probable", but *Luftwaffe* records have since confirmed that the plane was indeed shot down.

By midday the attacks were over. No ships had been hit or damaged. And, from the point of view of the Germans, the cost had been high. It is now known that no fewer than forty-eight Junkers of *Kampfgeschwader* 26 took-off that morning to attack the convoy. Only about half of them managed to find us. Of these seven were lost, four shot down over the convoy and three so badly damaged that they failed to make it back to their airfield.

The *Luftwaffe*, however, were not to give up easily, and that afternoon their shadowing aircraft were back. While there was still a hint of daylight our Wildcats were able to chase them away, but by four o'clock it was pitch dark. Our Wildcats were grounded and then the shadowers closed in. Hour after hour we could hear the not-quite-synchronized beat of their engines circling the convoy. McGrigor decided to try out his "Secret Weapon". This was an ancient Fulmar, overloaded with the latest air-to-air radar. *Nairana* had tried once before to use Fulmars as night fighters, with singular lack of success. Now it was *Campania's* turn. However, the night of 8 February was not an auspicious moment for her Fulmar's debut, for the seas were high, the clouds were thick and there was little light from stars, moon or Aurora Borealis. Nevertheless, at a few minutes to midnight the Fulmar was duly launched. She stayed airborne for the better part of two hours, but neither the skill of her pilot and observer nor the efforts of the FDOs of two carriers could enable her ˜to make an interception. In due course she was recalled. What happened next was predictable. She crashed on landing, nearly decapitating the batsman and ending up a mass of wreckage strewn all over the flight-deck. It was some time before *Campania* was able to operate her aircraft, which meant that we were saddled (yet again!) with an extra stint of night flying.

By the morning of 9 February, in worsening weather, we were past the 72nd parallel, more than 500 miles north of the Arctic Circle. Our aircraft patrolling at midday could see the distant glint of pack-ice. The convoy altered course to the east.

There were U-boats about, homed on to us by the circling reconnaissance planes, and it was now the turn of our Swordfish to keep our adversaries at bay. To quote John Godley:

> "It was intensely cold, the wind was consistently gale force, there was much movement on the ship, and for the Stringbags there was a serious danger of icing-up, not to mention the discomfort of flying in open cockpits. But we managed to keep flying. In the 72 hours between nightfall of the 7th and nightfall on the 10th over seventy Swordfish patrols were flown by the two carriers. Each lasted between ninety minutes and three hours; so on average two Stringbags were continually airborne day and night."

These patrols were unrewarded, but no one could say they were un-eventful.

At midnight on 9 February Provis and Rose landed heavily, shattering an oleo leg; their Swordfish slewed sideways across the flight-deck and ended up with its wheel six inches from the catwalk. A few hours later Rogers and Eames, landing-on in a blizzard, had their undercarriage wiped off by *Nairana*'s upflung stern; their Swordfish squelched on to the deck, breaking its back; Rogers and Eames clambered out unhurt, but the plane was a write-off and had to be heaved over the side. Within twenty minutes another Swordfish was taking-off.

The events of the next day, probably one of the most eventful in our squadron's history, are well described by Ian Cameron in *Wings of the Morning (The Story of the Fleet Air Arm in World War II)*.

"The 10th February dawned fine but bitterly cold, with heavy seas, scattered cloud and a strong-to-gale-force wind. Two of *Nairana*'s Swordfish had taken off at dawn on crocodile patrols and one of these planes was flying at about 900 feet between cloud and sea when the pilot, Lt-Cdr Godley, noticed a strange blur, like a thinly pencilled line, a little above the eastern horizon. The blur spread; it split into individual flecks of black; the flecks of black grew larger. And Godley suddenly realized what they were: about a dozen low-flying Junkers, in line abreast, heading straight for the convoy. And by a-thousand-to-one unlucky chance his Swordfish was slap in their path: a single slow and unarmed biplane face to face with a dozen fast, heavily-armed monoplanes. Godley shouted to his observer, George Strong, to warn the convoy, then he looked for cloud cover. But before he could make up his mind which way to turn, the Junkers had passed beneath him and the sky was empty. Strong got through a second time to the carrier, and Godley, taking care never to stray too far from cloud cover, resumed his patrol.

"Back in *Nairana* Strong's message was picked up at the same moment as a radar fix. The Wildcats on deck were started up, and the pair already airborne were vectored to intercept. Mearns and Moss were the pilots and they soon spotted the bombers coming in low and scattered on the convoy's beam. They prised one away and dived on it again and again in a succession of attacks pressed home to point-blank range. The Junkers cartwheeled this way and that; her turret guns flickered defiantly; but a ten-second burst from Moss set one of her engines on fire. She fell seaward. Mearns followed her down, gave her another short-range burst and saw her plunge into the sea and disintegrate. The Wildcats reformed and were vectored out to the convoy's bow where another group of bombers was coming in at sea level.

"By now four more of *Nairana*'s Wildcats were airborne: Armitage, Sargent, Blanco and Gordon, although the last-mentioned found his engine failing as soon as he left the deck and had to land on again in a hurry. The fighters made their interception about a dozen miles beyond the outer screen, and there followed a series of chaotic dog-fights fought out in the pale ribbon of sky between cloud and sea. The Junkers tried repeatedly to force their way through, but again and again they were broken up by *Nairana*'s fighters. For the better part of half an hour the Wildcats harried the Junkers round and round the perimeter of the convoy, forcing them to jettison their bombs and torpedoes and seek the safety of cloud. Several were damaged – three of them so badly, it was afterwards learned, that they never got back to Norway – and only once did a group of planes break through to make a coordinated attack. But this attack came within a hair's breadth of success and gave a hint of what would have happened to the convoy if it hadn't been for the Wildcats.

"A group of six Junkers in close formation managed to give the fighters the slip. They came diving down on the convoy, to be met by a terrific curtain of fire: first a box-barrage thrown up by the destroyers and corvettes of the screen, then a random eruption from the individual merchantmen, carriers and cruiser. The leader of the Junkers was a brave man. He flew low across the convoy's bow, drawing fire, while his companions peeled off one by one to make individual attacks. One plane was shot flaming into the sea; another, badly hit, was forced to seek shelter in cloud; another dropped his torpedo from too steep an angle and had the mortification of seeing it explode on impact. The other two made accurate attacks. One torpedo missed a merchantman by less than a dozen feet. The other came straight at *Nairana*. The carrier swung wildly to port, so wildly that her rudder jammed and for two complete circles she cavorted out of control in the convoy centre, scattering merchantmen and escorts left, right and centre. But the torpedo missed her, exploding in the churned-up froth of her wake. Then quite suddenly the sky was empty, and the torpedo-bombers were gone – though not before their leader, hit again and again by a hail of ack-ack, had fallen in flames among the merchantmen he had attacked so gallantly."

The main attack was over. However, a handful of Junkers continued to make individual efforts to break through and it was another of these that now fell to our fighters.

By 11.30 most of the German bombers were on their way back to Norway and most of our Wildcats had landed back aboard the *Nairana* to rearm and refuel. It was now that Al Burgham and Ken Atkinson were scrambled to provide a defensive shield against last-minute attacks. Only a few minutes after take-off Al spotted a solitary Junkers flying low towards the convoy. And the Junkers obviously spotted Al because it very hastily dropped its torpedo and started climbing for the safety of the clouds. Al can still remember exactly how he felt: "He's dropped his torpedo so he's no longer a threat to the convoy – and to protect the convoy is our first priority. On the other hand there don't seem to be any other aircraft about, and if I get him today he won't come back tomorrow." He broke to starboard, hoping to attack the climbing Junkers from high on its port quarter. But the Junkers proved unexpectedly fast and Al found himself chasing his quarry from almost dead astern. A few seconds before it reached cloud cover he got in a long accurate burst. For a moment the Junkers disappeared. Then it came plummeting out of the cloud-mass streaming smoke. It fell faster and faster until it plunged vertically into the sea. Al had barely had time to report "a kill" when he spotted another Junkers, also making a beeline for cloud. He managed to get in a long-range burst before this plane too disappeared into the swirling mass of cumulus. Al hopefully skirted the cloud base, but this time the Junkers failed to reappear. When *Nairana* reported that all enemy aircraft had left the vicinity of the convoy Al returned to the carrier and landed-on. He was amazed to find that he had been airborne no more than thirty minutes.

That night the German radio claimed nine ships in the convoy had been sunk. In fact not one had been so much as damaged. The Germans also admitted the loss of four torpedo bombers, but our intelligence men who monitored the Junkers' radio transmissions confirmed our impression that *Luftwaffe* losses had been far heavier. For of the twenty-six Junkers which had left Norway that morning it is now known that eleven failed to return, while another three had been so badly damaged that they crashed on landing.

It was, for our Wildcats, a famous victory, marred only by the fact that many of them had been repeatedly fired on by the very ships they were trying to defend. Indeed one of *Campania*'s fighters had been shot down and the pilot killed as he was trying to land on his own carrier.

All this happened a few days before 14 February and on Saint Valentine's day, by which time we had reached Kola Bay, our CO composed a Valentine card, illustrated by Jock Bevan, which was sent to the captains of all escorting warships:

It would be nice to think the message got through. Certainly on our voyage home none of our aircraft was fired at.

The last few days of JW64 were relatively uneventful, for us if not for *Campania*. U-boats were in the offing, now known to have been a pack of the *Rasmus Gruppe*, equipped with acoustic torpedoes. However, we managed to avoid them by hugging the edge of the pack-ice. During 11 and 12 February *Nairana* flew nine patrols, two of which had to be cut short because of sea mist. *Campania* flew seven patrols, the last three of which ended in disaster. On the night of 12 February one of her Swordfish went into the barrier and had to be written off. Another went over the side, injuring the batsman. Since *Campania*'s reserve batsman had also been injured, another of her Swordfish that was already on patrol had to land on *our* flight-deck, where it too ended up in the barrier! It was as well we were within sight of Kola Inlet, which we entered in the small hours of 13 February.

Our stay inside the protective belt of the Russian minefields was a brief one. After only three days we were again standing seaward to provide air cover for another homewardbound convoy.

It was sometimes the case with Russian convoys that the passage home was more eventful than the passage out, for the Germans knew exactly where we were and when we were leaving and had time to mass their forces.

This was certainly the case with JW and RA64. The homewardbound convoy consisted of thirty-seven merchantmen with their Commodore flying his flag in the *Samaritan*. The escort was the same as on the passage out. It was numbingly cold as, on the morning of 17 February, we headed out of Kola Inlet. The thermometer on *Nairana*'s bridge recorded 40° of frost, the flight-deck was white with rime and a rating whose hand accidentally brushed the metal wing of a Wildcat suffered third degree burns. We were expecting trouble. For, on the night before we sailed, a U-boat (*U452*, Kapitänleutnant Bentzien) had been sunk near the mouth of the Inlet. There had been a handful of survivors and we learned from them that a "pack" had recently arrived from Narvik and were lying in wait for us. Almost as soon as we were clear of the minefields there was a shattering explosion and HMS *Lark* was hit by an acoustic torpedo which blew off

# SAINT
## VALENTINE'S
### DAY
### 1945.

The single-engined Stringbag
  Has flown for quite a time,
Its prehistoric silhouette
  Is known in every clime—
How different the 88,
  With fuselage so slim—
A monoplane with motors two;
  Don't make mistakes with him!

Yet what a metamorphosis
  A bit of action brings,
When Junkers fly at 80 knots
  And grow some second wings;
And Stringbags, (clearly Nazified)
  And Wildcat sixes too,
Become the targets of all guns
  Whilst 88's fly through....

The leopard cannot change his spots,
  Nor I, (alas!) change mine:
Remember this, and I'll be pleased
  To be your Valentine.

her stern. She was towed back to the safety of Murmansk by a Russian tug. Conditions for flying became first difficult and then impossible, with mist gathering in a dense layer on the surface of the sea. This suited the U-boats, for their Schnorkels enabled them to stay at periscope depth near the edge of the pack-ice where it was almost impossible to detect them either visually or by radar. It didn't, however, suit the Swordfish, and, with visibility down to less than 100 yards, all planes were grounded.

It was now, while the convoy was bereft of air cover, that we suffered a tragic loss. A little after midday there was a sudden explosion, a sheet of flame and our guardship HMS *Bluebell*, which had been stationed only a couple of hundred yards on our port quarter, vanished. One moment she was there. Next moment an acoustic torpedo had struck her level with her magazines and she was pulverized in an instant to an acrid column of dust. Out of her ship's company of more than 120 there was only one survivor.

Then, providentially, the sea mist started to clear. By mid-afternoon our Swordfish were back in the air and the U-boats had lost their opportunity.

In the next twelve hours we flew thirteen patrols, some lasting more than three hours. This meant that there were always at least two aircraft circling the convoy. Conditions for flying were difficult. At first, the remains of the sea mist restricted visibility; then, as twilight gave way to total darkness, the wind increased and the waves steepened. By midnight it was blowing a full gale and *Nairana* was pitching and corkscrewing like a roller-coaster. Out of the thirteen aircraft to take-off four came or nearly came to grief. Supple and Lloyd had to return with their engine overheating and losing power. Rogers and Eames had to return with their ASV unserviceable. Paine and Roberts landed heavily, writing off their undercarriage, and, as their Swordfish slithered across the flight-deck, very nearly writing off the batsman as well.

Ron Brown and Jock Bevan had the narrowest escape of all. It was coming up to midnight as they were given the green Aldis light to take-off. *Nairana* was corkscrewing violently. And just as Ron fired his RATOG the carrier reared upwards and sideways, flinging the Swordfish not only into the air but straight towards the island. The plane hit the starboard oerlikon guns, did a spectacular half-roll, plunged near-vertical into the sea and sank like a stone. Aboard the carrier everyone who had seen what happened held his breath. For if Ron had activated his depth-charges that would have been the end not only of him and his observer but quite possibly of the *Nairana* as well. Half a ton of high explosive detonating on our waterline would have done us no good at all. The seconds ticked by. There was no explosion. And suddenly, and against all the odds, our lookouts saw that

Ron Brown and Jock Bevan had surfaced and were clambering into their dinghy, which had broken free as the Swordfish sank. They were swirled away into the night. One wouldn't have rated their chances of survival too highly. But after about fifteen minutes they were picked up by HMS *Onslaught*, commanded by Captain Pleydell-Bouverie, RN, who risked his ship and the lives of his ship's company to comb the sea for them with his searchlight. He was only just in time, for in those few minutes, in spite of their rubber-immersion-suits, Ron and Jock were frozen almost literally solid and in the last stages of hypothermia. To quote an official report, "Their limbs wouldn't bend and the clothes had to be cut away from their frozen bodies." Few aircrew survive a single ducking in the Arctic. Ron Brown survived two. And a torpedoing!

Two more patrols were flown that night: by the CO and John Rogers. Then conditions deteriorated still further and, by dawn on the 18th, the convoy was pitching into a full-scale Arctic hurricane. There was no question now of our fighting U-boats or Junkers, conditions were far too bad for them to survive in. Our adversary was the storm.

It is hard to find words that are adequate to describe the ferocity of the blizzard that now engulfed us. One of our pilots said it was "like being attacked by a wild animal". Equally telling is the matter-of-fact report in *"Convoys to Russia"*:

> "The weather that followed deserves the description of 'the great gale'. Other convoys suffered serious weather damage, but none so bad as this. The convoy was greatly scattered, numerous ships suffering severe weather damage. Several merchant ships were reduced to steering with block and tackle on the rudder-head and, on return to Britain, twelve warships had to be docked with weather damage."

Another report worth quoting is Mike Arrowsmith's met forecast:

"An intense depression centred over Spitzbergen continues to move rapidly east. Strong W'ly gale will continue today with low cloud and intermittent snow; wind increasing and backing this evening.

Grade 'C' Forecast until 2000/19
WIND: W'ly, averaging 70–80 knots but gusting considerably over
WEATHER: Cloudy with intermittent snow
CLOUD: 9/10–10/10 at 600 feet; patches at sea level

This forecast was pinned to the wardroom notice board, and beneath it some wag had written "Fly off ALL the Swordfish!"

The night brought no respite. Indeed conditions worsened. The maximum that our anemometer was able to record was eighty knots. In the small hours of the morning its needle reached this level and not once in the next twenty hours did it drop below it. And Arrowsmith reckons that many gusts were over 120 mph. The convoy slowed down: first to six knots, then to four. But even at this reduced speed, many of the merchantmen were continually shipping it green and in danger of foundering. McGrigor realized he could easily lose more ships to the storm than to the attacks of U-boats and Junkers. Early on 19 February he sent a signal to Surtees.

"*Nairana* from CS One. Am turning into wind and heaving to. Signal your intentions."

Godley was on the bridge with Surtees when the signal was handed to him. "Strawberry," he wrote, "didn't turn. Just a ghost of a smile. 'Reply as follows,' he said: 'CS One from *Nairana*. Am staying with the convoy'."

So RA64 split into two fragmented groups. *Campania*, with about half the merchantmen and escorts, hove-to into the wind. *Nairana*, with the other half, held course to the south at four knots. Several factors made a lot of the merchant captains reluctant to heave-to. Some didn't want to use up precious fuel without making headway towards their destination; some found that their vessels were easier to handle when they were under way and all wanted to put as much distance as possible between themselves and the north Norwegian airfields. For everyone realized that, the moment the weather cleared, the Junkers would be searching for us. It was this that made Surtees determined to stay with the convoy. For past experience had proved that, once a convoy was scattered and bereft of air cover, its individual merchantmen were easy prey for the German bombers. Our captain had no intention of deserting his charges. No matter what the risk or what the cost, he was determined that his aircraft would defend the convoy.

But there were times that night when it looked as though there might not be any aircraft left to protect the merchantmen. For in *Nairana*'s hangar, a little after midnight, a huge tractor weighing over a ton broke free of its lashings and, with every pitch and roll of the carrier, began to wreak havoc among the parked aircraft. It was, for the Squadron maintenance personnel, a nightmare scenario. Each aircraft had been trebly lashed down, and each lashing had been tied not just to one ring-bolt but to two. Every chock, drip-tray and oil drum had been doubly secured. Our electrically-powered tractor had of course been secured too, but with the ship rolling through 100 degrees, and one moment pitching bows-under and next moment dipping stern-under, a steel cable that had been fastened around the tractor began to work loose. Suddenly, under the strain of a particularly vicious roll, it parted. The tractor burst free of its lashings and went careering across the hangar, smashing into aircraft after aircraft. Squadron ratings risked their lives to fling themselves on to it and try to hold it down. But there were too few of them and the tractor was too heavy. Again and again it hurtled across the deck, crashing into the parked aircraft. The tannoy blared for reinforcements. John Godley appeared and helped to organize the teams trying to "net" the tractor. Nigel Ball appeared, lost his footing on the oil-coated deck, shot across the hangar on his backside and disappeared through a companionway. The situation was critical, with the tractor at last enmeshed like a huge bluebottle in a spider's web of ropes but not yet under control, when a joke did more to raise morale than a whole spate of orders and exhortations. About a dozen of the squadron maintenance personnel hadn't joined *Nairana*; they had been left behind at Burscough, a dull and unprepossessing airfield, where they had languished on reduced pay, reduced rum and reduced chances of promotion. They had moaned and moaned and moaned. And now, as a group of ratings scattered for their lives as the tractor bore down on them, one of them shouted, "Pity those poor buggers at Burscough!"

There was no doubt from that moment but that the runaway tractor would be brought under control. In the small hours of the morning Godley was able to report to Surtees that it had been secured. Three Swordfish, he told him, were a total loss and three had been badly damaged. But seven Swordfish and all the Wildcats were flyable.

Surtees, wedged into a corner of the bridge which he never seemed to leave, was concerned with one thing only. "The convoy," he told Godley, "is badly scattered. The moment the weather clears the enemy will be after us. We must be prepared to fly off any time. If need be at dawn."

Godley passed on the message to Chief Air Artificer Banham, and Banham and his maintenance crews worked flat out through the night, in about the most taxing conditions it would be possible to imagine, to repair the damage and bring order out of chaos. By dawn the hangar was back to normal and thirteen aircraft were ready to be flown off. It was the Wildcats that were needed.

During the night of the 19th/20th the weather moderated a little. As the eye of the storm went swirling away to the north-east the wind decreased from ninety knots to sixty knots, while the solid curtain of cloud broke up and its base lifted. But the seas remained mountainous – huge fifty-foot rollers, a mile from crest to crest, surging in endless succession over the western skyline. The convoy did its best to reassemble. Some ships, however, had been blown far out of position. By dawn four stragglers still hadn't returned to the fold and a German reconnaissance aircraft had found us and was shadowing us. We knew it wouldn't be long before the Junkers were back.

It seemed hardly possible that morning for our Wildcats to get airborne, and not possible at all – assuming they *did* get airborne – for them to have the slightest hope of landing back. However, it says much for the improved relations among *Nairana*'s top brass that there was now a meeting between Surtees, Nigel Ball, John Godley and Al Burgham and it was agreed that Al should decide if and when the Wildcats should be scrambled. Al was an experienced pilot, not given to taking risks, but he knew how much was at stake, knew that it would be no exaggeration to say the fate of many of the merchantmen rested on his fighters. At 0800 the order came through on the tannoy: "Range 4 Wildcats".

The ranging of four Wildcats would normally have taken less than ten minutes. That morning it took over an hour. The flight-deck handling parties were doubled. Even so, there were not enough men to hold the planes steady against the pitch and roll of the ship and the tug of the wind. The Wildcats glissaded this way and that over the ice-rimmed flight-deck, dragging with them whole rugger scrums of men as they clung to wings and heaved on securing wires. But at last the planes were manhandled into position and secured aft of the lift. Their engines were started. And four pilots – Armitage, Sargent, Gordon and Blanco – clambered into the cockpits.

At a little after ten o'clock "bogeys" appeared on the radar screen and the order was given to scramble.

*Nairana* laboured round into wind. An Aldis lamp flashed green from the bridge. The leading Wildcat revved up its engine. Chocks were whipped from under its wheels, gloved hands let go of its wings. For a second the plane slithered wildly; then, as it gathered speed, its tail rose and it was flung off the flight-deck through the spray of a fifty-foot wave. For a moment it hung half-stalling over the carrier's bow; then, picking up flying speed, it climbed into the comparative safety of the sky. Bill Armitage was airborne. His three colleagues also got off safely, in take-offs probably as hazardous as any ever made in the history of naval aviation. They formed up and were vectored towards the Junkers.

The Junkers weren't expecting them. German plans had been based on the assumption that the weather would be too bad for carrier-borne planes to be airborne and the sudden appearance of our fighters threw them into confusion. One group had planned a low-level torpedo attack, while the other group had planned to fly across the convoy's line of advance and drop mines. Both plans were now frustrated by our four Wildcats, who broke the formations up, harrying the German planes this way and that and forcing them to jettison their torpedoes and mines. The Junkers shied away. They had had a nightmare search for the convoy; they were at the very limit of their endurance (in more senses than one) and they had been mauled too savagely before by our Wildcats to have the stomach to try conclusions with them again. They dropped their torpedoes and mines at long range, more in hope than expectation, and made for the safety of the clouds. Most got away. But three, braver or less lucky than their companions, fell to the ack-ack of the warships. And two were shot down by our fighters, one by Gordon and Blanco, and one by Armitage and Sargent. (*Luftwaffe* records reveal that twenty-six Junkers took-off that morning to attack the convoy, but only nineteen returned. So it could be that our fighters so damaged two other planes that they failed to survive the flight home.)

It would not be wrong to say that our four Wildcats, that morning, saved the convoy. For, if the German planes had had to face ack-ack only, their attacks would undoubtedly have been more determined and more successful. But as our pilots came back and started to circle the carrier at 1,000 feet it looked as though they might well have to pay for their victory with their lives. For with our flight-deck corkscrewing this way and that, and rising and falling by anything up to fifty feet, one would have thought nothing short of a miracle would get them down safely. There was no miracle, just a combination of inspired batting and skilful flying; repeated four times.

Bob Mathé admitted afterwards that although he would have hoped to land Swordfish in such conditions, he never thought that the Wildcats would make it, for the monoplanes with their narrow undercarriage, high landing speed and shallow angle of approach were far more difficult to land than the accommodating biplanes. The first pilot, Bill Armitage, had to be waved-off twice. Waving-off was a nerve-racking experience, with the plane poised near-stalling above the round-down and the pilot longing to cut his throttle but having instead at the last moment to ram it full open and claw desperately for airspeed; but better an anxious wave-off than a disastrous touch down. The third time Bill approached *Nairana*'s stern obligingly swung up at the crucial moment, and the first Wildcat plummeted down, heavily but safely. The second plane had a lucky escape. Norman Sargent was given the signal to cut, but, at the last second, the flight-deck swung up sharply. Norman hit it hard, leapfrogged all six arrester-wires and was brought up short only inches from the barrier by the gale-force wind. Then the gale which had saved him very nearly proved his undoing. For the Wildcat, unhooked, was picked up almost bodily by the seventy-knot wind and bowled backwards across the ice-covered deck. To quote Norman:

"Rebounding from the barrier, I slithered across the deck on my wingtip. First, I was almost blown over the starboard side, then I was almost blown over the round-down. Much to their credit, a lot of the flight-deck-handling party tried to grab me as I slithered past them; but they hadn't a hope of stopping five tons of fast-moving Wildcat. I rammed open my throttle, managed to stop the glissade, and came to rest no more than a dozen feet from the round-down. From here I was hauled to safety."

Somehow, and against all the odds, the last two pilots – Gordon and Blanco – managed to get down in one piece.

These were not the last operational sorties carried out by the squadron – both Swordfish and Wildcats flew patrols during the final few days of RA64 and also during our last and once again aborted shipping strike – but they were the last really *meaningful* sorties. All that happened afterwards was something of an anticlimax.

There were no more attacks that afternoon, which was just as well because, almost as soon as the Wildcats landed, we were hit by another and almost equally violent storm and for the second time the convoy became scattered. Three extremely hazardous A/S patrols were flown in high winds and huge seas on 21 February, but conditions were too bad for the U-boats to operate and no contacts were made.

A couple of days later, as we were nearing the Faeroes, we flew our last sortie in defence of RA64. It was a sad occasion. Several stragglers had not yet managed to catch up with the convoy. Among them was the *Henry Bacon*, an American "Liberty Ship" which had aboard thirty-five members of the Norwegian Resistance who had been evacuated from Soroy Island to avoid German reprisals. On the afternoon of 23 February a formation of Junkers were searching for the main convoy, but found instead the solitary and defenceless merchantman. The *Henry Bacon* managed to get off a radio message and two of our Wildcats (flown by Armitage and Sargent) were flown off to go to her aid. However, by the time they found her her decks were awash and the Junkers were on their way back to Norway. Armitage and Sargent circled the sinking ship, watching the survivors take to their boats. The USN Armed Guard who were manning the *Henry Bacon* upheld the finest traditions of the sea; they gave up their places in the lifeboats to their passengers. All the Norwegians were saved, but twenty-six of the Armed Guard went down with their ship. There was nothing Armitage and Sargent could do except take an accurate fix on the lifeboats, circle them and fly low over them to make sure the survivors realized they were not being abandoned, then make their way back to *Nairana*.

The *Henry Bacon* was the only merchantman we ever lost. All told, we escorted twenty-one convoys consisting of something like 1,000 merchant vessels. To have lost only one ship, and she a straggler, was a record we could be proud of. Nonetheless it saddened us to think that on the very last day of our very last convoy lives had been lost.

During the final stages of our passage home air cover was provided by Coastal Command from their bases in Iceland and the Shetlands. The squadron was stood down and given a well deserved rest, until on 28 February we were flown ashore to Hatston – to find we were headline news.

The usual wartime restrictions had been lifted and the press had a field day.

> "Navy Saves Convoy in Arctic Battle", "Pilots Fought When Frozen to Their Cockpits", "Convoy Fights the Enemy in 80 mph Gale", Convoy Beats Planes, U-boats In 90 mph Gale".

There may have been a bit of hyperbole in this; but there was also some good factual reporting.

> "During the double passage," wrote *The Times*, "weather of exceptional severity was encountered, and in storms with gusts of over 100 mph all ships had difficulty keeping their stations. Twice under the stress of weather the convoy became scattered, but each time it was successfully reformed. . . . The finest achievement of the whole convoy was the flying of fighters from HMS *Nairana*, when her bows were dipping under huge waves and her screws cleared the water each time she tossed up her stern. Thanks to the able handling of the ship and the flying skill of the pilots, the planes got down safely."

And this is a good note to end on: "the able handling of the ship and the flying skill of the pilots". For it was this bonding of carrier and squadron which made *Nairana* and 835, by the end of the war in Europe, such an effective fighting unit. As I said in my Introduction: "She was our ship. We were her squadron." Like many a husband and wife, our relationship was not without its ups and downs, but when we pulled together we were, to quote *The Odyssey*, "a great comfort to our friends, and a great grief to our foes".

It was of course the drawing to an end of the war in Europe which heralded the end of 835 Squadron, for there was no way that our Swordfish could have been used against the Japanese in the Pacific. We stayed together for roughly another month, most of the time at Hatston, then briefly venturing again towards the Norwegian fjords with the idea of carrying out another shipping strike, only to find that this operation too had to be called off because of bad weather.

On our return from Norway, on 28 March, 1945, we received a signal that the Squadron was to be disbanded.

Although this was something that many of us had been half-expecting, it was nonetheless a shock to have it spelt out in black and white. We weren't sure whether to laugh or cry; laugh because we had come to the end of the road and were still alive, or cry because the friendships we had made and the *camaraderie* we had enjoyed were about to become things of the past.

There were some last rites: a last party in the wardroom, with Surtees, all *bonhomie*, singing "Fly off, fly off for Christ's sake, the Captain wants a gong!"; a last beat up of the Fleet at anchor in Scapa Flow, with the most pukkah warships singled out for our most outrageous low flying and acrobatics; and finally our Swordfish and Wildcats flown for the last time to Evanton or Abbot to be "mothballed". It was like saying goodbye to old friends. We disbanded on 1 April.

The evening before, we had packed our personal gear from our cabins in the *Nairana*, collected our flying gear for the last time from the Ready Room and had a last quick drink in the wardroom bar. The carrier was moored to the jetty at Greenock, off the Tail O' the Bank and next morning we went ashore to start a most welcome spell of indefinite leave before taking up our next appointments. When we got to Glasgow we couldn't think why all the church bells were ringing until we suddenly realized it was Easter Sunday. This seemed a bit symbolic, and a good many of us ended up in the Cathedral. After the Service we went our separate ways. And this, we told ourselves, must surely be the end of the Squadron story. We never thought there would be a postscript.

# 6

# *ENVOI*

Maybe old squadrons are like old soldiers – they never die, they only fade away. For here some of us are, exactly fifty years after the disbanding of 835 Naval Air Squadron having a reunion to celebrate the publishing of our story.

This gives me the excuse for some up-dates. After the defeat of Germany it was agreed that the spoils of war should be divided into three: a third to Great Britain, a third to the USA and a third to Russia. Included in these spoils were 156 U-boats which had surrendered to the Royal Navy. With the prospect of a "Cold War" already in the offing, Churchill was reluctant to hand over a third of these potentially dangerous U-boats to the Russians. It was therefore decided to destroy them. In an operation codenamed "Deadlight", the U-boats were towed 300 miles into the Atlantic and sunk by carrierborne aircraft. The carrier chosen for this somewhat macabre task was, ironically, the *Nairana*; "ironically" because she was about the only carrier in the Navy which *hadn't* sunk a U-boat throughout the whole of the war. She now sank 156 in three weeks! Soon after this she was transferred to the Royal Netherlands Navy where she served for three years as the *Karel Dorman*, before being converted to a cargo-carrying merchant ship, the MV *Port Victor*. Under this name she sailed for more than twenty years with the Port Line, latterly between Southampton and Wellington. Sometimes, as she lay at anchor in the harbour of New Zealand's capital city, a visitor would be welcomed aboard, an elderly man with a Scottish accent: Commander Edwardson was checking that "his" engines were still being well cared for.

Once she called at Dunedin, and my young son James and I went aboard to be warmly welcomed by the Captain. Among other things, he showed us a plaque in the main lounge which commemorated *Port Victor*'s wartime career as an escort-carrier. He also showed my son the ship's hooter and invited him to sound it. Since James was only six, he needed no urging and swung on the rope for a full twenty seconds – much to the consternation of the good citizens of Dunedin!

The *Nairana/Karel Dorman/Port Victor* ended her days, like many grand old vessels before her which had worn themselves out in service, in the shipbreakers' yards. On 21 July, 1971, she was delivered to British Breakers. By 7 August, 1971, all that remained of her were memories.

Perhaps Surtees ought to have an up-date too. He was awarded a bar to his DSO, and went on to fulfil a not unimportant role in naval operations in the Pacific. He remains an enigma. Many squadron aircrew whose judgement I respect are convinced he was unbalanced. That may be. Yet I am reminded of the words of the French poet, Alfred de Vigny: *"Il faut toujours exiger des hommes plus qu'ils peuvent faire afin d'en avoir"*, which could be roughly translated as "if you want men to do all that is possible, you must ask them to do the impossible." So I suppose you might argue that, by his unreasonable demands, Surtees brought out the best in us. At any rate, I prefer my last thoughts on him to be charitable. One of our observers, David Beal, subsequently met him in the Far East; they kept in touch and on 19 April, 1947, Surtees wrote in a letter to David:

"I hope you realize how much I admired 835 Squadron. Perhaps I did not always show it at the time, but so often I was worn out and worried which made me irritable. It is entirely due to you and the other lads that I got a bar to my DSO – and I realize it full well."

These are not, I suggest, the words of the devil incarnate.

I will spare my wartime friends their blushes by embarking on an update on *them*, but since this is their story, the last words should surely be theirs. I started writing *Alone in a Wide, Wide Sea* largely to satisfy myself. I had retired. I had time on my hands. I'd read books about the Air Arm I wasn't too happy with. I wanted to put the record straight, to get across what it was *really* like to fly in the Fleet Air Arm. My wartime colleagues buckled-to to help me. I've literally a suitcase full of letters, diaries, reminiscences and photographs sent from all over the world. When, a couple of years ago, I showed some of my friends my first draft, I was surprised not that they all thought it awful but that they all thought it awful for different reasons! "You should be more formal", wrote Hank Housser, "and give everyone their proper rank. We want this to be an official history." "Must you be so formal?" wrote Eric McEwan, "just get across that a lot of the time a lot of us simply had fun." Val Jones reckoned it ought to be stated categorically that our Captain was mad. "Personally," wrote George Sadler, "I always got on very well with Captain Surtees." It didn't take me long to realize that we all saw things differently. So what I have tried to do is chart a fair and balanced course between the minefields of many conflicting opinions. However, two of our aircrew, one an observer and one a pilot, made comments that we are all agreed on.

"We don't," Johnny Lloyd told me firmly, "want any heroics. Just tell people that we had a job to do and we did it and that was that."

"Looking back," John Cridland wrote, "I think we did a competent job – and that goes for both aircrew and groundcrew. As I remember it, 835 was a good squadron."

Let that be our epitaph.

# APPENDIX I

*Commanding Officers of 835 Squadron*

| | | |
|---|---|---|
| LtCdr. M. Johnstone, DSC, RN | ..... | Jan '42 – April '42 |
| Lt (then LtCdr.) J.R. Lang, RN | ..... | April '42 – July '43 |
| LtCdr. W.N. Waller, RN | ..... | July '43 – Dec '43 |
| LtCdr(A) T.T. Miller, RN | ..... | Dec '43 – Feb '44 |
| Lt(A) (then LtCdr) E.E. Barringer, RNVR | ..... | Feb '44 – Aug '44 |
| LtCdr(A) F.V. Jones, RNVR | ..... | Aug '44 – Jan '45 |
| LtCdr(A) J.R. Godley, RNVR | ..... | Jan '45 – March '45 |

# APPENDIX II

*Pilots and Observers serving in 835 Squadron*
(F = fighter pilot – Sea Hurricane or Wildcat: TBR = torpedo bomber
reconnaissance pilot – Swordfish)

*Pilots*

| *Name* | *Rank and date on joining* | *Rank and date on leaving* |
|---|---|---|
| C. Allen (F) | S/Lt(A)RNZVR Aug '43 | S/Lt(A)RNZVR Dec '43 |
| O.K. Armitage (F) | S/Lt(A)RNZVR Dec '43 | Lt(A)RNZVR March '45 |
| K.W. Atkinson (F) | S/Lt(A)RNVR June '44 | S/Lt(A)RNVR March '45 |
| P.H. Blanco (F) | S/Lt(A)RNVR June '44 | S/Lt(A)RNVR March '45 |
| R.H. Brown (TBR) | S/Lt(A)RNVR June '44 | S/Lt(A)RNVR March '45 |
| R. Bullen (F) | Mid(A)RNVR July '43 | S/Lt(A)RNVR Aug '43 |
| A.R. Burgham (F) | S/Lt(A)RNZVR July '43 | Lt(A)RNZVR March '45 |
| A. Costello (TBR) | S/Lt(A)RNVR April '43 | S/Lt(A)RNVR Feb '44 |
| S. Cowsill (TBR) | S/Lt(A)RNVR Oct '44 | S/Lt(A)RNVR March '45 |
| J. Cramp (TBR) | S/Lt(A)RNZVR Aug '42 | S/Lt(A)RNZVR March '43 |
| J.E. Cridland (TBR) | S/Lt(A)RNVR April '43 | S/Lt(A)RNVR March '45 |
| C. Cross (TBR) | S/Lt(A)RNVR April '43 | S/Lt(A)RNVR Sept '43 |
| J.F. Defrates (TBR) | S/Lt(A)RNVR July '44 | S/Lt(A)RNVR March '45 |
| D.J. Edwards (F) | S/Lt(A)RNVR Feb '45 | S/Lt(A)RNVR March '45 |
| W.E.F. Elliott (TBR) | S/Lt(A)RNVR March '43 | Lt(A)RNVR May '44 |
| J.R. Godley (TBR) | LtCdr(A)RNVR Jan '45 | LtCdr(A)RNVR March '45 |
| G.D. Gordon (F) | S/Lt(A)RNVR Dec '43 | S/Lt(A)RNVR March '45 |
| C.F. Gough (TBR) | S/Lt(A)RNVR Dec '44 | S/Lt(A)RNVR March '45 |
| J. Henshelwood (TBR) | S/Lt(A)RNVR March '45 | S/Lt(A)RNVR March '45 |
| H.C.K. Housser (TBR) | Lt(A)RCNVR May '42 | Lt(A)RCNVR June '43 |
| J. Hunt (TBR) | S/Lt(A)RNVR Jan '42 | Lt(A)RVNR June '44 |
| M. Johnstone (TBR) | LtCdr. RN Jan '42 | LtCdr. RN April '42 |
| H.G. Jones (TBR) | S/Lt(A)RNVR Jan '42 | Lt(A)RNVR April '43 |

| | | |
|---|---|---|
| W. Mayson (TBR) | S/Lt(A)RNVR March '45 | S/Lt(A)RNVR March '45 |
| E.H. McEwan (TBR) | S/Lt(A)RNVR July '43 | S/Lt(A)RNVR Jan '45 |
| R.G. McLaughlin (TBR) | S/Lt(A)RNZVR Aug '43 | S/Lt(A)RNZVR Sept '44 |
| S.A. Mearns (F) | S/Lt(A)RNVR July '43 | Lt(A)RNVR March '45 |
| D.B. Millar (TBR) | S/Lt(A)RNVR Jan '45 | S/Lt(A)RNVR March '45 |
| I.L.T. Miller (F) | S/Lt(A)RNVR June '44 | S/Lt(A)RNVR Dec '44 |
| J.T. Miller (TBR) | LtCdr(A)RN Dec '43 | LtCdr(A)RN Feb '44 |
| R. Moss (F) | S/Lt(A)RNVR Jan '45 | S/Lt(A)RNVR Jan '45 |
| E. McG. Murray (TBR) | S/Lt(A)RNZVR July '44 | S/Lt(A)RNZVR Jan '45 |
| L.W.H. Paine (TBR) | S/Lt(A)RNVR Jan '45 | S/Lt(A)RNVR March '45 |
| D.G. Payne (TBR) | S/Lt(A)RNVR Dec '44 | S/Lt(A)RNVR March '45 |
| P.H. Picot (F) | S/Lt(A)RNZVR July '43 | S/Lt(A)RNZVR Jan '44 |
| E. Pitts (TBR) | S/Lt(A)RNVR May '44 | S/Lt(A)RNVR Jan '45 |
| J. Provis (TBR) | S/Lt(A)RNVR July '44 | S/Lt(A)RNVR March '45 |
| C. Richardson (F) | S/Lt(A)RNVR Dec '43 | S/Lt(A)RNVR May '44 |
| J.P. Roffy (TBR) | S/Lt(A)RNVR Nov '44 | S/Lt(A)RNVR March '45 |
| J. Rogers (TBR) | S/Lt(A)RNVR Jan '45 | S/Lt(A)RNVR March '45 |
| G. Sadler (TBR) | S/Lt(A)RNVR April '42 | Lt(A)RNVR Nov '44 |
| N. Sargent (P) | S/Lt(A)RNVR Dec '43 | S/Lt(A)RNVR March '45 |
| R.P. Selley (TBR) | S/Lt(A)RNVR April '42 | Lt(A)RNVR March '45 |
| R. Shirley-Smith (TBR) | S/Lt(A)RNVR Jan '42 | Lt(A)RNVR Sept '43 |
| G.C. Summers (TBR) | Lt(A)RNVR Jan '45 | Lt(A)RNVR March '45 |
| J.S. Supple (TBR) | S/Lt(A)RNVR April '43 | S/Lt(A)RNVR March '45 |
| J.F. Urquhart (TBR) | S/Lt(A)RNVR May '42 | Lt(A)RNVR May '44 |
| P. Urwin (TBR) | Lt(A)RN July '44 | Lt(A)RN March '45 |
| W.N. Waller (F) | Lt.RN July '43 | LtCdrRN Dec '43 |
| F. Wallis (F) | S/Lt(A)RNVR May '44 | S/Lt(A)RNVR July '44 |
| K. Warren (TBR) | S/Lt(A)RNVR March '44 | S/Lt(A)RNVR July '44 |
| D.W. Whittick (TBR) | S/Lt(A)RNVR Oct '44 | S/Lt(A)RNVR March '45 |
| K. Wilmot (TBR) | S/Lt(A)RNVR Sept '43 | S/Lt(A)RNVR March '44 |
| H.R.D. Wilson (TBR) | S/Lt(A)RNVR Sept '43 | S/Lt(A)RNVR Jan '45 |
| D. Yate (F) | S/Lt(A)RNVR July '43 | S/Lt(A)RNVR Aug '43 |

## Observers

| Name | Rank and date on joining | Rank and date on leaving |
|---|---|---|
| G. Arber | S/Lt(A)RNVR Sept '43 | S/Lt(A)RNVR March '44 |
| E.E. Barringer | S/Lt(A)RNVR Jan '42 | LtCdr(A)RNVR Aug '44 |
| D.W. Beal | S/Lt(A)RNVR July '44 | S/Lt(A)RNVR March '45 |
| J.S. Bevan | S/Lt(A)RNVR June '44 | S/Lt(A)RNVR March '45 |
| W. Buckie | Lt(A)RNVR April '43 | Lt(A)RNVR July '44 |

| | | |
|---|---|---|
| W. Cairns | S/Lt(A)RNVR Aug '43 | S/Lt(A)RNVR March '44 |
| G. Clewett | S/Lt(A)RNVR March '45 | S/Lt(A)RNVR March '45 |
| J. Dalton | S/Lt(A)RNVR April '43 | S/Lt(A)RNVR Feb '44 |
| J.V.H. Eames | S/Lt(A)RNVR July '44 | S/Lt(A)RNVR March '45 |
| P. Grady | Lt(A)RCNVR Feb '45 | Lt(A)RCNVR March '45 |
| K. Hall | S/Lt(A)RNVR June '43 | S/Lt(A)RNVR Feb '45 |
| R.F. Hankin | S/Lt(A)RNVR March '44 | S/Lt(A)RNVR March '45 |
| R. Henshall | S/Lt(A)RNVR March '43 | S/Lt(A)RNVR May '43 |
| L.M. Holley | S/Lt(A)RNVR Oct '44 | S/Lt(A)RNVR March '45 |
| R.V. Jones | LtCdr(A)RNVR July '44 | LtCdr(A)RNVR July '44 |
| J.R. Lang | Lt.RN April '42 | LtCdr.RN Sept '43 |
| R. Legood | Lt(A)RNVR Aug '44 | Lt(A)RNVR Jan '45 |
| A.R.J. Lloyd | S/Lt(A)RNVR May '43 | S/Lt(A)RNVR March '45 |
| J.M. McCormick | S/Lt(A)RNVR Aug '42 | S/Lt(A)RNVR March '43 |
| J.L. McEwan | S/Lt(A)RNVR July '44 | S/Lt(A)RNVR March '45 |
| D.O'D. Newbery | Mid(A)RNVR May '42 | S/Lt(A)RNVR Nov '44 |
| J. Parker | S/Lt(A)RNVR Jan '42 | S/Lt(A)RNVR March '43 |
| D.J. Ravenhill | S/Lt(A)RNVR May '44 | S/Lt(A)RNVR March '45 |
| J.S. Robert | S/Lt(A)RNVR Jan '45 | S/Lt(A)RNVR March '45 |
| G. Rose | S/Lt(A)RNVR July '44 | S/Lt(A)RNVR March '45 |
| S. Smith | S/Lt(A)RNVR April '43 | S/Lt(A)RNVR Sept '43 |
| R.A. Stiff | S/Lt(A)RNVR Nov '44 | S/Lt(A)RNVR March '45 |
| S.G. Strong | S/Lt(A)RNVR Sept '43 | S/Lt(A)RNVR March '45 |
| J.G. Teesdale | S/Lt(A)RNVR Jan '42 | Lt(A)RNVR July '44 |
| E.V. Thomas | S/Lt(A)RNVR April '44 | S/Lt(A)RNVR Oct '44 |
| S.H. Thomas | S/Lt(A)RNVR Jan '42 | Lt(A)RNVR June '44 |
| J.B. Winstanley | S/Lt(A)RNVR May '42 | S/Lt(A)RNVR April '44 |
| P.F. Worrell | S/Lt(A)RNVR Oct '44 | S/Lt(A)RNVR March '45 |
| N. Wylie | S/Lt(A)RNVR Jan '45 | S/Lt(A)RNVR Feb '45 |

# APPENDIX III

## AWARDS TO 835 NAVAL AIR SQUADRON
## AND TO THE AIR DEPARTMENT OF HMS NAIRANA

| Name and Rank | Award | Date | Citation |
|---|---|---|---|
| O.K. Armitage S/Lt(A)RNZVR | DSC | 19.6.45 | A |
| H.W.C. Banham, AA3 | MID* | 20.3.45 | H |
| D.W. Beal, S/Lt(A)RNVR | MID | 20.3.45 | B |
| P.H. Blanco, S/Lt(A)RNVR | MID | 19.6.45 | A |
| A.R. Burgham, S/Lt(A)RNZVR | MID | 17.10.44 | C |
| " " | DSC | 20.3.45 | D |
| J.F. Defrates, S/Lt(A)RNVR | MID | 20.3.45 | B |
| R.E. George, PO Airman | MID | 20.3.45 | H |
| J.R. Godley, Lt CdrRNVR | DSC | 24.4.45 | E |
| G.D. Gordon, S/Lt(A)RNVR | MID | 20.3.45 | F |
| " " | DSC | 19.6.45 | A |
| J.G. Gowan, T1 Air Mch O | MID | 19.6.45 | A |
| R.G. King, AA4 | MID | 19.6.45 | A |
| R.C. Mathé, Lt(A)RNVR | DSC | 14.6.45 | I |
| " " | DSC | 19.6.45 | A |
| S.A. Mearns, Lt(A)RNVR | MID | 17.10.44 | C |
| " " | DSC | 19.6.45 | A |
| W.D. Merryfield, PO Rad Mech | MID | 19.6.45 | A |
| I.L.T. Miller, S/Lt(A)RNVR | MID(Posth) | 20.3.45 | G |
| R. Moss, S/Lt(A)RNVR | MID | 19.6.45 | A |
| H.W. Perrett, Sgt., RAF | DSM | 19.6.45 | A |
| C.W.G. Richardson, S/Lt(A)RNVR | MID(Posth) | 17.10.44 | C |
| N.W. Sargent, S/Lt(A)RNVR | MID | 19.6.45 | A |
| T.W. Snowdon, Wt Acft Off | MID | 20.3.45 | H |
| S.G. Strong, Lt(A)RNVR | MID | 24.4.45 | E |
| F. Wallis, S/Lt(A)RNVR | MID | 17.10.44 | C |

| | | | |
|---|---|---|---|
| F. Westwater, Air Mech IE | MID | 19.6.45 | A |
| D.W. White, S/Lt(A)RNVR | DSC | 11.12.45 | J |

*Mentioned in Despatches

A    Operation "Hotbed", North Russian Convoy in February 1945
B    For the attack on and probable destruction of a U-boat on 14.12.44
C    For defence against air attacks in the Western Approaches, May 1944
D    For attacking enemy aircraft on 12th December 1944
E    For a night attack on enemy shipping off Norway on 29.1.45
F    For an attack on a Blohm und Voss 138 aircraft on 14.12.44
G    For convoy duty and attacking enemy aircraft in December, 1944
H    For services during an Arctic passage in December 1944
I    Birthday Honours List, 1945
J    Wind-up of the war in Europe

Battle Honours awarded to 835 Squadron and HMS *Nairana*

| | |
|---|---|
| Atlantic | 1943/44 |
| Arctic | 1944/45 |

# APPENDIX IV

*Aircraft flown on carrier based operations*

## SEA HURRICANE

*Technical Data*

*Description*: Single-seat carrier-borne fighter. Metal construction with metal and fabric covering.
*Manufacturers*: Hawker Aircraft Ltd., Kingston-on-Thames; conversion by General Aircraft Ltd.
*Power Plant*: One 1.460 Rolls Royce Merlin XX.
*Dimensions*: Span 40 feet; length 32 ft. 3"; height 13 ft. 3"; wing area 258 sq. ft. The Sea Hurricane's wings could not be folded; this was a serious disadvantage when operating from a carrier.
*Weight*: Empty 5,800 lbs; loaded 7,800 lbs.
*Armament*: Four 20mm cannon in wings.
*Performance*: maximum speed 300 mph at 21,000 ft; cruising 200–220 mph; climb to 20,000 ft. 9½mts; range 460 miles (normal) 960 miles (with auxiliary tanks); service ceiling 28,000 ft.

Throughout the whole of the Second World War the Air Arm never had an adequate purpose-built British fighter. In 1945 its squadrons were equipped with:

(a) British-built twin-seater fighters of inherently low performance (Fulmars and Fireflies): 8%.

(b) Adapted RAF fighters which *per se* were excellent planes but which had serious shortcomings when it came to operating from a carrier (Sea Hurricanes and Seafires): 20%.

(c) Fighters designed and built for the US Navy and bought from America (Wildcats, Hellcats and Corsairs): 72%.

Of the British-built fighters Sea Hurricanes were arguably the best. (Fulmars and Fireflies were often slower than the bombers they were expected to intercept and shoot down, while Seafires, with their narrow undercarriage and long-bladed propeller, were too fragile and had too short a range for the rough and tumble of work from a carrier. For every Seafire lost through enemy action twenty were lost taking-off or landing-on.) Sea Hurricanes were more robust, although they too had shortcomings; by the time they reached the Navy most were already old, survivors from the Battle of Britain, and their wings couldn't be folded, which meant they took up an inordinate amount of room and were difficult to manoeuvre between flight-deck and hangar.

In spite of these limitations, Sea Hurricanes did sterling work with the Air Arm, particularly in the Atlantic. At a time when the war at sea was going badly, they provided much-needed air cover for our convoys, by operating from escort carriers, MAC ships (Merchant Aircraft Carriers) and CAM ships (Catapult Aircraft Merchantmen). Flying from the latter was particularly hazardous; a pilot would be catapulted off in mid-ocean, knowing he had no hope of landing, but that having made his interception he would have to bail out and hope to be rescued by one of the ships in convoy.

Al Burgham, who was among the first fighter pilots to join 835 Squadron, writes of the Hurricane: "It was a plane I developed a great affection for. It was robust, reliable, manoeuvrable and forgiving, and I felt very comfortable flying it. Not being designed for carrier-operations, one had to land it in a nose-up attitude, which meant that one couldn't see the batsman because of the engine-cowling; however, once one had mastered the technique of landing off a curved approach, deck-landings became fairly routine in most weather conditions."

Hurricanes were a stop-gap. They filled the void between the time when old and obsolete British fighters (like the Sea Gladiator, Skua and Fulmar) were withdrawn from service and the time new and effective American fighters (like the Wildcat, Hellcat and Corsair) came into service. They did all that could have been expected of them. And more.

★　　★　　★　　★　　★

# SWORDFISH

## *Technical Data*

*Description*: Carrier-based, torpedo-bomber-reconnaissance biplane: metal structure covered with fabric. Crew of 2 or 3.
*Manufacturers*: Fairey Aviation Co. Ltd., Hayes, Middlesex; subcontracted to Blackburn Aircraft.
*Power Plant*: One Bristol Pegasus III or XXX (690 or 750 h.p.)
*Dimensions*: Span 45 ft. 6 in; length 36 ft. 4 in; height 12 ft. 10 in; wing area 607 sq. ft.
*Weight*: 5,200 lb empty; 9,250 lb loaded.
*Armament*: One Vickers gun aft; one 18 in. torpedo or one 1,500 lb mine or bomb; or four depth charges or eight 60 lb rockets.
*Performance*: Maximum speed 95–110 kts; range 550 miles; endurance 5 hours; service ceiling 10,000 ft.

The Swordfish was one of the great planes in the history of aerial warfare. Judged by its appearance and performance, it should have been obsolete at the outbreak of war, yet such were its handling qualities and its reliability that it outlived a whole series of intended successors and was the only aircraft of any of the combatants to be both "in at the beginning of the war in Europe and in at the end". Indeed more Swordfish were operational on the last day of hostilities than on the first.

Its longevity is testimony to the excellence of its design, the story of which is told in Chapter 1, pages oo and oo. In a rapidly changing field, in which most aircraft had a useful life-span of two or at the most three years, the "Stringbag" remained operational for a whole decade. In 1934 the first Swordfish (No. K4190) made its first successful test flight. In 1944 the last Swordfish (No. NS205) left the sub-contractors' factory at Brough. The latter had a slightly more powerful engine (a 750 hp Pegasus XXX rather than a 690 hp Pegasus III), its two rear cockpits had been merged into one, and it was festooned with sophisticated weaponry (ASVX, RATOG and RP etc); apart from this the two aircraft were so similar as to be virtually identical.

In the intervening decade 2,399 "Stringbags" were delivered to the Air Arm. Between them they flew more hours than any other type of allied aircraft and sank a greater tonnage of enemy shipping – substantially over a million tons. And what is perhaps more pertinent, they undoubtedly *saved* a large number of merchant seamen and merchant vessels from a watery grave. For they were, above all else, protectors of convoys. Once the war at sea had been fully joined, most of the Air Arm's twenty-odd Swordfish squadrons were employed on convoy escort duty and it was the contribution of these archaic-looking but robust and dependable biplanes which, at a critical moment in the Atlantic, turned the possibility of defeat into the certainty of victory.

★    ★    ★    ★    ★

## WILDCAT

### Technical Data

*Description*: Single-seat, carrier-borne fighter; all metal, stressed-skin construction.

*Manufacturers*: Grumman Aircraft Engineering Corporation, Bethpage, Long Island, N.Y.

*Power Plant*: One 1,200-hp Pratt and Whitney Twin Wasp S3C4-G.

*Dimensions*: Span 38 ft; length 28 ft 10 in; height 9' 2½"; wing area 260 sq ft.

*Weight*: Empty 4,650 lb; loaded 6,100 lb.

*Armament*: Six 0.50-calibre guns in wings.

*Performance*: Maximum speed 290 mph; cruising speed 240 mph; climb 3,300 ft per minute; range 1,150 miles; endurance 4 hrs 10 mts; service ceiling 28,000 ft.

Wildcat was the nickname of the Grumman Martlet, the standard fighter used by the US Navy and Marine Corps when America entered the war. They were tough, tubby, highly manoeuvrable little planes which bore the brunt of the initial flying in the Pacific, where they gave a good account of themselves. In particular a handful of Wildcats from Marine Fighting Squadron 211 defended Wake Island against the same sort of overwhelming odds that faced the Sea Gladiators "Faith", "Hope" and "Charity" on Malta.

Wildcats first saw service with the Royal Navy towards the end of 1940. They were used for the defence of Scapa Flow and on Christmas Day, 1940, a Wildcat of 804 Squadron became the first American-built fighter to shoot down an enemy plane – a JU88. They were first used at sea in the autumn of 1941, when Wildcats and Swordfish operating from HMS *Audacity* proved in no uncertain manner the value of carrier-borne aircraft for protecting convoys against both U-boats and long-range bombers. They provided air cover for convoys to Malta and Russia, and helped to cover

*190*

Allied landings in North Africa, Madagascar, Italy and Normandy; they also saw service in the Western Desert. But their greatest contribution to victory was their work in the Atlantic. Here, operating from MAC ships and escort carriers, they not only kept enemy shadowers and bombers at bay, but, working in conjunction with Swordfish, they prevented U-boats from operating on the surface.

Ken Atkinson, who flew both Sea Hurricanes and Wildcats with 835, compares the two aircraft. "The Wildcat was superior in all respects but two. The Hurricane had a broad undercarriage, and was very stable on take-off and landing, and when moving about the flight-deck. The Wildcat, on the other hand, had a narrow undercarriage and was much more unstable and prone to swing. This instability was particularly noticeable when the plane was parked with its wings folded, and it was not unknown, in heavy weather, for Wildcats to break their lashings and topple over the side. Their other disadvantage was that their undercarriage had to be raised by hand, by operating a crank-handle. Since this was positioned on the right-hand side of the cockpit, a pilot had, immediately after take-off, to hold the control column with his left hand – for those of us who were not left-handed a hazardous few moments. It was also advisable, when raising your undercarriage, to make sure that the RT leads from your helmet were well out of the way; otherwise with every turn of the crank-handle you wound your head progressively lower!"

In spite of these shortcomings, and in spite of the fact that by the end of the war in Europe it was short of both speed and firepower, the Wildcat was generally popular with its pilots. It was particularly liked for its manoeuvrability, its endurance (almost double that of a Seafire), and its rate-of-climb (almost double that of a Sea Hurricane), the latter attribute being especially important when it came to making interceptions from the deck of a carrier.

# BIBLIOGRAPHY

My principal source of information has been the *835 Squadron Fair Flying Log* which records every flight made by every aircraft in the Squadron from the day we were formed until the day we were disbanded. In addition, many aircrew have made contributions based on their own flying log books, letters home and personal recollections. Without their help my task would have been a labour of Hercules, not a labour of love. The publications listed below have provided additional source material.

Admiralty Records, *The Development of British Naval Aviation 1919–1945* Vols I–IV, Historical Section, Admiralty, 1954 *et seq.*

Appleyard, J., *Elements of Convoy Defence in Submarine Warfare*, Historical Section, Admiralty, 1917

Beaver, P., *The British Aircraft Carrier*, Patrick Stevens, 1982 (2nd edn., 1984)

Behrens, C.B.A., *Merchant Shipping and the Demands of War*, HMSO, 1955

Broome, Captain J., *Convoy is to Scatter*, William Kimber, 1972

Cameron, Ian, *Wings of the Morning*, Hodder & Stoughton, 1962

Campbell, Vice-Admiral Sir Ian and Captain D. McIntyre, *The Kola Run*, Muller, 1958

Churchill, Sir Winston, *The Second World War*, Vols I–IV, Cassell, 1948–52

Costello, J, and T. Hughes, *The Battle of the Atlantic*, Collins, 1977

Cremer, Peter, *U-333: The Story of a U-Boat Ace*, Bodley Head, 1984

Cunningham, Admiral Sir Andrew, *A Sailor's Odyssey*, Hutchinson, 1951

Doenitz, Admiral Karl, *Handbook for U-Boat Commanders*, German Admiralty, 1937; *Ten Years and Twenty Days*, Weidenfeld & Nicolson, 1959

Gretton, Vice-Admiral Sir Peter, *Convoy Escort Commander*, Cassell, 1964; *Crisis Convoy*, Peter Davies, 1974

Hough, Richard, *The Longest Battle: the War at Sea 1939–45*, Weidenfeld & Nicolson, 1986

Irving, David, *The Destruction of PQ 17*, William Kimber, 1980

Jones, Geoffrey, *Autumn of the U-Boats*, William Kimber, 1984; *Defeat of the Wolf Packs*, WIlliam Kimber, 1986

Kemp, P.K., *Victory at Sea*, Muller, 1957

Kilbracken, Lord, (formerly John Godley), *Bring back my Stringbag*, Peter Davies, 1979

Lamb, Commander C., *War in a Stringbag*, Cassell, 1977

Lewin, R., *Ultra goes to War*, Hutchinson, 1978

Lewis, M.L., *History of the British Navy*, Penguin, 1957

Macintyre, Captain Donald, *The Battle of the Atlantic*, Batsford, 1961

Middlebrook, M., *Convoy*, Morrow, 1976

Ministry of Information, *Merchantmen at War*, HMSO, 1944; *The Battle of the Atlantic*, HMSO, 1946

Morrison, S.E., *U.S. Naval Operations in World War II*, 15 vols., Little Brown, 1948–62; Vol. VII, *The Battle of the Atlantic*

Poolman, Kenneth, *Armed Merchant Cruisers*, Leo Cooper, 1985; *The Catafighters and Merchant Aircraft Carriers*, William Kimber, 1970; *Escort Carrier*, Ian Allan, 1972

Price, R., *Aircraft and Submarine*, Naval Institute Press, 1973

Robertson, Terrence, *Walker RN*, Evans, 1956

Roskill, Captain S.W., *The War at Sea*, HMSO, 1959; *The Navy at War, 1939–1945*, Collins, 1960

Ruegg, Bob, and Arnold Hague, *Convoys to Russia 1941–1945*, World Ship Society, 1992

Schoefield, Admiral B.B., *The Russian Convoys*, Batsford, 1964

Slader, John, *The Red Duster at War*, William Kimber, 1988; *The Fourth Service*, Hale, 1994

Sturtivant, R., *The Squadrons of the Fleet Air Arm*, Air Britain (Tonbridge) 1984

Terraine, John, *The Right of the Line*, Hodder & Stoughton, 1985; *Business in Great Waters*, Leo Cooper, 1989

Till, Geoffrey, *Air Power and the Royal Navy, 1914–1945*, Jane's Publishing, 1979

Van der Vat, Dan, *The Atlantic Campaign*, Hodder & Stoughton, 1988

Waters, S.D., *New Zealand in World War II*, Official War History, New Zealand Government printer

Winton, John, *The Defence of Sea Trade*, Michael Joseph, 1983; *Freedom's Battle: The War at Sea 1939–45*, Hutchinson, 1967

Wragg, David, *Wings Over the Sea*, David & Charles, 1979

Young, John M., *A Diary of Ship Losses 1939–1945*, Patrick Stephens, 1989

# INDEX

## A

Abbotsinch, RNAS, 63, 64, 118, 177

*Activity*, HMS, (ex SS *Telemachus*), 42, 44, 45, 81, 84, 86, 90

Adder patrols, 126

Allen, S/Lt C, 81, 182

Alligator patrols, 126

*Allister*, SS, 23–25, 27

*Andalusia Star*, SS, 12, 13, 15, 23

Arber, S/Lt G. ("Albert"), 12, 81, 91, 183

Arbroath, RNAS, 37, 39, 67, 112, 157

Archangel, 121, 122

*Archer*, HMS, 49

Arctic Circle, 126, 128, 141, 163

*Argus*, HMS, reported as "dismasted hulk", 6; used for deck-landing training, 44; 62, 63

*Ark Royal*, HMS, 6, 67, 75

Armitage, Lt O.K. ("Bill"), 64, 81, 84, 93, 102, 137, 146, 160, 162, 165, 173; shoots down Ju88 and lands-on in Arctic hurricane, 174; 175, 176, 182, 185

Armstrong, PO J.W. ("Willy"), his part in locating the *Bismark*, 65–67; 86–88, 108

Arran, Ise of, 61–63

Arrowsmith, Lt Mike, describes work as Met Officer *Nairana*, 76, 77; 99, 123, 155; forecast for the great storm, 170, 171

Asdic (Sonar), 15, 17, 85, 86, 94, 122, 137

ASV and ASVX (Air to surface-vessel radar), 18; fitted to Swordfish, 39; 49; importance of in Battle of the Atlantic, 75, 76; 90, 97, 98, 100; fitting more sophisticated ASVX to Swordfish, 107, 108; 110, 132, 137, 138, 142, 150, 189

Atkinson, S/Lt Ken, 106, 118, 166, 182, 191

*Audacity*, HMS, 190

*Aurora Borealis*, 125, 163

118

Godley, Lt/Cdr John, joins
squadron as CO, 157, 158;
describes attack on shipping
in Norwegian fjords, 158,
159; 160; establishes rapport
with Surtees, 161; describes
patrol north of Arctic Circle,
163; 164; his Valentine's day
card, 168; 170–173, 181,
182, 185

Gordon S/Lt George, 84, 94,
101, 102, 114, 129; shoots
down Blohm and Voss on his
21st birthday, 146; 165, 173;
shoots down Ju88 and lands-
on in Arctic hurricane, 174,
175, 181, 182, 185

Gough, S/Lt Charles, 153,
159, 182

Gowan, Air Mech. O, J.G.,
185

Grady, Lt. P., 184

Greenock, 48, 63, 89, 134, 177

# H

Hall, S/Lt K. ("Paddy"), 59,
81, 92, 138, 150, 157, 184

Hankin, S/Lt R.F., 138, 184

Hatston, RNAS, 39, 41, 42,
67, 153, 161, 176, 177

Havana, 23, 26, 27

Hawkins, Capt., 23

Healey, Cdr (BBCs "Uncle
Mac"), appointed to
*Nairana*, 73, 93; and
German prisoners of war, 94;
135

Hellcats, Grumman, 58, 188

*Henry Bacon*, SS, 175, 176

Henshall, S/Lt R., 183

Henshelwood, S/Lt J., 182

Hepp, Kapitan, 86

*Highlander*, HMS, 104–105

Hjelke Fjord, 66

Holley, S/Lt L.M., 126, 138,
150, 184

Hollings, Lt S., gunnery officer
*Nairana*, 71; and ship's
motto, 72, 107, 129

Housser, Lt H.C.K., ("Hank"
or "Harry"), 36, 40, 46, 47,
53, 55, 59, 179, 182

Howe, Capt, RNAS
Machrinhanish, 156

Hunt, Lt J, ("Johnny"), 11, 13,
22, 32, 45, 55, 81, 87, 101,
182

# I

IFF (Identification friend or
foe) 21, 83, 142, 145

*Illustrious*, HMS, 1, 6, 75

# J

Jacksonville, 23–27

Jamaica, 13, 24, 33

Jeschke, Kapitan-leutnant, 82

Johnstone, Lt/Cdr Mervyn
("Johnnie"), joins squadron
as CO, 11, 12, 14, 23, 26,
27, 29, 33, 181, 182

Jones, Lt/Cdr F.V. ("Val"),
joins squadron as CO, 111;
112; his character compared
with that of Surtees, 117;
118, 124, 126, 128, 132,
136, 138; at odds with
Surtees, 139; 140 and 149;

McLaughlin, S/Lt R.G., 81, 82, 82–84, 183

Machrihanish, RNAS, 33, 43–48, 50, 135, 156, 158

*Magpie*, HMS, 81, 86

Mallett, Lt/Cdr Dick, Senior Operations Officer, *Nairana*, recalls wartime experiences, 77, 78; 142, 155, 158

Marylands (target-towing bombers), 66, 67

Mathé Lt R.C. ("Bob"), batsman aboard *Nairana*; debt owed to him by squadron aircrew, 75; 112, 143, 145, 156; successfully lands-on Wildcats in Arctic hurricane, 174, 175; 185

*Maxeffell*, SS, 53

Mayson, S/Lt W., 183

Mearns, Lt S.A., ("Sam"), 58, 59, 84, 101, 102, 104; describes trip to Casablanca, 115, 116; 147, 162; shoots down Ju88, 164, 165, 183, 185

Merryfield, PO Rad.Mch., W.D., 185

meterological Officer (see also Lt Arrowsmith), 73, 76, 77

metox (U-boat radar), 20, 97, 101

Miami, 26, 27

Millar, S/Lt D.B., 183

Miller, S/Lt I.L.T. ("Dusty"), 106, 112, 147; shot down, 148; 149, 161, 185

Miller, Lt/Cdr T.T., joins squadron as CO, 67, 81, 86; near fatal crah on landing; 87; 88, 89, 133, 181

Moss, S/Lt R., 161, 162; helps shoot down Ju88, 164, 183, 185

*Mounsey*, HMS, sunk by U-boat, 130

Mull of Kintyre, 43, 50, 119, 134

Murmansk, 71, 118, 119, 121, 122; description of, 128; subjected to the worst bombing in the war, 129; 140, 154, 161, 169

Murray, S/Lt E. McG. ("Mick"), 112; describes hazardous working up, 113; describes passage of convoy MKF34, 113–114; describes Aurora Borealis, 125; 127, 128, 157, 183

# N

*Nairana*, HMS, 2, 9; 68–186 *passim*; general description of, 69–72; specification, 69; comparison with US escort carriers, 70, 71; duties of her air department, 73–79; official commisioning, 79, 80; sails on first operation, 81; with escort groups in mid-Atlantic, 82–89, 97–105; with Gibraltar convoys, 89–97, 105–107, 113–117; with Russian convoys, 123–154, 160–176; with shipping strikes in Norwegian fjords, 154–156, 158–160; postwar history, 178, 179

Nairana (Tasmanian eagle),

# U

U-boats, 7, 12, 13; our job to
prevent their attacking
merchantmen in convoy, 14;
their strength in 1939, 15;
their first "happy time", 16;
their second "happy time",
17; development of "wolf
packs", 17; 22, 24, 25, 30,
32; our use of ASV against,
37, 38; 40; their success in
the North Atlantic in 1942,
45; use of convoys against,
53, 54; use of fighter aircraft
against, 57, 58; their success
in the North Atlantic in
1943, 64; in running battle
with Walker's 2nd Escort
Group, 81–88; 90; passage
of U-boat prisoners to UK,
94, 95; terrible death for
those lost in Battle of the
Atlantic, 94, 95; 97; sighted
and attacked by our
Swordfish and Hurricanes,
101, 102; 106, 107; our use
of ASVX against, 108; our
use of Glow Worm against,
112, 114; their threat to
Russian convoys, 121, 122;
ineffectiveness of Asdic in
Arctic conditions, 122, 123;
126–130, 136, 138, 141,
143–145; attacked by Supple
and Lloyd, attacked by
Wilson and Strong; sunk by
*Campania*'s 813 Squadron,
149, 150; attacked by
Defrates and Beal, 150,
151–154, 163; torpedo *Lark*,

167; torpedo *Bluebell*, 169;
170, 175, 176; captured U-
boats sunk in Operation
Deadlight, 178.
*U-238*, torpedoes *Magpie*, 86
*U-295*, torpedoes *Mounsey*,
130
*U-365*, torpedoes *Cassandra*,
144
*U-387*, sunk by *Banborough
Castle*, 144
*U-403*, torpedoes *Bonneville*,
53
*U-452*, sunk off Kila Inlet, 167
*U-502*, sunk by *Starling* and
*Wild Goose*, 82
*U-509*, torpedoes *Stentor*, 53
*U-734*, sunk by *Woodpecker*, 85
*U-762*, sunk by *Wild Goose* and
*Woodpecker*, 85
Urquhart, Lt J.F., ("Jimmy"),
36, 50, 55, 81, 183
Urwin, Lt, P. ("Pat"), joins
squadron as Senior pilot,
112, 126, 138, 157, 183

# V

Vaenga, 140
*Ville de Tamatave*, SS, capsizes,
53
*Vindex*, HMS, 69, 111, 123,
124, 128, 130–134, 136,
153

# W

Walker, Capt John, and
Second Escort Group, 81,
82, 85, 86
Waller, Lt/Cdr Wilfred, joins

squadron as CO, 58, 59; 63,
  64, 67, 181, 183
Wallis, S/Lt Frank, 104, 183,
  185
Walrus, 58
*Warspite*, HMS, 92
Waterman, Lt/Cdr, Senior
  Medical Officer, *Nairana*,
  138; discusses Surtees'
  sanity, 140, 141
Westwater, Air Mech IE, F.,
  186
White, S/Lt D.W., 186
Whittick, S/Lt D., 126, 133,
  138, 183

Wildcat VIs, Grumman
  Martlet, 33, 75; replace
  Hurricane IIcs, 118; 131,
  132, 133, 135, 145–149,
  153, 155, 160, 162, 163,
  165; save convoy and land-
  on in Arctic hurricane,
  173–175, 177; technical data
  and evaluation, 190, 191

# Y

Yate, S/Lt F., 183
Yeovilton, RNAS, 75, 118